◀ CONTENTS ▶

Ian Riley's immaculate Stanier 5MT 4-6-0 No. 44871 departs from Summerseat with a service from Rawtenstall to Heywood on March 13, 2016. LIAM BARNES

ACKNOWLEDGEMENTS

Over the duration of the past 50 years more than 1000 people have worked hard to make the East Lancashire Railway the successful heritage railway it is today. This bookazine is dedicated to everyone who has been part of the railway in the past, present or future.

Sincere thanks to all the people who have assisted me in putting this publication together, with special thanks to Peter Duncan, Mike Kelly, David Layland, David Wright, Tracey Parkinson, John Stephens, Andi Moyes, Joanne Crompton, Nigel Valentine, Kevin Delaney, Terry Eyres, Liam Barnes, Emma Seddon, Fred Collinge, Neil Harvey, Mike Taylor and Tim Grimshaw.

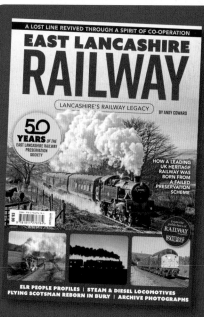

A LOST LINE REVIVED THROUGH A SPIRIT OF CO-OPERATION

EAST LANCASHIRE RAILWAY

LANCASHIRE'S RAILWAY LEGACY BY ANDY COWARD

50 YEARS OF THE EAST LANCASHIRE RAILWAY PRESERVATION SOCIETY

HOW A LEADING UK HERITAGE RAILWAY WAS BORN FROM A FAILED PRESERVATION SCHEME

from the publishers of RAILWAY

ELR PEOPLE PROFILES | STEAM & DIESEL LOCOMOTIVES
FLYING SCOTSMAN REBORN IN BURY | ARCHIVE PHOTOGRAPHS

MAIN PIC: BR Standard 2-6-4T No. 80080 heads a winter service through Horncliffe, heading towards Rawtenstall on January 28, 2012. NIGEL VALENTINE

LOWER LEFT: Ex-Manchester Ship Canal 0-6-0T No. 32 *Gothenburg* and Ex-Meaford Power Station 0-6-0 ELR No. 1 heads the inaugural ELR reopening train to Rawtenstall through Townsend Fold on April 27, 1991. MIKE TAYLOR

LOWER MIDDLE: Stanier 5MT 4-6-0 No. 45407 passes through Burrs as the sun sets on January 10, 1999, with a service to Rawtenstall. NEIL HARVEY

LOWER RIGHT: 40106 *Atlantic Conveyor* heads towards Burrs Country Halt station on October 29, 2017, with Holcombe Hill and the Peel Monument clearly visible in the background. NIGEL VALENTINE

◀ MEET THE TEAM ▶

EDITOR:
Andy Coward

DESIGN:
Craig Lamb, Kriele Ltd

COVER DESIGN:
Charlotte Fairman

REPROGRAPHICS:
Jonathan Schofield,
Paul Fincham

PRODUCTION EDITOR:
Pauline Hawkins

PUBLISHER:
Steve O'Hara

PUBLISHING DIRECTOR:
Dan Savage

MARKETING MANAGER:
Charlotte Park

COMMERCIAL DIRECTOR:
Nigel Hole

PUBLISHED BY:
Mortons Media Group Ltd,
Media Centre,
Morton Way,
Horncastle,
Lincolnshire
LN9 6JR.
Tel: 01507 529529

PRINTED BY:
William Gibbons and Sons,
Wolverhampton

ISBN:
978-1-911276-78-4

COPYRIGHT:
Mortons Media Group Ltd,
2018 All rights reserved.

MORTONS
MEDIA GROUP LTD

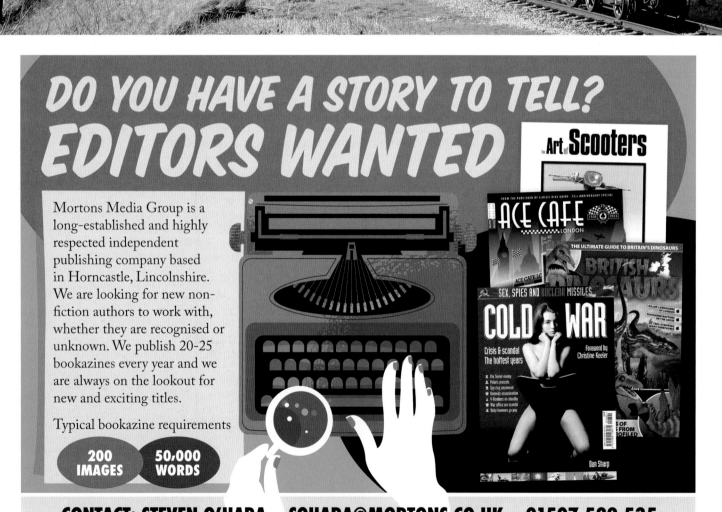

Stanier 5MT 4-6-0 No. 45407 has been closely associated with the ELR for the past 25 years, whilst owned by both the late Paddy Smith and then locomotive engineer Ian Riley. With a hardy frost on the ground, the ever-reliable Black 5 arrives at Irwell Vale on January 2, 2017. LIAM BARNES

The year 1968 proved to be very significant in the history of Britain's railways. While British Railways was dispensing with its final steam locomotives, the railway preservation movement was still in its infancy. Railways such as the Bluebell and Ffestiniog were up and running under private ownership and services on the Keighley and Worth Valley Railway were relaunched during the course of the year.

Compared to many of the more established heritage railways in the UK, the East Lancashire Railway is a relative newcomer to the movement, having only started passenger operations between Bury Bolton Street and Ramsbottom in July 1987. However, from rather humble and basic beginnings, the railway has grown to become one of the leading tourist attractions in the North West and one of the most popular heritage lines in the UK.

The East Lancashire Railway Preservation Society was formed in 1968 by a small group of enthusiasts and local residents at the quiet village station in Helmshore on the now-closed Stubbins Junction to Accrington line. The preservationists aimed to reopen part of the line between Stubbins and Haslingden Grane Road as a heritage line, linking with the British Rail Bury to Rawtenstall line services, which were still operational at the time, but under threat of closure. That original aim subsequently came to nothing, with BR unwilling to sell the land for an affordable sum and with an unsupportive local council also pouring cold water on the preservationists' plans.

When it become obvious that the Stubbins to Haslingden reopening could not happen, the ELRPS volunteers relocated to the former ELR Goods Warehouse at Castlecroft. An initial 12-month lease from Bury Council was the start of a very positive relationship between the railway and the council, a cooperative that has grown throughout the time that has ensued.

Partnership between the preservationists and the supporting local authorities has been one of the key success stories of the modern-day ELR, with the railway forging close

An atmospheric image, as Great Western Railway 'Manor' 4-6-0 No. 7828 *Odney Manor* and 'Castle' 4-6-0 No. 5029 *Nunney Castle* keep LMS 4F 0-6-0 No. 4422 company at Castlecroft shed on the evening of January 30, 1993. KEITH SANDERS

relationships between themselves and the councils of Bury, Rossendale and Rochdale. The railway would simply not exist had it not been for the help and cooperation of the local authorities that recognised the potential and economic benefits of having a heritage railway operating through their area.

After the initial opening to Ramsbottom in July 1987, the ELR was extended to Rawtenstall in April 1991 and then an easterly extension from Bury to Heywood was brought back into passenger use in September 2003, taking the overall running length of the railway to just over 12 miles. With around 200,000 visitors travelling on the railway every year, it has helped to improve the area that it serves, with the main towns of Heywood, Bury, Ramsbottom and Rawtenstall all thriving when a lot of other towns are finding the economic outlook to be tough.

And the ELR is not stopping there. A further extension of the Heywood line to Castleton is planned over the next few years, a project that will provide a direct interchange facility with rail services on the Manchester to Leeds 'Calder Valley' line.

The ELR has hosted hundreds of steam and diesel locomotives of all sizes throughout its history and has organised many groundbreaking and memorable events that have placed it firmly on the map as Greater Manchester's second most popular paid-for attraction, behind the Manchester United tour. Come along and enjoy the journey.

Andy Coward
Editor

A brief history of the railways around Bury and Rossendale

The line now operated by the East Lancashire Railway was originally part of two separate railway routes, with the Bury to Rawtenstall section of the route once continuing towards Bacup, while the Bury to Heywood line was once part of the Bolton to Rochdale line. While the Bury to Bacup line was built by the original East Lancashire Railway, the Bolton to Rochdale line was a product of the competing Lancashire & Yorkshire Railway.

The Bury to Rawtenstall line was originally part of the 12½-mile Bury to Bacup line, the origins of which come from the formation of the Manchester, Bury and Rossendale Railway in 1843. The company wanted to build a railway from Clifton Junction (on the Manchester to Bolton line) to Bury, with a single track extension from Bury, through to Ramsbottom and Rawtenstall.

The Manchester, Bury and Rossendale Railway subsequently changed its name to the East Lancashire Railway in 1845 and the newly named company was already working on plans for an extension to the Bury to Rawtenstall line, which would see a main line route built to connect the new line with Accrington, with the extension diverging from the Rawtenstall line at Stubbins Junction, about one mile north of Ramsbottom.

The ELR planned to have its main line route between Manchester and Accrington and this decision meant the Bury to Stubbins Junction section would now be built as a double-track route, with the Rawtenstall service from Stubbins Junction operated as a single-track branch line.

The biggest engineering challenges on the line were the large number of river crossings that were required to carry the route over the snaking nature of the River Irwell. Additionally, between Summerseat and Ramsbottom, two tunnels were constructed to carry the line through hills.

The line between Bury and Rawtenstall was opened by the ELR on September 28, 1846, with stations located at Bury Bolton Street, Summerseat, Ramsbottom, Stubbins, Ewood Bridge & Edenfield and Rawtenstall.

However, the railway mania period meant that the various railway

companies were constantly looking at possible new routes where they could extend and two months before passenger services started operating to Rawtenstall, the decision had been taken by the ELR to extend the Rawtenstall branch through to Bacup.

Construction of the Bacup extension was swift, with the first section of the route opening to Newchurch (later known as Waterfoot) on March 27, 1848, before the full line to Bacup was completed and opened on October 1, 1852. The Bacup extension saw stations located at Cloughfold, Newchurch, Stacksteads and Bacup.

In 1857, a second track was added to the Stubbins Junction to Rawtenstall section of the line and the decision was also taken to double-track the full line through to Bacup. The construction of a formation for the second track through to Bacup was complicated due to the need to bore another tunnel through The Glen at Waterfoot, where two single track tunnels had been built for the original single-track line during

The view from a Bolton-bound DMU leaving Bury Knowsley Street on February 16, 1960. Immediately at the end of the station platforms was a bridge which carried Knowsley Street over the railway, while the sharp curve around to Bury Bolton Street can be seen on the right hand side. The Bolton line continued straight ahead through the left-hand bridge, with these bridges carrying Manchester Road over the railway. Beyond that in the distance can be seen another bridge, which carried the railway from Manchester to Bury over the Bolton line. RICHARD GREENWOOD

the original construction of the line. A third tunnel was built through solid rock alongside the two original tunnels, with the new Thrutch Tunnel openings being adjacent to the entrance of Newchurch No. 1 Tunnel and the exit to Newchurch No. 2 Tunnel.

The ELR built its headquarters at Bury Bolton Street and the imposing building was located alongside Platform 2 at the station, surviving until it was demolished by BR in January 1974,

having been out of use for many years.

The second station in Bury was located on Knowsley Street and while few passenger services operated between the two stations, there was a rail link provided to connect them as part of the wider rail network. The station at Knowsley Street was served by fewer passenger services than the neighbouring Bolton Street, but there was a much bigger freight yard at Knowsley Street.

Bury Knowsley Street was opened by the Lancashire & Yorkshire Railway in 1848. The station has four through tracks, with two fast lines which weren't served by platforms. On May 26, 1962, LNER B1 4-6-0 No. 61274 hauls an excursion train through Bury Knowsley Street, while a Metropolitan Cammell DMU stands in the adjacent platform with a service to Bolton Trinity Street. RICHARD GREENWOOD

The first section of the Bolton to Rochdale line opened in 1841 as a branch off the Manchester and Leeds Railway from Blue Pitts (later renamed Castleton) to Heywood. In May 1848 the line was extended to Bury Knowsley Street and six months later in November 1848 it reached Bolton, by which time the M&LR was known as the Lancashire & Yorkshire Railway. Many services operating on the Bolton to Rochdale line originated from Liverpool and Merseyside under the L&YR. The ELR subsequently amalgamated with the L&YR in 1859, with the L&YR controlling all services that operated in and around Bury.

The Bury to Castleton section of the line featured a large goods yard and warehouses on land adjacent to Bury Knowsley Street station, with the line the crossing over the River Roch by the seven arch brick-built Roch Viaduct (known locally as Seven Arches). Shortly after Roch Viaduct was Heap Bridge Junction, where a branch line diverged to a nearby paper mill, Yates Duxbury, which had its own internal rail system and small fleet of industrial steam locomotives and wagons.

The line then continued for about a mile in a deep cutting with the gradient rising steadily towards Broadfield station, which was located alongside Pilsworth Road to serve the local residential community and mills. A mile after leaving Broadfield trains arrived at Heywood, which also featured a number of sidings and good facilities and the station was built on a sharp curve which could be challenging for the crews of lengthy trains.

After crossing Green Lane Level crossing the line continued for about three-quarters of a mile before reaching Castleton Junction, where the line joined the Manchester to Leeds line.

By the time the Victorian rail building mania period had come to an end, the town of Bury was served very well by

The view from the footplate of L&YR 0-6-0T No. 52523 on July 28, 1962, as the train approached Stacksteads on the line between Bury and Bacup. The locomotive was being used on a charter organised by the Roch Valley Railway Society, the 'Salford Hundred Railtour'. IAN G HOLT

the railways with a myriad of lines emanating to and from the town.

While the Bolton to Rochdale line saw many express and stopping services running along the route, many originating from Liverpool and Merseyside, the Bury to Bacup line was mainly operated as a steam push-pull style of service until the line pioneered diesel traction from 1956.

THE BACUP BRANCH DMU TAKEOVER

At the start of the 1950s, British Railways (BR) began to adopt modern diesel technology as a way of replacing some of the elderly steam locomotives which still operated on large parts of the railway network. Trials of various new designs of diesel locomotives and diesel multiple units (DMU) became a regular sight around the country, as BR believed diesel traction could offer significant cost savings against the steam locomotives, while also improving journey times and service frequencies.

While the vast majority of diesel locomotive and multiple unit designs were built as a result of the BR

Modernisation Plan of 1955, the development of diesel traction had begun some time beforehand.

The Bury to Bacup branch operated between 16 and 19 return services each day using steam locomotives on push pull workings and the branch was suffering from declining passenger numbers, due to the level of competition from local bus operators. While car ownership was growing in popularity, it was still an unaffordable luxury to many people who relied on the trains and buses for commuting and for leisure activities.

Running through some heavily populated local communities, the Bury to Bacup branch was an ideal line to use as a test bed for a DMU service and BR decided to see if improved and faster services on the route was a way of reversing decline and improving patronage on the line.

The first hint that the elderly steam locomotives on the line could be on their way out came on November 22, 1954, when a brand new two-car Derby Lightweight DMU was employed to run two return trips from Bury to Bacup,

The large stone station building on the Up platform at Rawtenstall, pictured in 1962. The building was constructed by the East Lancashire Railway and featured its curved stone windows. On the opposite platform was a much more basic wooden structure, which was added at a later date. FRED COLLINGE

Bury North Junction, pictured in the 1950s, showing sidings going off towards Castlecroft Goods Yard on the right-hand side. Immediately before the tunnel is Bury North signal box, while Bolton Street station can be seen on the other side of Bury EL Tunnel. The third rail electrification was in place for trains serving the Bury to Holcombe Brook line, although the electric services to Holcombe Brook were discontinued in 1951. FRED COLLINGE

Passing over immaculately maintained trackwork, a Metropolitan Cammell DMU departs from Summerseat, working a service to Bury on April 19, 1963. By the time this photo was taken, it was known that the future of the Bury to Bacup line was in doubt. IAN G HOLT

On March 26, 1963, the sole Derby Lightweight DMU allocated to Bury approaches Waterfoot with a Bury to Bacup service. IAN G HOLT

as BR tested the new technology on the route. Those trials on the line had proved successful and as BR began a programme of DMU building it was decided that the Bury to Bacup line would be the first line in Lancashire to have its steam services replaced with DMUs. An order was placed with Birmingham train builder Metropolitan Cammell to build 36 new two-car lightweight DMUs, of which seven sets were earmarked for the Bury to Bacup service.

Although built to a different design to the Derby Lightweight that had been trialled on the line, the Metro Cammell units were the first DMUs built by a non-BR Works to a design that would subsequently be modified and eventually become the basis of the hugely successful Class 101 DMU design.

The seven DMUs built for the Bury to Bacup line were the first to be completed and the first completed example underwent testing in October 1955 around the Birmingham area. Another was sent to London in December for inspection by railway officials, before the seven new sets were delivered to Bury in preparation for commissioning prior to their introduction into service.

With the new DMUs now at Bury and commissioned, BR announced the new half-hourly timetable would start from February 6, 1956.

The new timetable would deliver the most frequent service on the line in its 110-year history and journey times would be cut by several minutes as the new generation DMUs were able to achieve better acceleration and deceleration than the steam services

they were replacing. The most noticeable aspect was that with a regular 30-minute service frequency throughout the day there would be 37 trains each weekday travelling towards Bacup and 35 to Bury, which was a huge improvement on the previous timetable.

And so began the best level of service experienced on the Bury to Bacup line. The seven dedicated Metro Cammell DMUs, along with a solitary Derby Lightweight DMU, operated the services on the route almost exclusively for the

BELOW: Although the final 10 years of services to Bacup were principally operated by DMUs, steam did still venture on the line for various specials and for freight purposes. On June 10, 1966, a DMU stands in the station platform while Stanier 5MT 4-6-0 No. 44728 shunts a brake van in the goods yard. IAN G HOLT

Following the removal of the original canopy over Platform 2 at Bury Bolton Street, the East Lancashire Railway headquarters building is shown to good effect on June 3, 1972, the day that passenger services between Bury and Rawtenstall ended. This imposing building was demolished in January 1974. ANDY COWARD COLLECTION

On March 26, a Metro Cammell DMU crosses over Hareholme Viaduct between Cloughfold and Waterfoot, while working a Bury to Bacup service. IAN G HOLT

next five years, until a new fleet of 25 'Cravens' DMUs (later designated as Class 105) were introduced into the area to operate services and from the early 1960s it was these units which became the most common sight on the route.

The start of DMU operation and the new timetable service saw a huge increase in passenger levels on the branch, with an increase in passenger numbers of around 135% during the first few months, proving that such initiatives could revive the fortunes of some declining steam-operated local routes.

It was reported that some 23,000 passengers used the new service during its first week of operation, compared to 8000 passengers for the corresponding week using the steam service the previous year, although undoubtedly a

proportion of these passenger numbers would be local residents trying out the service.

However, the seven Metropolitan Cammell DMUs were not deemed to have been as successful as the services they operated. The units suffered from poor ride quality and frequent complaints were received from traincrew and passengers about the hard ride experienced on the units when they were travelling at speed on the line. The coupling arrangements on the Bury to Bacup DMUs were also not compatible with other DMU designs that had subsequently been introduced into service.

As such, the units were classed as non-standard and by the late 1960s they had all been withdrawn and scrapped.

The other 29 DMUs built from the same order for the Eastern Region were also retired after only a few years in service. None of the units survived into preservation, although many examples of the similar-looking, but numerous examples of the much more successful Class 101 Metropolitan Cammell DMU's can still be found on various heritage railways around the UK.

DMU development by BR became widespread throughout the 1960s and most local services went over to DMU operation from the mid-1960s, with steam locomotives used mostly for express passenger services and freight, prior to BR eliminating steam traction from their network in August 1968, with the North West being the final domain of steam locomotives on BR.

One of the Metro Cammell DMUs negotiates Rawtenstall East Level Crossing over Bury Road on March 26, 1963, while working a Bacup to Bury service. IAN G HOLT

Decline and CLOSURE

The Reshaping of British Railways report

British Railways had been closing less-popular lines long before the publication of *The Reshaping of British Railways* report in March 1963. However, when the controversial report recommended the closure of the majority of lines through Bury and the complete loss of passenger services in the Rossendale Valley, it sent shock waves through the area.

On March 26, 1963, a Derby Lightweight DMU arrives at Waterfoot station with a Bacup to Bury service. The day after this photograph was taken, *The Reshaping of British Railways* report would be released, recommending the closure of this line and countless others all across the country. IAN G HOLT

The publication of the infamous *The Reshaping of British Railways* report, commissioned by the British Railways Board Chairman Dr Richard Beeching, on March 27, 1963, had a huge impact on almost the whole of the British Railways network, but locally its recommendations were savage and brutal.

The services listed for closure in the Bury and Rossendale areas were the Bury to Manchester electric line, the Bury to Bacup route through Ramsbottom and Rawtenstall, along with the loss of the Manchester to Accrington service which would see the original East Lancashire Railway main line route closed. These closures would leave the Bolton to Rochdale service as the sole-surviving rail route serving Bury, and even that was not assured a safe future.

The wholesale nature of the cuts took residents, commuters and politicians somewhat by surprise. Both the Bury to Manchester line and the Bury to Bacup line had benefited from the introduction

of new train fleets less than a decade earlier and both were relatively busy routes, especially during the traditional weekday peak periods.

The report quickly became a huge political issue. It was acknowledged that there were parts of the rail network that were unprofitable and inefficient, but many felt the proposals went too far and there was outrage from many communities across the country that faced isolation because of the closures.

The publication of the report made headline news all across the country and very few areas would be exempt from Dr Beeching's 'Axe', as the press chose to describe the closure proposals.

In the local area services had already been withdrawn on the Bury to Holcombe Brook and the Bacup to Rochdale lines, and the stations at Haslingden and Baxenden on the Stubbins to Accrington section of line had both been closed for a number of years.

Prior to its publication, few could have guessed just how far *The*

BRB Chairman Dr Richard Beeching with his report.

Reshaping of British Railways report would go in its recommendations. Although the railways needed work to save costs, it was still a huge shock to see the scores of stations and lines listed for closure across the country.

At a time when some British manufacturing industries were suffering from declining fortunes, the prospect of adding thousands of railway workers to the unemployment statistics was also not an easy pill to swallow.

While local press reporters went into overdrive about the closure proposals, in terms of the Bury and Rossendale areas,

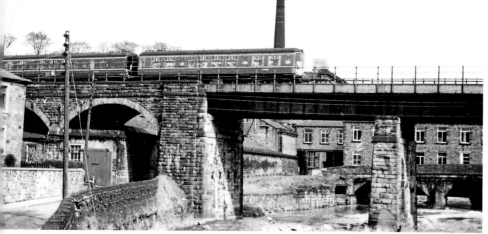

On April 19, 1963 a DMU heads across Brooksbottom Viaduct in Summerseat, with Hoyles Cotton Mill prominent in the background. It would be the village of Summerseat that dominated the campaign against closure of the line, which was an essential lifeline for people living there. IAN G HOLT

it was the decimation of all passenger services in and around Rossendale that brought about the fiercest criticism from the newspapers.

In the seven years since DMU services had been introduced on the Bury to Bacup line, the route had been seen as having a secure future. The line was the first in Lancashire to receive new DMUs, and the introduction of a half-hourly service throughout the day had transformed the line from the days when it was operated by elderly L&YR steam locomotives.

There was also an element of disbelief at the proposals to close the popular Manchester to Bury electric line, which was relied on by thousands of local commuters to get into Manchester, the route having seen considerable investment just four years earlier, with the major redevelopment of Radcliffe Central station in 1959 and a brand new electric train fleet the same year.

The Bury to Manchester line subsequently saw a reprieve from the Minister of Transport in 1964, who agreed its closure could not be justified, and the route now forms part of the successful Metrolink tram network. A common misconception is that the lines were closed on the instructions of Dr Beeching, whereas this was not the case. The report he commissioned

highlighted those unprofitable lines he believed should be removed from the network to create a leaner, more profitable, rail network. The ultimate decision as to whether a line was to be closed or reprieved rested with the Government, through the offices of the Minister of Transport.

SHOCK REACTION

The hit-listed lines would be closed unless the local community could prove the loss of their rail services would cause hardship in the community. The Transport Act 1962 had made provision for the Transport Users' Consultative Committee (TUCC) to hear any cases where people believed the loss of services would result in hardship. Objections to closures would need to be lodged with the TUCC, who would then consider those objections and make recommendations to the Minister of Transport, with the Minister then making the final decision as to whether to reprieve a service or allow the closure to go ahead.

The Government of the day, through Minister of Transport Ernest Marples MP, had a pro-road transport policy, but the rail closures would undoubtedly increase the amount of people privately owning cars and this would do little to aid the already congested road network

of the 1960s. While new motorways were being built across the country, much of the existing road infrastructure would struggle to cope with so many people being displaced from the railways. The assumption that most would simply go from train to bus was an optimistic suggestion.

Almost as soon as the findings and recommendations of the report were published, the local press set about getting opinions from people who would be affected by the closures. Naturally, there was a great deal of shock that the cuts could be so swingeing and a spokesman for the Rossendale branch of the National Union of Railwaymen told the press: "We never expected anything like this. We had heard all sorts of rumours but nobody ever suggested that the Valley lines would close completely. Skilled men on the railways will only be labourers, as far as industry is concerned."

The chairman of Bacup Transport Committee, Alderman J B Whalley, also reacted angrily to the report, saying: "To close the railway to make a profit is a very short-sighted policy. The line runs through a very heavily populated district and to put more traffic on our already congested roads is a step in the wrong direction. I feel the best way out is to develop the area and cut down unemployment which would, in turn, make for increased railway traffic. To strangle development for the sake of profit is definitely wrong."

Even during the 1960s the Rossendale Valley was still an important manufacturing heartland, with the main industries being cotton and shoe manufacture, although competition from overseas was starting to have an effect on some of the industries that dominated the area. Many people living in the area worked in the scores of mills that dotted the towns in the Rossendale Valley and most of these workers relied on the trains to get them to work, with car ownership generally reserved for

LMS Stanier 5MT No. 45101 hauls a Liverpool Exchange to Rochdale express service through Bury Knowsley Street station on February 27, 1962. The Bolton to Rochdale line was initially thought to be safe from closure under the Beeching proposals, but was subsequently identified as a line to be closed and another fight was launched to try and save the route. RICHARD GREENWOOD

LMS Stanier 5MT No. 44757 passes through the attractive station at Broadfield, located between Bury Knowsley Street and Heywood, on the Bolton to Rochdale line while hauling a Southport to Rochdale service on June 3, 1965. RICHARD GREENWOOD

people on larger incomes.

Local councillors and MPs were also keen to add their voices in response to the report, and with a General Election due to take place the following year, it quickly became apparent that the Beeching Report and the railway closures would become a major political issue and could have quite an impact on the Conservative Government of the day, who had effectively commissioned the report by calling for the railways to become more cost-effective.

Rossendale MP Anthony Greenwood was quoted as saying: "The closing of the Bacup to Bury line, coming on top of the increasingly serious unemployment situation in parts of the area would be another grave blow to Rossendale and must be resisted by every legitimate means. The railways should be a public service, catering for the needs of the community as a whole and providing security of employment for those who have devoted their lives to the industry. Only an integrated transport service, co-ordinating rail and road transport, can save the railways and stop further congestion on the roads. Having seriously damaged our local industry the Government now want to deny us our line of communication. Our chances of putting the Valley back on its feet again will be seriously reduced if more and more of our local amenities are going to be destroyed in this foolish, wanton way."

The local press took a balanced viewpoint when it came to analysing why the railways were not making the sort of money they should be, with reporters highlighting how many off-peak services were lightly loaded and there was a feeling that many people took the railways for granted and expected the trains to be run, irrespective of cost.

Clearly savings could be made by pruning these lightly used services and making more use of unstaffed stations with tickets being sold on the trains, rather than the expense of maintaining staffed booking offices at stations that only generated relatively modest amounts of revenue, particularly outside the peak periods.

The reaction to the closures in Bury was similar to that of their neighbours in Rossendale, but the greatest shock among the proposals was the threat to the popular Bury to Manchester electric railway, which was used by thousands of commuters each week. When the report was first published in 1963, Bury Council and its neighbouring authorities set about fighting to retain both the Bury to Manchester line and the Bury to Bacup line, both of which were seen as being essential to the local community and their loss would cause long-term damage to the prosperity of the town and the surrounding areas.

A 'Cravens' DMU departs from Rawtenstall, heading towards Bacup, shortly before the line was closed. The level crossing at Rawtenstall East was located on Bury Road in the town and was frequently the source of many complaints from motorists about the amount of time cars were delayed at the crossing while trains crossed. A dual carriageway bypass was subsequently built, but by the time it opened the trains and the level crossing were gone. KEITH ROSE

The village of Summerseat was very much a case in point. The village, which contained a large cotton mill and mill-worker community, had poor road access and didn't have a bus service due to the condition of the roads leading to it, with some substantial upgrading of the roads required to make them suitable for a bus service.

FIGHTING FOR SURVIVAL

This potential hardship on the people of Summerseat went on to become one of the main focuses of the fight to save the Bury to Bacup line, with the railway providing an essential social lifeline for many of the people in the village. As such local residents got together to form the Summerseat Rail Action Committee, and decided they would do all they could to help the local authority at Bury fight to save their local line.

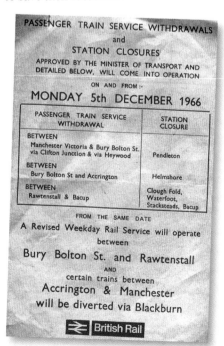

Closure Notice for Stubbins to Accrington and Rawtenstall to Bacup line

After the initial shock of the report's publication, the various town councils, unions, trade associations, commuters and local residents all went away to prepare for the long fight to save their various local lines, some of which would be successful, while others would end in defeat and line closures.

As the various local authorities planned their cases against the closures they decided to carry out a huge census on June 6, 1964. The census would survey rail users on the threatened lines between Manchester and Bury, Manchester and Accrington, and also the Bury to Bacup routes. This census, supported by a total of 14 local authorities across the region, was organised to establish the effect of closures on rail users should the various lines see their passenger services withdrawn, with questions tailored to find out the impact the closures would have on the community.

The results of the census would then be used to compile a detailed report which would be presented to the TUCC as part of a formal objection to BR's plans to close the lines. On the Bury to Bacup line, council-employed teams worked throughout the day, from before the first train in the morning until the last train at night, handing out forms to travellers. There were also specially created questionnaires for school children, with the questions on these forms specifically dealing with rail travel in connection with schools.

A Bury Town Hall spokesman told the local press: "The idea is to get an accurate picture of how the closures would affect the lives of members of the public in the area who use the present services. We are hoping that all passengers will co-operate by filling in the forms and returning them. We are particularly anxious to obtain details of any special cases of hardship that will result from closure of the lines."

A pair of DMUs pass each other in late 1966. To the right can be seen the overgrown Castlecroft Goods Yard, part of which went on to become the home of the East Lancashire Railway Preservation Society six years later. KEITH ROSE

BR's case for closure of the Bury to Bacup line was submitted to the TUCC with the company stating that if the line was closed, local bus operators would need to purchase an additional six 56-seater buses at an estimated cost of £29,640, with an expected return of around £20,600 should two-thirds of the rail passengers transfer to bus services. They claimed keeping the line open would cost around £130,000 each year, but would only generate a return of £40,300, resulting in a loss of £89,700. Renewals of infrastructure over a five-year period could also total £72,350. The document submitted by BR also gave details of the number of people boarding and alighting from trains at the various stations along the line, along with comparisons between existing bus and rail fares and details of alternative services currently available.

At the end of October 1964 BR, in accordance with the Transport Act 1962, published its intentions to close the Bury to Bacup line on January 4, 1965. The formal closure procedure required a period of six weeks between November 6 and December 21, 1964, for objections to be lodged, and upon receipt of just one formal objection the closure date would be postponed until the TUCC

had been given the chance to review the objections and submit a report to the Minister of Transport for the final decision.

The following month there was confusion as to whether any of the threatened services would actually be withdrawn, following the October 1964 General Election. The change of Government from Conservative to Labour had seen Tom Fraser MP appointed as Minister of Transport, and he had stated there would be no more major rail closures until a full review could be carried out. However, the situation with lines that were already subject to a formal closure notice, including the Bury to Bacup line, was less clear. A spokesman for the TUCC said: "So far as we are concerned, nothing has changed. We are carrying on as usual until we hear anything to the contrary."

BACUP LINE INQUIRY

Mr Fraser subsequently decided the closures of the local lines should continue to follow the formal closure procedures implemented before the new Government came to power and a public inquiry into the closure of the Bury to Bacup line, the linked services

to Manchester via Clifton Junction was organised by the TUCC, would be held in Bury on September 30, 1965.

There was a huge response to the closure proposals and a number of objections were lodged with the TUCC, along with two petitions. The reasons for the objections were many and varied, but it was clear that if the Bury to Bacup line closed it would cause great inconvenience and hardship to local people who relied on it.

Of the objections received, nine claimed the closure would add even more traffic on to the already congested roads, while another six cited the severe winter weather in the Rossendale Valley that often left roads badly affected, with motorists having to use the trains for commuting during the wintry weather. Other road-related objections were about the additional time it would take travellers on local buses and the number of changes which would have to be made for journeys that were relatively straightforward by train.

In relation to the issue of bus travel, BR claimed existing and proposed bus services would be more than suitable for the displaced rail passengers, with regular bus services from Rawtenstall to Bury, where they could join the electric train services at Bury Bolton Street for Manchester. BR did, however, acknowledge that passengers using the bus services from Bacup would need to change buses at Rawtenstall.

The prospect of replacement bus services was of cold comfort to the people of Summerseat and many objections to the closure had come from people living in the village. Residents faced a 20-minute walk from the railway station to the closest bus stop and a walk of around 30 minutes for some of the residents living in outlying parts of the village.

Other objections were raised by Rawtenstall Cricket Club, who claimed the closure would reduce the number of members joining the club and have

On November 26, 1966, LMS 3F 0-6-0 Nos. 47202 and 47383 stand on Platform 2 at Bury Bolton Street, ready to haul the Manchester Rail Travel Society's 'Three Counties Special' from Bury to Stockport Edgeley, while a Bury Manchester EMU awaits departure from Platform 1. Stanier 4P, 2-6-4T No. 42644 had earlier worked the train from Manchester to Bacup and then back to Bury. COLOUR RAIL

Now relegated from its glory days as a terminus for two routes, a Class 105 'Cravens' DMU stands at a deserted Bacup station, awaiting departure for Bury shortly before the line was closed. While the line was well used during the main rush hour periods, usage during the daytime was often sparse. KEITH ROSE

a detrimental effect on the number of spectators attending to watch matches. The Rossendale Girl Guides Association stated that training courses and meetings were often held at their headquarters in Bury and for people living in the Bacup and Waterfoot areas the train was the most convenient method of getting to Bury.

The Workers Educational Association said the closure would affect the quality of the classes held in Rossendale, as many of the tutors travelled from Manchester and the loss of the trains would make their journeys more complicated.

Finally, the Rossendale Valley Textile Workers Association was concerned about the effect the closure would have on shift workers, many of whom started work at 6am. It was feared some workers might lose their jobs, as they would be unable to reach their workplace for the start of the early shift.

The public inquiry also heard from various schools and educational bodies who stated that schoolchildren would suffer hardship, as the trains were used by many local scholars.

Bacup Council said the closure would hit the future prosperity of the town, while Ramsbottom Council feared house builders might move away from the area, with the town becoming less desirable for commuters from Manchester.

The public inquiry had heard many convincing arguments why the train services should be retained and, with the public inquiry finished, the TUCC went away to prepare their report for the Minister of Transport.

By 1966, the neighbouring Blackburn MP, Barbara Castle, had become Minister of Transport and, therefore, it was to be her decision about the future of the lines. With Mrs Castle knowing the area around Bury and Rossendale, many hoped that she might show some sympathy to their plight.

The news rail users of Rossendale had been waiting for finally came

In dramatic lighting Stanier 4P 2-6-4T No. 42644 leads Ivatt 2MT 2-6-0 No. 46437 negotiating the junction pointwork at Stubbins hauling 'The Rossendale Forester' railtour towards Bacup on December 3, 1966. This tour took in all the local lines that would be closed later in the day, as well as other routes in the East Lancashire area. ANDY COWARD COLLECTION

through in September 1966, but it wasn't what most people had been hoping for. While the campaign by Bury Council and the villagers of Summerseat had proven that viable alternative public transport into the village was not yet available and the closure would cause them hardship, it was still a surprise when Mrs Castle announced she was only going to reprieve the Bury to Rawtenstall section of the Bacup line, and that the line between Rawtenstall and Bacup, along with the former ELR main line route between Stubbins Junction and Accrington, would be closed.

In announcing her decision, Mrs Castle said: "The common section of line north of Bury has now been reprieved to Ramsbottom because bus alternatives would not be satisfactory. The reprieve of the line to Rawtenstall will allow bus-rail co-ordination for inhabitants of Haslingden and the Rossendale Valley beyond Rawtenstall to Bacup. Detailed examination showed that some of the closure proposals would have thrown considerable numbers of commuters on to the roads and added to congestion. Cases in point included the services between Rawtenstall and Bury (for Manchester). But where we can make sensible savings I want to make them."

It would only take a month before BR announced its intention to withdraw direct services between Manchester and Accrington, incorporating the closure of the Stubbins Junction to Accrington line, and the closure of the Bacup to Rawtenstall section of line as from Monday, December 5, with the final trains running on the previous Saturday evening, December 3, 1966.

SERVICE ALTERATIONS
The provision of additional bus services to compensate for the loss of the trains was one of the requirements of the Minister of Transport when she authorised the closures, and these details were provided in the official closure notice issued by BR.

To compensate for the loss of rail services between Bacup and Rawtenstall, an additional four morning and four afternoon peak period bus services were to be provided each weekday in both directions. Additionally, Haslingden Council announced it would provide three morning and three evening bus services from Helmshore to Ewood Bridge station, to link with the surviving train services on the Bury to Rawtenstall line.

Shortly afterwards BR announced

Looking immaculate, Stanier 4P 2-6-4T No. 42644 stands in Platform 2 at Bury Bolton Street station on December 3, 1966, while working 'The Rossendale Forester' railtour. THE LATE COLIN WHITFIELD/RAIL PHOTOPRINTS

The Locomotive Club of Great Britain tour of local railway lines on December 3, 1966, 'The Rossendale Forester' departs from Bacup station at lunchtime on that fateful last day. COLOUR RAIL

The attractive stone station building at Summerseat was built to a typical East Lancashire Railway design, but became unstaffed in 1968 and was subsequently demolished in 1970. The villagers of Summerseat were instrumental in the fight to keep train services operating on the line, due to the poor nature of the roads leading in and out of the village. ANDY COWARD COLLECTION

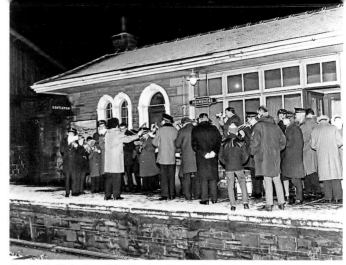

Members of Helmshore Prize Band perform on the platform at Helmshore on the evening of the final trains through the village. The residents of Helmshore worked hard to ensure the train service passed into history with due ceremony. HELMSHORE LOCAL HISTORY SOCIETY

it was introducing a new timetable on the surviving Bury and Rawtenstall line from Monday, December 5, 1966. This timetable offered a greatly reduced level of service on the route, with 15 trains operating in each direction on weekdays, 17 trains on Saturdays and no Sunday service.

Having enjoyed a mainly 30-minute interval between trains since the DMUs were introduced on to the line 10 years earlier, the timetable was far less flexible, with gaps of more than two hours between trains in some cases during the day. Campaigners who had fought to retain the service saw this as BR's latest attempt to make the surviving Bury to Rawtenstall line unattractive to travellers.

With the end of passenger operations between Bacup and Rawtenstall approaching, there was hope that the line may be retained for freight operations, but in November 1966 BR confirmed freight services were also being withdrawn from the line at the same time as passenger services, meaning the surviving goods yards beyond Rawtenstall would also close.

The fight was now over and as December 3, 1966, arrived the communities around Rossendale prepared to bid their much-loved train services a fond farewell.

While there were plans to hold suitable festivities at Helmshore station on the Accrington line, there were no such arrangements for the Rawtenstall to Bacup line, although it was inevitable that local people would turn out in force to travel on the last trains running on both lines.

On the final day of services a farewell railtour, 'The Rossendale Forester', had been organised by the Locomotive Club of Great Britain. Steam-hauled by Ivatt 2MT 2-6-0 No. 46437 and Stanier 4P 2-6-4T No. 42644, the tour originated from Manchester Victoria at 10am, travelling through Cheetham Hill Junction to Castleton, where the train then traversed the Rochdale to Bolton line between Castleton and Bolton, before travelling to Clifton Junction for a trip along the doomed ELR line to Bury.

The railtour then continued from Bury Bolton Street to Bacup before returning to Bury, where the train then returned north for Stubbins Junction and on to Accrington, taking the tour through the soon-to-be-closed Helmshore station, before continuing on to other lines in East Lancashire, with the train returning to Manchester Victoria at 5.47pm. The operation of a farewell railtour created a lot of interest and many local people turned out to watch it pass through.

THE LAST TRAINS RUN

As the evening arrived, the focus of attention first fell on the Accrington line and Helmshore station, which witnessed huge crowds of people throughout the evening. Helmshore Prize Band played The Excursion Train Galop, composed in 1844 during the railway building mania era, with Helmshore Local History Society securing a copy of the score from the British Museum. The timetable for the last train had gone adrift and it was nearly 9.50pm before the train, a four-coach DMU, pulled into Helmshore station to the sound of exploding detonators, which had been placed on the track in respect of a railway tradition to mark the end of a service. The final train had been delayed while BR staff strengthened it to four coaches at Accrington to cope with the demand from passengers.

The front of the train, driven by Arthur Middlehurst, carried a

On December 3, 1966, a DMU approaches a snow-covered Waterfoot station with a Bury to Bacup service. This was the final day of services on the section of line between Rawtenstall and Bacup. FRED COLLINGE

An Accrington to Manchester DMU calls at Helmshore station on the last day of services on the line between Stubbins Junction and Accrington, December 3, 1966. FRED COLLINGE

As the last train departs, a member of station staff at Helmshore station turns out the gas lamps on the station for the final time on the evening of December 3, 1966. HELMSHORE LOCAL HISTORY SOCIETY

At the same time demolition trains were operating between Rawtenstall and Bacup in October 1968, the opportunity was also taken to demolish the wooden platform buildings from what was the Bacup-bound platform at Rawtenstall station. FRED COLLINGE

commemorative headboard with a top centre crest of a red rose surrounded by the words 'East Lancashire Railway' and underneath it bore the words 'Last train Accrington – Bury – Accrington, 3 December 1966.' The headboard had been made by local enthusiast Albert Wilkinson.

By the time the train returned to Helmshore from Bury, the crowds that had descended on the station to welcome it dwarfed those that had watched it depart earlier, with an estimated 500 people awaiting its return towards Accrington. After another performance from Helmshore Prize Band the train departed for Accrington for the final time, again with detonators placed liberally on the tracks to ensure a lively send-off for a service which had served the village for over 118 years.

It was then the turn of the Bacup line to see the end of its train service between Rawtenstall and Bacup. Again, detonators exploded at various places along the route as the train passed through, but there was not the level of commemorations that had been witnessed earlier in the evening in nearby Helmshore. The last train to Bacup was well patronised though, with plenty of local residents joining the enthusiasts who had come out to witness the line pass into the history books.

With the northern section of the line now closed and Rawtenstall the new terminus, BR installed new buffer stops at Rawtenstall the following week, as well as a new set of points which directed all trains on to the Up platform. The only trains that would now venture beyond Rawtenstall were the demolition trains, although it would be some time before they operated.

SUMMERSEAT TAKES ON BR

Summerseat seems an unlikely location for rebellious residents, but the attempts by BR to close their railway line and the subsequent service reductions saw the villagers launch a protest against BR's tactics in the strongest way possible.

The residents of Summerseat had been particularly vocal in their support for the retention of their railway service when it was originally announced that the Bury to Bacup line would be closed. Over the next three-and-a-half years, active campaigning had taken place by the villagers to get the recommendation to close the line reversed.

While the announcement in September 1966 that the Bury to Rawtenstall line would remain open was down to active campaigning by many people and organisations, the local residents of the small village to the north of Bury had been instrumental in the campaign and were jubilant when the reprieve was announced by Minister of Transport, Barbara Castle. However, their initial joy was to be short-lived and as soon as the revised timetable for the truncated line was published the residents of Summerseat decided to take action against BR, who had introduced a much-reduced service frequency on the line. The publication of the new drastically reduced timetable seemed to be BR's way of exacting revenge on the communities along the line who had fought to keep their train service.

On a cold Saturday in January

The last ever service to work over the ELR line to Accrington prepares to depart from Platform 3 at Bury Bolton Street on the evening of December 3, 1966, carrying a suitable commemorative headboard and showing an incorrect destination on the destination blind. THE LATE DAVE DYSON, COURTESY OF TIM GRIMSHAW

1967, an organised crowd of about 150 residents descended on the usually tranquil station at Summerseat to demonstrate against the service cuts, with the ensuing protests resulting in two residents from the village being arrested for deliberately obstructing the passage of a train.

The protesters' aim was to stop one of the trains on the line by obstructing its path, to demonstrate that BR's new timetable was unacceptable to rail users, particularly in the village which relied so heavily on a regular and reliable train service. The protests had been organised in secret village meetings and although police officers were in attendance to ensure that the demonstration passed off peacefully, they didn't realise how the villagers intended to show their ill feelings towards BR.

While it was clear that residents were angry, a local councillor from Ramsbottom appealed to villagers that illegal actions could lose the support of the wider community and urged them to keep their protests peaceful. However, after the councillor had left the platform, the protest began as the time of the train's arrival at the station approached.

The chosen train which the protesters were planning to stop was due at Summerseat from Rawtenstall at 2.16pm, and as the time drew nearer a small number of residents carrying placards started to walk on to the tracks, before police officers quickly removed them and returned them to the platform. Following this, the platform was cleared of protesters for fear of a repeat episode when the train arrived.

Undaunted, more residents appeared further down the track by a foot crossing close to the station on the Bury side and then started walking up the track towards the platforms and the waiting police officers. The train from Rawtenstall was running late but finally arrived at 2.25pm and the police made sure the track was clear before allowing it to depart. However, it was soon delayed again by protesters appearing on the tracks as it departed and the police were forced to remove them before it could continue. While the train had only been delayed by a few minutes, the residents had made their point and believed they had forced BR to take notice of their feelings.

However, the hoped-for improvements to the timetable were not forthcoming, with the exception of the restoration of two later evening services, and there would be further negative modifications to the timetable over the following five-and-a-half years, as BR sought to rid itself of passenger services on the line.

Another BR cost-saving exercise had seen the stations on the line, apart from Bury Bolton Street, become unstaffed from March 1968. All the station buildings along the line were subsequently demolished, apart from Ewood Bridge which survived in a badly vandalised and derelict condition until after passenger services had been withdrawn.

Almost two years after the last trains had run on the route, trains were once again running on the Rawtenstall to Bacup line in mid-October 1968, although only as far as Stacksteads, due to a break in the line between Stacksteads and Bacup.

Demolition trains were operated to recover the redundant scrap track and other remaining scrap materials from the line. The work took several weeks to complete, with more of the railway disappearing every day as the train made its way back towards Rawtenstall.

By 1969, it was becoming increasingly clear that the line was under threat again. Operating with the assistance of a social grant awarded by the Minister of Transport at a rate of £130,000 in 1969, and reduced to £104,000 for 1970, the future for the line was far from certain and the local councils and the Summerseat Rail Action Committee were preparing for another fight, even though it was clear that many of the passengers who had previously used the

Closure Notice for Bury to Rawtenstall line.

trains had now found alternative forms of transport to get them around.

It came as little surprise when BR announced its formal intentions to close the line in January 1970 and efforts to save the service were back on again.

Further evidence of the ongoing decline followed a few months later, when BR began single line operations on the route, with the disused second line lifted for scrap, although this was not unexpected as the timetable now meant twin-tracks were no longer required to handle the level of services operating.

The TUCC announced their intention to hold another public inquiry in Bury on October 29, 1970, revealing a total of 73 objections had been received, along with a petition calling for the line to be kept open.

ANOTHER PUBLIC INQUIRY
At the public inquiry it was the hardship that would be caused to the residents of Summerseat that was a key component of the arguments to retain the services. The focus of the argument was once

again the condition of the roads into the village, particularly during bad weather conditions. Other communities along the line would suffer from the loss of the train service, but nowhere near as much as those living in Summerseat.

However, it was also revealed at the meeting that the council was spending £35,600 on road improvements into the village from the Holcombe Brook side. This move would clearly undermine the case for retaining the rail services, as the road improvements would finally allow buses to access the village and the lack of a bus service was the main reason the trains needed to be retained. While Bury Council wanted the train service to be retained, councillors had accepted that BR seemed determined to close the route and the upgrading of the roads was being done as the closure now seemed inevitable.

Grant funding for the line was only guaranteed until the end of 1971, meaning further grants would be required if the service was to be retained into 1972 and beyond. The decision now rested with the Minister of Transport, who would need to decide whether to retain the service after the funding expired at the end of 1971 and, if so, what level of grant assistance would be required to operate the service.

In January 1972 it was announced that permission had been granted for passenger services on the line to be withdrawn. The Minister had approved the closure proposals, due mainly to the requirement for a £95,000 grant to keep the service running. The SELNEC Passenger Transport Authority was planning on introducing a bus service through Summerseat during 1972 and this would finally remove the residents' claims of hardship if the trains were withdrawn.

However, the Minister said that the line would not be closed prior to May 31, 1972, to allow SELNEC time to get a road licence for the new bus service through the village. Improvements had by now been made to the roads accessing the

LEFT: By August 1969, the station at Ramsbottom was unstaffed but remained in good condition. A decent crowd of waiting passengers prepare to board the Bury-bound DMU entering the station. ANDY COWARD COLLECTION

RIGHT: Ramsbottom station building devoid of windows, as contractors begin work on demolishing the buildings from the station. Following the removal of the buildings, the only waiting facilities on the platforms would be bus-stop waiting shelters. ANDY COWARD COLLECTION

FAR RIGHT: Ramsbottom station during the demolition of the station buildings and canopies in 1970. The now-redundant Bury-bound platform has been cleared, while work is under way on the removal of the remaining canopy, prior to the main station building being demolished. ANDY COWARD COLLECTION

village, but the narrow roads around the village itself were still a cause of some concern when introducing bus services in place of the trains.

The closure announcement brought little surprise when it came. Both the line and its service frequency bore little resemblance to how it had been back in 1966, before the Rawtenstall to Bacup and Stubbins to Accrington lines had closed. The withdrawal of staff from stations and the subsequent demolition of most of the station buildings had made the platforms an unwelcome place to wait for a train and the changes in the operating timetable had made it impracticable for many people to use the line outside of the usual peak hour journeys.

BR immediately gave four months' notice of its intention to close the line to passenger services, with the stations at Summerseat, Ramsbottom, Stubbins, Ewood Bridge and Rawtenstall all scheduled to close. When the official Closure Notices were posted it was revealed that the line would be closed to passenger services from Monday, June 5, 1972, with the final trains operating on Saturday, June 3.

The one glimmer of hope was that the line was being retained for freight services, with coal trains still operating several times a week to the coal depot that had been built in the goods yard alongside Rawtenstall station.

Although staffing levels on the line were nowhere near what they had been in the past, for the few remaining BR staff who still worked on the line, some of them faced an uncertain future. One such person was Rossendale councillor Gaythorne Bland, who worked as a signalman at Rawtenstall West, and who was to be made redundant after the passage of the last train.

As the last day of services arrived, local people and enthusiasts set out for the now-traditional process of marking the closure of yet another railway line. Having suffered declining passenger numbers over the previous few years,

On October 21, 1968, contractors work on removing the redundant trackwork between Newchurch No. 1 and Newchurch No. 2 tunnels at The Glen in Waterfoot. Over the course of a few weeks during the autumn of 1968, demolition trains steadily worked their way down the line, removing all scrap assets from the former railway line. KEITH ROSE

it was necessary for the final trains to be strengthened to a four-car DMU to accommodate all the people expected to come out to say goodbye to the service.

Having given up on their aspirations to take over the Stubbins Junction to Haslingden Grane Road section of the now-closed line to Accrington, volunteers from the East Lancashire Railway Preservation Society had moved their headquarters and collection of exhibits and railway artefacts to the goods yard at Castlecroft, in Bury, and made it clear the focus of their efforts was now to reopen the Bury to Rawtenstall line for passenger services. ELRPS volunteers joined other local enthusiasts and residents who travelled on the 9.05pm service from Bury to Rawtenstall, which was the last scheduled passenger train to work along the line.

More than nine years had passed since the Bury to Rawtenstall line had been listed as one to be closed under the Beeching Report, but ultimately the final decline of the railway had begun after the Bacup section of the line had been closed in December 1966. And so, as the final train from Rawtenstall made its way down the line, more than 126 years of passenger services through the Rossendale Valley came to an end.

COAL TRAINS RETAINED

While passenger services had been lost, the establishment of a coal depot in the goods yard at Rawtenstall, as recently as 1966, had guaranteed the medium-term survival of the Bury to Rawtenstall line as a freight artery. Coal was still very much in demand throughout the 1960s and 1970s, with the fuel used extensively by manufacturing businesses and also for heating domestic properties.

The coal depot had the capacity to handle 80,000 tons of coal each year, with the fuel being brought to the depot by train before distribution around the Rossendale Valley by road.

It was off-loaded from trains into huge storage bunkers and was then moved from the bunkers by conveyor belt to one of eight 25-ton capacity bagging hoppers. A loading platform was provided where sacks were filled and control equipment enabled the sacks to be filled at a rate of one cwt every five seconds, before they were transferred directly on to delivery lorries.

The process was an efficient way of managing the distribution of coal and, although the coal had to be distributed from the depot by road, bringing it in by train greatly eased the overall number of large vehicles on the Rossendale Valley roads.

The trains were hauled by diesel locomotives, with the most common types being Class 25s and Class 40s, although occasionally other locomotives such as Class 47s worked the trains.

The Rawtenstall coal trains continued running throughout the 1970s, largely unnoticed, although as other forms of fuel were becoming more popular, the number of trains running along the line were reduced to one or two each week.

On Monday, August 1, 1977, tragedy occurred when one of the coal trains, hauled by locomotive 40027, was involved in a tragic collision with a car while crossing Townsend Fold level crossing, killing the front-seat passenger in the car and seriously injuring the

Shortly before the station buildings and concrete footbridge were demolished, a Bury-bound DMU stands in the station at Rawtenstall in August 1969. The buffer stops in the background were installed following the closure of the section through to Bacup in December 1966. ANDY COWARD COLLECTION

driver and two other occupants of the road vehicle.

Since the passenger services on the line had been withdrawn, the signal boxes at Ramsbottom, Townsend Fold and Rawtenstall West were not staffed, with travelling shunters assuming responsibility for ensuring the level crossing gates were closed to road traffic, although following the accident BR confirmed the gates at Townsend Fold had been damaged by another train four months earlier and had not yet been repaired.

The damage to the level crossing gates had seen emergency procedures put into place for the operation of Townsend Fold crossing, with a travelling shunter supposed to get off the train when it stopped before he closed the remaining serviceable crossing gate and stopped road traffic on the other side of the crossing using a red flag, before waving the train through the crossing.

On Saturday October 3, 1970, the final train from Bolton to Rochdale arrives at Bury Knowsley Street station, becoming the last passenger service to call at Bury's second railway station, which was officially closed on the same evening. As with other stations in the area, Bury Knowsley Street had become very rundown during its final few months. ANDY COWARD COLLECTION

The train driver and travelling shunter were both accused of manslaughter and the subsequent trial in December 1977 eventually found both men not guilty. The court heard that the train driver failed to stop, as he was supposed to, and the train hit the road vehicle as the car driver did not see or hear the train approaching.

The court also heard the driver had an exemplary previous record and his failure to stop had been his first indiscretion in a career of more than 30 years on the railway. The travelling shunter was also cleared, when BR officials confirmed that his duties did not start until the train had come to a stand and as the train driver had failed to stop there was little the shunter could have done to prevent the accident from happening.

With the rise in gas for heating and the coal trains down to just one a week by 1980, it seemed that the future of the coal trains along the line could be in doubt. The closure of Bury Bolton Street station in March 1980 had seen the last remaining passenger services to Manchester transferred to the new combined bus and rail interchange in Kay Gardens at Bury, rendering the old station redundant. However, following the closure of the station, the coal trains continued to run through the station, operating on the one remaining through line alongside the former Platform 2.

BR eventually announced that the final coal train to operate between Castleton and Rawtenstall would run on December 5, 1980, eight-and-a-half years after passenger services had ended, with 40098 given the honour of being the final locomotive to haul a revenue-earning coal service along the remaining section of line through Heywood, Bury and Ramsbottom, before terminating at Rawtenstall. After the wagons had been emptied, the train made its way back down the line, bringing down the curtain on BR operations on the line.

By this stage, the ELRPS had set their sights firmly on restoring passenger services to the line and,

unlike their early days at Helmshore, the preservationists had widespread support from the local authorities who could see the benefits of reviving the line for tourists and enthusiasts.

The local authorities of Bury and Rossendale, along with Greater Manchester Council, urged BR not to remove the track from the line, as the removal of trackwork would make the reinstatement of the line much more difficult. Thankfully BR agreed to leave the track in place while negotiations for the purchase of the Bury to Rawtenstall line proceeded.

At this stage the ELR had no plans to preserve the Bury to Castleton section of line and while BR also left the track in place on this line, its fate appeared to be sealed between Bury and Heywood, although the Standard Wagon Works at Heywood ensured that trains continued to operate between Heywood and the connection on to the Calder Valley line at Castleton Junction.

AN UNWANTED UPGRADING

With regards to the Bolton to Rochdale line, which included the section of line between Bury and Castleton, the story could have been very different, but it too was another casualty of the infamous Beeching report, despite initial suggestions that it could have escaped the axe.

When *The Reshaping of British Railways* report was published, the Bolton to Rochdale line was not mentioned in the list of numerous lines highlighted for closure, meaning that potentially it could have been the only surviving passenger service to operate through Bury, if all the other local passenger services had all been withdrawn, as recommended.

However, the line was listed in the Section 2 list of the report, which were classified as 'Services to be modified'. This meant services on the line would be subject to a more detailed survey by railway officials, and if the results of that survey showed the line was not financially viable, it would be added to the list of lines to be closed.

Upgrading of a service from the Section 2 list was not a particularly welcome move for rail users and, when this inevitably happened in August 1964 to the Bolton to Rochdale line, yet another fight began to keep trains running on this line, in addition to the ongoing efforts to save other local routes at the time.

The Bolton to Rochdale line had been the subject of an operational and cost survey and the news that the line was now being considered for closure meant that Bury was now on the brink of being wiped off the railway map entirely.

BR immediately began rationalising services on the line, announcing plans to withdraw Sunday services from the

Bury Bolton Street station closed on March 14, 1980, when the only remaining passenger services, the electric trains to Manchester Victoria, were transferred to a newly built bus and rail interchange station in Kay Gardens, Bury. The new facilities were a big improvement for passengers, with Bolton Street station presenting a run-down and decrepit appearance during its final few years. Shortly before closure, an electric train prepares to depart from Platform 3. RICHARD GREENWOOD

By the time the Bury to Rawtenstall line closed to passengers on June 3, 1972, the station facilities were basic, with buildings, canopies and all the previous passenger amenities swept away. On the final day of services, a coupled pair of Class 105 'Cravens' DMUs depart from Ramsbottom, heading towards Rawtenstall. ANDY COWARD COLLECTION

winter 1964 timetable, with a formal closure announcement to follow at a later date. The withdrawal of Sunday services was part of a cost-cutting exercise, with BR claiming Sunday services were expensive to operate and traffic levels were much less during the winter.

As part of the formal closure process, BR announced in November 1964 its intention to withdraw passenger services on the line from January 4, 1965. It was inevitable this date would be postponed, as the process for closure meant the date would be deferred should any objections be received by the TUCC, and it was clear the Bolton to Rochdale closure was just as controversial as the other local closure proposals.

By the beginning of December 1964 the TUCC had already received 149 objections from individuals and a further 13 from organised bodies. It seemed highly likely that with this level of opposition, a public inquiry would be held.

With numerous objections received, BR was forced to abandon its plans to withdraw services while the evidence was studied to allow a decision to be taken, although it would take more than 18 months before a decision was made.

A TEMPORARY REPRIEVE

In September 1966, the Minister of Transport, Barbara Castle MP, announced she was not willing to close the line in view of the extreme hardship caused to some users. Sadly the celebrations were not to last long though, as within two years its future was once again in doubt.

Bury Knowsley Street goods depot and yard had once been a thriving hub for goods traffic coming from local companies in Bury, Tottington and Ramsbottom, with many freight services utilising the large yard. However, the general run-down of rail services in the area, along with the need to save costs and the decline in some of the local manufacturing industries saw the extensive yard and its huge Lancashire

and Yorkshire Railway goods warehouse closed in June 1967, displacing more than 50 staff employed there.

In May 1968, the line played host to the Royal Train, as Her Royal Highness Queen Elizabeth II travelled by train to Bradley Fold, as part of her 'Operation Spring Clean' tour. In preparation the station was repainted, presenting a much fresher appearance than the other stations along the line.

In September 1968, BR once again gave advance notice of its intention to withdraw passenger services on the Bolton to Rochdale line. The move followed discussions between BR and the Regional Economic Planning Council, which revealed the line was unlikely to form part of the long-term passenger rail network for the area. The railway board said it would provide the Ministry with up-to-date reports showing heavy losses on the service.

Grant aid funding provision for some loss-making railway lines was how the Government now supported uneconomic railway services under the Transport Bill and, in November 1968, the Government announced £62 million of grant aid was available for a number of unprofitable lines. Although the Bury to Manchester and Bury to Rawtenstall lines were included in the list to receive grant aid funding for 1969, the Bolton to Rochdale line was not.

Grant funding for the line was subsequently agreed on a short-term basis, but as it was the subject of unresolved closure proposals on January 1, 1969, BR insisted it had to publish further closure proposals before the end of the year, as the line was uneconomic to run without Government aid.

At the time a number of new Passenger Transport Authorities were being set up to oversee and manage the operation of public transport services in various parts of the country. The Bolton to Rochdale line lay within the area under the control of the SELNEC PTA. It was hoped the new organisation would be consulted before a final decision on

the closure was made, as they would ultimately be responsible for managing alternative bus services.

By the end of October 1968, Bury Council announced its intention to fight for the retention of the line, joining forces with other local authorities that would be affected by the proposals. The councils of Bury, Bolton, Rochdale, Heywood, Radcliffe, Little Lever, with Lancashire County Council, all agreed that the line should be retained and gave their support to efforts to save the route from closure.

By January 1969 the TUCC had received 24 objections from individuals, two from affected local authorities and a petition containing 33 signatures,

Closure Notice for the Bolton to Rochdale line.

with a few weeks still remaining for objections to be received, the deadline for objections being February 1, 1969.

The main grounds for objections to the closure included hardship to passengers who relied on the inter-town service, the probability of widespread rail redundancies and damage to shopping and other businesses in the towns linked by the line.

Another initiative designed to save money was announced by BR in September 1969, when it stated the stations at Bradley Fold, Radcliffe Black Lane, Bury Knowsley Street, Broadfield and Heywood would become unstaffed, with fare collection taking place on board the trains by conductors using portable ticket machines. Rochdale, Castleton and Bolton stations, which also served other lines, would all retain staffed booking offices and tickets could still be purchased from booking offices at these stations. Bus shelter style waiting facilities would replace the station waiting rooms that had previously provided rail passengers with much-needed warmth and shelter from the unpredictable Lancashire weather and the redundant station buildings along the line would be demolished.

ANOTHER CLOSURE APPROVED

While campaigners hoped this move could help ensure the line's future, a BR spokesman was quick to pour cold water on this, saying: "This is something we would have done in any case. It has nothing to do with proposals to close the line. These same schemes are being operated in other areas where we have small stations that are not paying their way. Staff at the stations are being offered alternative employment and in some cases workers nearing retirement will be given the chance of leaving before their time – with compensation."

The annual passenger timetable for the route was issued on May 4, 1970, and detailed the service frequency on the line for the period up until May 2, 1971. The timetable showed 17 trains between Rochdale and Bolton each weekday, with 19 trains in the Bolton to Rochdale

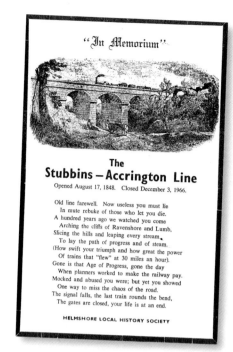

Helmshore Local History Society
Accrington line memorial card.

direction, reduced to 18 on Saturdays.

However, the publication of a timetable until May 1971 didn't necessarily mean that BR intended the line to survive until 1971 and the railway authorities were still actively pursuing the closure of the line. Therefore, it was with some irony that the same month the new timetable was issued, the final decision into the future of the line was announced. The Minister for Transport had approved BR's plans to withdraw services from the line, bringing to an end more than six years of campaigning by local authorities, rail unions, concerned commuters and local residents.

The Government had been supporting the service with grant aid funding of up to £156,000 per year, which was not deemed as being sustainable. While acknowledging the closure would create a degree of hardship and inconvenience for rail users, the Minister considered existing bus services could provide an adequate alternative over most sections of the line, although a single direct bus service between Bolton and Rochdale

did not exist and passengers wishing to make such a journey would need to change buses during their trip. After the final closure decision had been announced, and with arrangements for alternative bus services now in place, it was only a matter of time before the closure date was announced and this came in September 1970, when BR stated the closure date for the line would be the following month, on October 5, 1970.

The closure of the Rochdale to Bolton line meant that the only surviving passenger services through Bury would be the popular Bury to Manchester electric commuter line, itself reprieved from closure by government, along with the Bury to Rawtenstall line, which was still under threat of closure and its long-term survival could certainly not be guaranteed. The last trains ran from Bolton to Rochdale on Saturday, October 3, 1970, and once again scores of enthusiasts turned out to travel over the line for the last time.

As had become traditional, the last train was packed with local people and railway enthusiasts who marked the occasion with suitable ceremony. More than 300 passengers joined the final train, the 8.14pm service from Bolton to Rochdale, which had been strengthened to six coaches to cater for the number of people who wished to take part in the journey. As other lines in the area were still open, Castleton and Rochdale stations remained open, as did Bolton Trinity Street. At Heywood, the Standard Wagon Works remained active for the construction and maintenance of railway wagons, with its works close to Green Lane level crossing. Coal traffic to the depot at Rawtenstall also continued and these trains used the line between Castleton and Bury, before using the spur line from Knowsley Street station through to Bury Bolton Street and then on to Rawtenstall.

However, between Bury and Bolton there was no requirement to retain the line for freight services and the lines were quickly lifted, the demolition trains once again being the final trains to operate on the line. With the exception of the Bury to Manchester electric service, Dr Beeching's closure axe had swung savagely in Bury and Rossendale, leaving the future of the freight route from Bury to Rawtenstall in the hands of the preservationists who sought to reopen it.

LEFT: Following the closure of Bury Bolton Street station on March 14, 1980, the only services to operate through the redundant station were the weekly coal trains to Rawtenstall, which ran through the tracks alongside the former Platform 2. An unidentified Class 25 hauls a train of empties back through the station from Rawtenstall. The coal trains would only outlast the station by a further nine months before they ceased operating. THE LATE COLIN WHITFIELD/RAIL PHOTOPRINTS

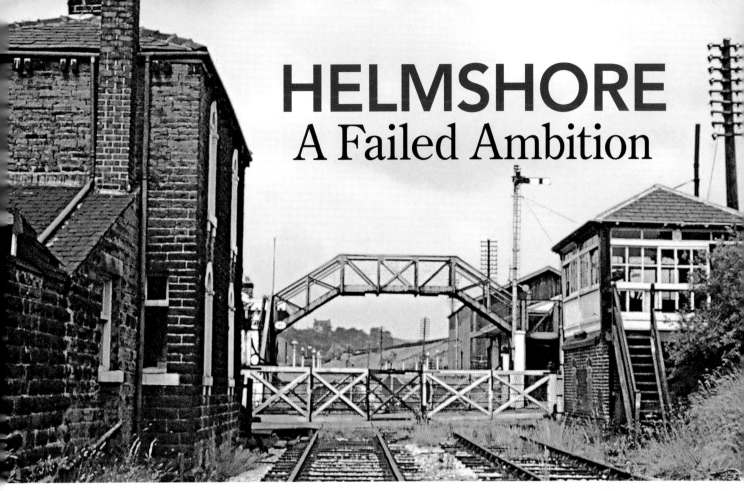

HELMSHORE
A Failed Ambition

The existence of the East Lancashire Railway can arguably be attributed to a disgruntled group of local businessmen and commuters who lost their train service following the publication of *The Reshaping of British Railways* report in March 1963. However, while the preservationists went on to restore and reopen the Bury to Rawtenstall section of the Bury to Bacup line and the Bury to Heywood section of the Bolton to Rochdale route, the original aim had been to restore commuter services on a neighbouring railway line which is now long gone.

Helmshore is an attractive and popular village located about eight miles to the north of Bury, and the railway station that served the village was the only surviving intermediate station on the section of line between Stubbins Junction and Accrington at the time of closure. Built by the original East Lancashire Railway (ELR) and opened in August 1848 as part of their 'main line' between Accrington and Manchester, the route from Stubbins to Accrington was often referred to as the ELR's 'Alpine Line', due to the number of challenging gradients and numerous viaducts that had to be constructed to carry the railway line.

Services between Accrington and Manchester ran from Accrington along the line through Helmshore to Stubbins Junction, where they then shared space with services on the Bacup to Bury line, before continuing towards Manchester on the ELR's route from Bury to Manchester, via Radcliffe Bridge, before joining the Bolton to Manchester line at Clifton Junction for the final section

TOP: A view of the station master's house, signal box and level crossing at Helmshore, pictured in 1968. The station master's house has since been extensively extended and is now a luxury private house. ANDY COWARD COLLECTION

of the route on the approach into Manchester Victoria.

The Stubbins Junction to Accrington section of the route originally had three intermediate stations located at Helmshore, Haslingden and Baxenden, although the latter two had been closed by British Railways (BR) before the line itself was recommended for closure by the infamous Beeching report, *The Reshaping of British Railways*.

As with countless other communities all across the country there were active campaigns and protests against the closure proposals from local residents, commuters and politicians, but it was confirmed in September 1966 that the Minister of Transport, Barbara Castle, had approved the discontinuation of the Manchester to Accrington services, which would include the complete closure of the ELR's Clifton Junction to Bury and Stubbins Junction to Accrington lines.

At the same time, Mrs Castle refused permission to close the neighbouring line between Bury and Rawtenstall due to the undue hardship experienced by the residents of Summerseat, although the northern section of that line, between Rawtenstall and Bacup, would also be lost. Local bus services would run between Helmshore and Ewood

Bridge, to connect with the surviving train service on the Bury to Rawtenstall line. The final date of services on the Stubbins Junction to Accrington, Rawtenstall to Bacup and the ELR Bury to Clifton Junction lines was announced by BR as being Saturday, December 3, 1966, with official closure as from December 5, 1966.

A CHANCE FOR SURVIVAL
However, a number of local Helmshore businessmen, commuters and residents decided that they still didn't want to lose their train service and planned to reopen part of the line as soon as possible after closure. Just a few weeks before the line was due to be closed the Helmshore and District Railway Preservation Society (H&DRPS) was formed, with its aims being to return weekday commuter services to the route, with the possibility of steam-hauled services for enthusiasts and visitors at weekends. However, with closure of the line now imminent, they would have to act fast to gain public and political support for their ambitions.

A public meeting was organised for November 25, 1966, to discuss their plans, which were essentially to try and initially reinstate services as quickly as possible between Helmshore and Stubbins Junction to link with the

On November 19, 1966, a Class 105 Cravens DMU calls at Helmshore with an Accrington to Manchester service. Two weeks after this photograph was taken the final BR services were operated along the route. KEITH ROSE

The Station public house, which is located on Helmshore Road and used to be situated next to the station good yards has a pub sign depicting a steam locomotive in a cartoon style, although the artist has clearly researched the former station at Helmshore, as the building shown on the pub sign is clearly one of the long-lost station buildings. ANDY COWARD

On the bitterly cold evening of December 3, 1966, the final BR service from Bury to Accrington stands at Helmshore station. The train was running late due to BR having to couple another Class 105 unit to form a four-car unit, due to the number of passengers turning up to travel on the last train, with an estimated 400 people making the journey. THE LATE DAVE DYSON, COURTESY OF TIM GRIMSHAW

BELOW: A view of the Up side station building at Helmshore in 1966, shortly before the line was closed by BR. FRED COLLINGE

Rawtenstall to Bury line. The main problem with this idea was that the station at Stubbins only served trains on the Rawtenstall route and did not have platforms serving the Accrington line, so a new platform would need to be built if Stubbins was to be used as an interchange between the two routes, as it was almost impossible to imagine that BR would allow trains from Helmshore to share their line into Ramsbottom and Bury with a private enterprise railway.

They stated that at a later date they hoped to reinstate the full line through to Accrington, but initially they would concentrate on the relatively short section between Helmshore and Stubbins. The original committee of the H&DRPS consisted of eight people, which included three councillors from Haslingden Council, who were also concerned about the impending loss of their train service.

The evening of December 3, 1966, soon arrived, with scores of local people and enthusiasts coming out in force to travel on the last BR-operated train, which had to be strengthened from two to four coaches to cope with the demand to travel on the final train, to ensure the BR service passed into history with due ceremony.

On the night of the closure society

secretary, Stanley Snelgrove, told the local press: "We are investigating the possibility of running the line from Helmshore to Stubbins Junction, where it joins the Rawtenstall to Bury line, by private enterprise. This has been done in other parts of the country and we have asked British Rail to lease Helmshore station premises temporarily as our headquarters. We hope to follow this by purchasing the whole line for daily commuter services."

As the final train made its way back towards Accrington, the crowds of people who had descended at Helmshore made their way home in the snow and the reign of BR on the line passed into history. Thousands of commuters would now need to amend their travel arrangements, transferring to either private cars or buses.

However, despite their good intentions, it quickly became clear that negotiating to take over the line was not going to be as straightforward as they may have first thought. Over the following 15 months, despite numerous communications with BR and the Ministry of Transport, little actual progress was made in their efforts to bring trains back to the line.

THE ELRPS IS BORN
In April 1968 a meeting was called where it was acknowledged that their plans had not succeeded and the H&DRPS was formally wound up.

It was acknowledged that the commuters who had previously relied on the rail services had now found alternative travel arrangements and the demand for commuter rail services to be reinstated on the line had all but gone. Changes introduced to the timetable on the Bury to Rawtenstall line from 1967 had seen services on that route significantly reduced by BR from the levels they had been prior to the closure of the Rawtenstall to Bacup section in December 1966, meaning that

The wooden Goods Warehouse and yard were located on the Up side of the station. The Goods Warehouse was the last remaining part of the station on the Accrington side of the level crossing to be demolished in 2002, many years after it had ceased to be used for railway purposes. FRED COLLINGE

LEFT: A general view of the station at Helmshore in 1968, taken from the level crossing towards the Up side buildings and platforms. ANDY COWARD COLLECTION

providing a connection with trains on the Rawtenstall line was also no longer an attractive or practical proposition.

A local press article on April 13, 1968, said the H&DRPS had been "frustrated at every corner". Despite writing more than 60 letters to various officials, chairman Robert Spiby said any replies he had received were curt and unhelpful in their response.

They claimed Haslingden Council had not done enough to keep the line open originally when it was first proposed for closure by BR and the council had subsequently been more than happy when a road scheme was announced that involved building a major new bypass over the railway formation between Haslingden and Baxenden. "I personally am of the opinion that someone, somewhere in a position of high authority could at a very early stage have told us of these proposals by the county council," said Stanley Snelgrove.

However, a number of the people who had been involved in the H&DRPS weren't quite ready to give up on the idea of returning trains to the line and they decided to form a new organisation to try and reopen the three-and-a-half-mile line between Stubbins Junction and Haslingden Grane Road solely as a heritage railway.

Construction of the new Haslingden bypass had breached the railway just beyond Haslingden Grane Road, with the section of line between there and Accrington lost forever. The new organisation was named the East Lancashire Railway Preservation Society (ELRPS) and like the H&DRPS they also hoped to link their services with the Bury to Rawtenstall line at Stubbins Junction, even though it was clear the future of passenger services on that line, reprieved from closure by Barbara Castle as recently as 1966, was far from certain with BR actively running down services on that line.

In June 1968 the chairman of the

newly formed ELRPS, Walter Baker, told the local press about the society's new aims to reopen the railway between Haslingden Grane Road and Stubbins, with Helmshore once again proposed as the headquarters for the new organisation: "We have formed a society whose aim is to negotiate with British Rail with a view to purchasing the three-and-a-half miles of track between Grane Road and Stubbins Junction. Should our negotiations be successful, we hope to run a service of trains between Haslingden and Stubbins Junction at weekends. These would be worked by steam locomotives and for the benefit of railway enthusiasts, schoolchildren for educational purposes, and for the thousands of tourists that such a venture would attract. If we are able to establish this working tribute to the steam

August Bank Holiday Weekend 1970 and Stanier 5MT No. 44806 stands in the Accrington-bound platform at Helmshore station. The locomotive belonged to the late Kenneth Aldcroft, an ELRPS member, but due to there being no covered accommodation for the locomotive it was unable to stay at Helmshore on a long term basis and it subsequently moved to the Lakeside and Haverthwaite Railway. ANDY COWARD COLLECTION

locomotives, it would turn Haslingden and Helmshore into a tourist centre."

LOCAL COUNCIL OPPOSITION

The new society was keen to establish itself as a tourist attraction, rather than a commuter-style operation, and its members were also keen to distance themselves from the now-defunct H&DRPS, despite some society officials having been involved in both organisations.

Within a couple of months of its formation, the society had reached agreement with British Rail to take out a temporary lease on the station premises at Helmshore, where they planned to establish a museum in one of the station buildings and a refreshment room in another, along with plans to host various open days and special events to promote their scheme for reopening the line.

However, while Haslingden Council had been initially relatively supportive of the H&DRPS in its aims to reopen the line for commuter trains, it was far less supportive of the new venture and a number of councillors were openly hostile and publicly critical of the society's efforts to reinstate train services on the truncated route for enthusiasts and tourists.

In September 1968 a local newspaper report carried the headline '*Rail Society's head-on crash with council*' and reported on a letter that had been sent to Haslingden Council by ELRPS chairman, Walter Baker, stating the society's intentions. In his letter to the council, Mr Baker said: "May I say it has never been the intention of the society to override the aims of any local authority. We too are public spirited, and far from the hoodlum crowd that we are considered. On the contrary, members consist of architects, surveyors, clergymen, chemists and students, to name but a few, who reside in many places, such as Woking, Tunbridge Wells, Cambridge, Sheffield, Manchester and the whole of the North West. And they are ever mindful of their duties to the local populace. The intention is to be helpful at all times.

"The consensus of opinion is that we definitely have something to offer, and in this connection would prefer to add a little gaiety, colour and charm to both the Haslingden and Helmshore end of the township, as opposed to creating difficulties."

The council had a number of concerns about the potential reopening of the line and the potential liabilities that could occur should the scheme fail, with numerous viaducts on the line, along with the busy level crossing at Helmshore station. In the same article Coun Donald Butterworth was quoted as saying: "I don't think there has been any misunderstanding. There has been correspondence with our MP, the Ministry of Transport, and British Rail, and in one of the letters it says it is the duty of the local authority to make the most advantageous use of the land in the public interest, and this is what we are trying to do. I am very worried about the responsibilities in this, as they are very great on this stretch of line, and it is very important that the people who get hold of this are able to handle those responsibilities."

Another councillor for Haslingden Council, Ervin Russell, was more direct in his criticism for the preservationists, stating: "In my opinion they are crack pots and they just want to play at being railwaymen. They are playing like a lot of children and this is a lot of nonsense. They are interfering with progress in the town. I hear they are collecting trading stamps to help save the station – god knows how many stamps they will need. They are a pack of loonies and in my opinion a blithering nuisance."

Haslingden Council feared the preservationists would not be able to

The trains have gone and the preservationists have moved to Bury, leaving Helmshore station to return to nature. The station is pictured in 1975, with the buildings still intact, although the level crossing gates and footbridge have been removed. There were a couple of attempts to restore the station buildings as private houses, but these were subsequently demolished and a pair of bungalows were built across the trackbed where the platforms and buildings had been located. A new housing estate has since been built on the former goods yard and the rest of the station site. FRED COLLINGE

maintain the structures on the line, leaving them with the financial liability. They were also opposed to the prospect of road traffic being held up while the level crossing gates were opened to allow trains to cross Helmshore Road, even though any level of service operated by the preservationists would be considerably less than they had been during BR operations.

While discussions about the future of the line continued, volunteers had been working hard tidying up the disused Helmshore station site, which they were now renting from BR. In August 1969 the society opened a museum in one of the station waiting rooms. The work required to upgrade the former waiting room for its new function included re-plastering the walls, renewing the ceiling and replacing a number of windows that had been damaged by vandals. The new museum was used to display the society's growing collection of railway memorabilia,

most of which came from the local area, including various station signs, locomotive number plates, books, maps, photographs and other items of railway equipment.

BUILDING MOMENTUM

The society was keen to promote its activities among visitors and the local community. In 1970 it organised a couple of high-profile open days at the station to allow visitors to see the exhibits the society had amassed and to learn more about the proposed reopening project. An open day, organised during the Easter weekend in 1970, attracted more than 1200 visitors despite the event being plagued by poor weather. Speaking to the local press, a society spokesman commented: "Despite the weather we feel the open day was very successful and we are very grateful to everyone who helped to make it a success. It has boosted our funds towards the reopening of the railway from Haslingden Grane Road to Stubbins Junction, and we intend to organise more similar events."

The biggest open day organised by the ELR during its time at Helmshore took place during the August bank holiday weekend in 1970. The event featured visiting LMS Stanier 4-6-0 5MT No. 44806, which had been purchased by a member of the society, Kenneth Aldcroft, and a BR Class 25 diesel locomotive, with both moving around the station site throughout the weekend. In addition to the visiting locomotives, the open weekend also featured various fairground rides, miniature train rides and offered a chance for local residents and enthusiasts to see what the ELRPS wanted to do.

More than 3500 visitors attended throughout the weekend, although due to a lack of covered accommodation the visiting 'Black 5' (which was actually painted in an unauthentic but attractive

On March 24, 1989, the signal box at Helmshore stands awaiting its fate, still in reasonable condition more than 22 years since it had last been used to control train movements around the station. Shortly after this picture was taken it was demolished to allow a new one-bedroom house to be built in its place. DAVID A INGHAM

BR lined green livery at the time) was hauled away following the event and subsequently moved to a new home on the Lakeside and Haverthwaite Railway.

In late 1970, BR once again proposed the closure of the Bury to Rawtenstall line. With rolling stock for Helmshore capable of being delivered by rail using the Bury to Rawtenstall route, it was essential that this line was not lost and society officials started to investigate the possibility of also preserving the Bury to Rawtenstall line, even though negotiations with BR over the purchase of the line to Haslingden Grane Road were proving to be complicated and difficult.

In spring 1971 the realisation that reopening the Stubbins Junction to Haslingden line was not going to succeed finally came when BR announced that it wanted £28,000 for the line and the station premises at Helmshore – a huge sum at the time for such an organisation to raise. BR also refused to let the society purchase the line by staged instalments over a number of years, even though this method of purchase had been agreed to other preservation schemes elsewhere in the country when they had been negotiating to purchase their routes. This unrealistic demand forced the society to re-evaluate its plans and at an extraordinary general meeting members decided to look at other sites away from Helmshore for the establishment of a railway centre.

As if to reinforce the fact that efforts to reopen the Stubbins to Haslingden route were lost, BR had begun the task of lifting the redundant track along the line, leaving the society's rolling stock isolated on a few short lengths of track in the station goods yard at Helmshore. Reinstating the trackwork on the line would greatly add to the cost of reopening the line and the dream of reopening the line was over.

TIME TO SAY GOODBYE
Over the following months the society looked at a number of sites around the area before settling on the former East

The simple plaque attached to the surviving level crossing gate post, denoting the opening and closing dates of the railway through Helmshore. The survival of the gate post and concrete level crossing lamp post is remarkable some 52 years after the line closed. ANDY COWARD

Lancashire Railway Goods Warehouse at Castlecroft in Bury, which had been used as a depot for contractors working on the construction of a new ring-road around the town. This site was also ideally situated, as it too was alongside the Bury to Rawtenstall line, which was by that stage due to lose its passenger service within months.

Bury Council agreed to grant a 12 month lease to the preservationists. During the first half of 1972 the ELRPS relocated its collection of exhibits and rolling stock from Helmshore to its new home and the keys to Helmshore station were returned to BR on June 21, 1972.

And so Helmshore was left to join the countless other abandoned railway stations around the country that were decaying and gradually returning to nature. After a number of years in increasingly derelict condition and with a couple of failed restoration attempts behind them, the main station buildings at Helmshore were demolished and a pair of bungalows were built on the former station site. Remarkably, the wooden goods shed survived until 2002, when it too was demolished and a new housing estate was built in the former goods yard and part of the former station area.

On the Bury side of the level crossing, the station master's house was bought as a private residence and has been extended and developed into a luxury home. The signalbox opposite the

stationmaster's house remained in semi-derelict condition, being used as a small workshop, before it was demolished in 1989. A brand new one-bedroom home was built in stone on the footprint of the signalbox and to a similar design, providing an attractive reminder of where the railway once ran through the village. One of the wooden level crossing gate posts survives with a plaque attached to it detailing the history of the site and a concrete lamp post which once lit the level crossing is now used to display hanging baskets.

The ELR's move to Bury in 1972 proved to be transformative for the railway, as the local authorities of Bury and Rossendale, along with the now-defunct Greater Manchester Council, and more recently Rochdale Council, all recognised the economic and tourism benefit of having a heritage railway on their doorstep. Rather than standing in the way of the preservationists, the councils entered into a partnership with them to ensure that the railway between Bury and Rawtenstall, and then Bury to Heywood, could be successfully reopened as a viable and important part of the local community and economy.

The support from Bury Council was a positive contrast to the experience of the ELR with the local council responsible for Helmshore, Haslingden Council (ironically, now part of ELR Trust partner Rossendale Council), who saw the preservationists as an inconvenient bunch of amateurs wanting to play trains and offered little, if any, support to their aims and ambitions.

Quite how the present-day ELR would have differed from the current operation had they successfully reopened the Stubbins to Haslingden Grane Road line is open for conjecture, but it probably would have been a very different heritage line to that which has been established a few miles away from Helmshore. Helmshore station and the Stubbins to Accrington line may now be long gone from the railway map, but their place in the history of the ELRPS will never be forgotten.

In 1990, a new one-bedroom home was built on the footprint of the former signalbox to a sympathetic design by local stonemason Allan Dunn. The attractive small home is pictured on May 29, 2018. ANDY COWARD

Looking across the former level crossing towards Bury on May 29, 2018, with the new signalbox house and station master's house on either side of the former trackbed. The station platforms were located behind the photographer, but the site is now occupied by a pair of bungalows, while a modern housing estate occupies the former goods yard and the remainder of the station site. ANDY COWARD

The station master's house at Helmshore survives and has been extended significantly from how it was in BR days, to provide a luxury house. ANDY COWARD

The Long Wait

After the disappointment of losing the fight to reopen the Stubbins Junction to Haslingden route, the ELRPS volunteers brushed themselves off and set about seeking a new home, before settling on the former East Lancashire Railway Goods Warehouse at Castlecroft, Bury. With an eye on the possibility of reopening the Bury to Rawtenstall line to passenger services, the volunteers set up a transport museum while waiting for their chance.

With the society and its members having accepted the scheme to reopen the Stubbins Junction to Haslingden line was a lost cause, they spent the first half of 1972 relocating their collection from Helmshore to Castlecroft Goods Warehouse at Bury, following visits to a number of possible new home bases over the past few months. The building at Castlecroft was in a reasonable, if rather run-down condition, having been used by contractors building the adjacent Peel Way dual carriageway.

However, for the ELRPS their new home had bags of potential and opportunities. The building would comfortably accommodate the society's small collection of locomotives and rolling stock, with the yard to the front of a suitable size for outside exhibitions and special events. The move to Bury brought a new optimism to the volunteers who were now setting up a transport museum in the Goods Warehouse, while keeping an eye on the Bury to Rawtenstall line which was tantalisingly visible from the bottom of the yard. By the time the ELRPS was moving into its new home the closure of the Bury to Rawtenstall line to passenger services had already been announced, with the last day of services scheduled to run on June 3, 1972.

However, while BR had achieved its objectives of closing the line to passengers, there was no immediate prospect the coal trains would be withdrawn, so the line would remain an operational part of the BR network. The establishment of a coal depot in the goods yard at Rawtenstall had been part of the rationale that led to the town becoming the new terminus of the line when the section to Bacup closed in December 1966.

To avoid having to use the busy Bury to Manchester commuter line to access the Rawtenstall line, the coal trains travelled along part of the former Rochdale to Bolton line, which itself had closed to passengers in October 1970, between Castleton, Heywood and Bury. Coal trains then travelled through the remains of the closed Bury Knowsley Street station, before negotiating the sharp curve into Bury Bolton Street and then on to Rawtenstall.

The loss of passenger services on the Bury to Rawtenstall line gave

Bury Bolton Street station was closed by BR on March 14, 1980, with services transferred to Bury Interchange the following Monday. Following the closure of the Bury to Rawtenstall line to passengers in June 1972, the only passenger services to operate from the station had been the electric trains to Manchester Victoria. Shortly before closure 504458 departs from Platform 3 with a service to Manchester. DAVID A INGHAM

the ELRPS an immediate aim. While busily establishing the new Bury Transport Museum at Castlecroft Goods Warehouse, it was clear that if the preservationists were going to achieve their original aims of operating a heritage railway service, then the Bury to Rawtenstall line was the obvious choice for their attentions.

The ELR approached BR about operating passenger services on the line when coal trains were not running at the weekends. However, BR would not entertain any ELR-operated trains running on the Bury to Rawtenstall line while BR still owned it and it was made clear to the preservationists that their request would not be permitted.

The station layout at Bury Bolton Street was remodelled shortly after the loss of passenger services to Rawtenstall, with coal trains using the track through the former Platform 2, while the trains for Manchester Victoria used the island Platforms 3 and 4, with buffer stops installed at the north end of the station adjacent to the station staircases on both sides of the island platform.

With no immediate prospect of being able to operate trains, the ELRPS continued to develop its museum, including the addition of a number of road vehicles. A cafe, shop and small exhibits museum were set up inside the building and the railway's impressive

collection of railway signs and other railwayana was displayed on the walls for visitors to admire. After months of preparation and hard work by the volunteers, Bury Transport Museum was officially opened on August 26, 1972.

FOSTERING RELATIONS

Even in those early days at Bury, the ELRPS quickly noticed a dramatic contrast in the attitudes of the local council, which owned the building and land they were occupying. Bury Council had initially agreed a 12-month lease on the Castlecroft site when the society approached the council about the possibility of using the site and councillors were interested in what the preservationists were trying to do.

Having not previously enjoyed the best of relations with Haslingden Council when based at Helmshore, the positive attitude from Bury Council was a breath of fresh air and the relationship with the supporting local councils has remained extremely positive and supportive ever since.

One problem the society sought to resolve soon after moving to Bury was the need to secure land for a short running line which could be linked to the museum yard. The intention was that the new line could be used for testing locomotives and, subject to agreement from BR, they also hoped to operate passenger train rides along the short

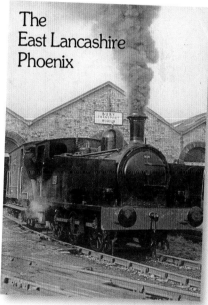

The East Lancashire Phoenix brochure.

section of line.

A suitable section of land was identified alongside the Bury to Rawtenstall line, which had formerly been occupied by railway tracks towards the site of Tottington Junction, where the long-closed branch line to Holcombe Brook diverged from the Bury to Bacup line. The section of land was just over a quarter of a mile in length and the society took out a lease from BR and began amassing rails and sleepers to

Ex-Burnley Gas Works Andrew Barclay 0-4-0T North Western Gas Board No. 1 was one of the mainstays of steam operations during the early days of Bury Transport Museum. The locomotive is displayed in the museum yard during 1978. PETER M DUNCAN

The passenger running line that never was. NWGB No. 1 departs with a train up the Quarter Mile siding during 1979. Despite plans by the ELRPS to run passenger trains on the short demonstration line, BR would not sanction this and it was destined to never carry passengers. PETER M DUNCAN

40115 heads away from Bury Bolton Street towards Heywood following the successful delivery of D832 and D1041 to Bury Transport Museum on February 11, 1981. Beyond the second bridge was the site of Bury Knowsley Street station and this location was subsequently filled in with earth after closure. PETER M DUNCAN

Ex-Manchester Ship Canal Hudswell Clarke 0-6-0T No. 70 stands inside Bury Transport Museum during the late 1970s. The building was used to display various road and rail vehicles, along with an extensive collection of railwayana. PETER M DUNCAN

allow track to be re-laid on what would become known as the Quarter Mile.

It would be more than two years before the whole Quarter Mile was reinstated, but subsequent discussions with BR over the possible operation of passenger services on the short demonstration line came to nothing, with the land owner refusing to allow any passenger operations over the track while the land belonged to them.

The Quarter Mile was used for demonstration purposes at open days and special events, but BR's refusal to allow passenger services to run on the line meant it was destined to never carry a passenger on it and the short wooden platform that had been constructed to allow passengers to join Quarter Mile trains became simply a viewing point.

Having impressed its local authority landlords with its aims and ambitions, the society was given a further two-year lease on the Castlecroft site by Bury Council in early 1974. The Goods Warehouse was now in a much better condition than it had been when the ELRPS moved in and the council was happy that it had a tenant that wanted to become part of the local attractions around the town.

During those early days, the regular steaming days brought in larger numbers of visitors than a normal opening day with the funds generated by visitors reinvested into things the preservationists needed to further their aims. Fundraising was a crucial aspect of the society, with raffles, newspaper collections and various other initiatives carried out to bring in much-needed additional funds.

A FUTURE FOR BOLTON STREET?

Each month a steaming day was organised with visitors permitted on to the locomotive footplate for a short ride in the museum yard. However, an incident on another heritage railway in 1976 saw the Railway Inspectorate introduce a ban on footplate rides for members of the public. This development saw a drop in the number of visitors attending the steaming days, which was not helped by the unwillingness of BR to allow the ELR to run passenger trips along the Quarter Mile.

At the end of October 1976, ex-Manchester Ship Canal Hudswell Clarke 0-6-0T No. 32 was renamed *Gothenburg* in a ceremony at the museum. The

locomotive had carried the name prior to the start of the First World War, but the nameplates were removed by the MSC at the start of the war and were not returned afterwards. The locomotive had been repainted into lined green, with the paint and materials supplied free of charge by Crown Paints.

In May 1978 volunteers joined a DMU which had been hired to take members and other passengers from Bury to the North Yorkshire Moors Railway. The DMU charter only generated a modest profit for the organisation but was done partly as a celebration of the society's 10th anniversary.

The following month, confirmation came through that a new bus and rail interchange was to be built in Bury, spelling the end of Bury Bolton Street as the only surviving passenger rail services to Manchester Victoria would be transferred to the new station. The new interchange would be located on the other side of Bury town centre, alongside Kay Gardens on the site of what had been the market hall, prior to it being destroyed by fire several years beforehand.

The route of the new line would diverge from its existing route at Bury Loco Junction and travel along a disused section of trackbed, which once directly linked Bury Loco Junction with the Bolton to Rochdale line, before cutting through part of the former Bury Knowsley Street station and terminating at low level below the new bus station. As the coal trains were still operating at the time, a flat crossing was installed to allow the coal services to cross the new passenger route out of the town.

In March 1980, work on the new bus and rail interchange was completed. The final trains from Bury Bolton Street operated on March 14, with work to slew trackwork on to a revised formation to the south of Bury Loco Junction carried out over the weekend, in time for the new station to come into use from Monday, March 17, 1980.

'The Rossendale Farewell' charter on February 14, 1981, was the first passenger train to traverse the Bury to Rawtenstall line since it had closed in June 1972 and was organised by a local enthusiast following the cessation of coal traffic on the line in December 1980. The train is pictured at Rawtenstall. DAVID A INGHAM

The East Lancashire Phoenix headboard.

RIGHT: 'The East Lancashire Phoenix' train stands in Platform 2 at Bury Bolton Street on March 27, 1982, ready to work a train to Rawtenstall. During the day three trains ran from Bury to Rawtenstall, carrying 1300 happy passengers along the line. PETER M DUNCAN

Prior to the closure of Bury Bolton Street, Bury Council entered into discussions with BR about the possibility of purchasing the station and sought to secure a lease on the station premises, pending a sale. Agreement to grant a temporary licence to Bury Council for the station premises came through in June 1980, with the preservationists given access to the now-closed station. The station would be crucial to the ELR's aim of operating passenger trains from Bury to Rawtenstall and neither the railway or Bury Council wanted to see the buildings demolished.

Having officially become caretakers of the building, the ELRPS worked hard to tidy up the station site, while also boarding up the unsecured platform-level buildings and the two staircases leading up from the platforms to the booking hall. The British Rail signage was quickly taken down from the front of the building and an East Lancashire Railway sign was put in its place. Information about the ELRPS and Bury Transport Museum was also prominently displayed in the windows of the station.

PROGRESS AT LAST!
Coal trains on the Bury to Rawtenstall line continued until December 1980, with the final train leaving Rawtenstall behind 40098 on December 5. The loss of the coal traffic now left the line completely redundant and BR now had effectively no use for the railway between Heywood and Rawtenstall, which had been retained purely for the Rawtenstall coal trains.

Although interest in reviving the Bury to Rawtenstall line by the ELR was gaining more support at the start of 1981, there were still many obstacles to overcome and absolutely no guarantees that the preservationists would succeed in their aims of returning passenger trains to Rawtenstall. The future of the Bury to Heywood line was very much

in doubt, with the preservationists concentrating their efforts on securing the Bury to Rawtenstall route.

Rossendale resident David Isherwood wanted to give people a chance to travel on the line for what could have been the final time and he chartered a special train from BR to run from Manchester Victoria to Rawtenstall, covering the whole section of the line from Castleton to Rawtenstall. Although the Standard Wagon Works was still active at Heywood, the line beyond Heywood was now officially out of use following the final coal train to Rawtenstall the previous December.

Almost nine years after the last passenger train had traversed the line, 'The Rossendale Farewell' tour ran on Saturday, February 14, 1981, and the train quickly sold out all 300 seats on the six-coach DMU. The charter was an ideal opportunity for the ELR to highlight its efforts to reopen the line, and an hour's stop-off at Bury was arranged during the tour to allow passengers a chance to visit Bury Transport Museum.

Three days previously, the ELR

had seen the delivery of its first ex-BR main line diesel locomotives, with Western Region diesel-hydraulics D832 *Onslaught* and D1041 *Western Prince* delivered by rail to Castlecroft, the two new arrivals being accommodated in a newly constructed three-road shed located at the bottom of the yard, alongside the Bury to Rawtenstall line.

The popularity and success of 'The Rossendale Farewell' in February 1981 had been observed closely by ELR officials and they subsequently approached BR about hiring a diesel multiple unit and operating a series of chartered trips along the line from Bury to Rawtenstall, in conjunction with the supporting local councils and Greater Manchester Council, to publicise their efforts to preserve the line.

BR agreed to the request and on March 27-28, 1982, the ELR held what was its biggest open weekend to date at Bury Transport Museum, with the highlight being three passenger trains from Bury to Rawtenstall on the Saturday, using an eight-coach DMU chartered from BR.

During the ELR Phoenix event weekend, ex-Manchester Ship Canal 0-6-0T No. 70, newly named as *Phoenix*, operates a brake van ride in the Bury Transport Museum yard. PETER M DUNCAN

Ex-Manchester Ship Canal Hudswell Clarke 0-6-0T No. 70 *Phoenix* operating a passenger shuttle between Bury Bolton Street and Buckley Wells on May 28, 1984, passing over the trackbed of the former Bolton to Rochdale line. The track on the Bolton line beyond Bury had been lifted shortly after closure in October 1970. DAVID A INGHAM

Speaking in the special East Lancashire Phoenix brochure produced to mark the occasion, Coun P Scott, the chairman of Greater Manchester Council's planning committee wrote: "Greater Manchester Council is an enthusiastic supporter of the plan to re-establish a railway service on the Bury to Rawtenstall line. We particularly welcome the opportunity given to us, on March 27, to run the three special excursion trains so that the general public can appreciate the beauties of the line in the Upper Irwell Valley, part of the Croal-Irwell Valley scheme. GMC, together with Rossendale Borough Council, is doing all in its power to obtain the line for public use, and to make sure that not only the steam enthusiasts, but also other members of the public, will be able to appreciate the beauties of this particularly scenic area. Additionally it is felt that the preservation of the railway will help the general development of tourism in the area, which our council believes, in turn, will be an important factor in creating jobs for the future."

The same weekend saw ex-Manchester Ship Canal 0-6-0T No. 70 officially named *Phoenix* to publicise the initiative, with the locomotive appearing in steam at the museum throughout the event. More than 2000 visitors were reported to have visited the museum over the course of what had been a very successful weekend, in addition to the 1300 people who had been lucky enough to travel on one of the special trains, and it had shown the potential that a preserved Bury to Rawtenstall train service could bring to the area.

THE HARD WORK BEGINS

Negotiations between the councils, ELR officials and BR had seen a commitment given to not lift the track from the Bury to Rawtenstall line, pending its purchase. During the final few months the ELRPS had been based at Helmshore, they had watched helplessly as BR staff tore up the double-track formation around them, and there was no intention of letting history repeat itself with the Bury to Rawtenstall line.

Throughout the next couple of years, more diesel and steam locomotives arrived on the railway, including the first ex-BR main line steam locomotives – which had been purchased from the famous scrapyard in Barry, South Wales – for long-term restoration to working order. A number of coaches were also purchased, as the railway geared up for the day when it would be able to operate its own train services.

It is no secret that much of the success behind the purchase of the line was due to grant funding. In spring 1984, the Department for the Environment awarded a Derelict Land Grant of £435,000 to Greater Manchester Council (which acted as the lead council on behalf of Bury Council) and Rossendale Council to fund the purchase of the line from BR. Although the process of buying the land would not be concluded quickly, it was now clear that the Bury to Rawtenstall line would be reopened as an operational railway.

For the May 1984 Transport Extravaganza, permission was sought from BR to operate a short steam-hauled shuttle service during the event from Bury Bolton Street station to Buckley Wells. The shuttle would consist of No. 70 *Phoenix*, a single passenger carriage and a brake van. BR agreed to the request subject to the vehicles passing an inspection, which they subsequently did. The event proved to be very successful, with a good turnout of visitors taking the advantage of a short ride to Buckley Wells behind a steam locomotive. However, shortly after the event BR had a change of heart and instructed the ELR that no further movements could take place around Bury Bolton Street while BR retained the ownership of the land.

The movement ban was subsequently lifted the following year, but only to allow certain approved locomotives to shunt the growing quantity of rolling stock around the site.

In 1984 the East Lancashire Railway Trust was established. The organisation was set up to manage the assets of the local authorities and representatives of the ELR operating company, the East Lancashire Light Railway Company Ltd, Rossendale Council and Greater Manchester Council formed the trustees of the new joint organisation. Bury Council and Lancashire County Council representatives were also invited to join the ELR Trust.

In early 1986, the Light Railway Order needed for the ELR to operate services was granted, but the purchase of the railway from BR had not yet been completed and was further complicated when GMC was abolished. GMC had been incredibly supportive of the railway and, thankfully, its powers in relation to the railway were transferred to the equally supportive Bury Council.

On May 22, 1985, BR Standard 4 2-6-4T No. 80097 is unloaded at Bury following its rescue from Woodhams scrapyard in Barry, South Wales. The locomotive had been bought by a consortium of ELRPS volunteers under the Bury Standard Four Group name. No. 80097 is expected to enter service on the ELR during 2018 following a 30 year restoration. PETER M DUNCAN

Another Derelict Land Grant was awarded during 1986 to Bury and Rossendale Councils, this time for £600,000. The money was provided to allow structures along the line to be refurbished, where necessary. This money would allow work on the upgrading of bridges and tunnels to take place as soon as the railway had been purchased from BR.

While some work was needed on the Bury to Ramsbottom section, it had been identified that three river bridges and one road bridge would need to be replaced with new structures between Ramsbottom and Rawtenstall and the money would allow their replacement.

In autumn 1986, all of the legal works had been completed and the Bury to Rawtenstall line was formally signed over from BR to the two local authorities, who would then lease the line to the East Lancashire Light Railway Co Ltd, which was the operating company of the ELRPS and would be the organisation granted the Light Railway Order to allow it to operate passenger services on the line.

After 18 years and countless setbacks, the ELRPS and its volunteers had finally achieved their ambition, but there was still a great deal of work to be done before passenger trains could return to the line.

SECURED FOR PRESERVATION

Due to the need for more major civil engineering on the Ramsbottom to Rawtenstall section, it was decided that the railway would be reopened in two stages, with Bury to Ramsbottom first with a proposed reopening date of June 6, 1987, announced. This would be followed by the Rawtenstall section around two years later, although this target proved to be somewhat optimistic and it did not reopen to passengers until April 1991.

On December 27, 1986, the first works train to operate along the line under ELR operation ventured out of Bury

Volunteers assemble on December 27, 1986, ready to take the first works train up the line from Bury to Summerseat, where the track was to be ballasted and packed. PETER M DUNCAN

towards Summerseat, where volunteers worked on ballasting and packing a section of track that was known to suffer from historic slippage and would need attention before regular trains could begin running.

The train then ventured further north and over the following weeks the trains got nearer to Ramsbottom, although the removal of a viaduct and its replacement by a new embankment immediately to the south of the station meant it would be a few more months before trains could enter the station platform.

Having only taken formal possession of the railway a few months beforehand there was a phenomenal amount of work left to do at many locations, but volunteers were assisted by a number of government Manpower Services teams, which were schemes designed to help the long-term unemployed gain new skills and get back into work.

A visit by the Railway Inspectorate in April 1986 resulted in the railway announcing that the reopening of the line to Ramsbottom had been put back by six weeks, with a new reopening

date set for July 25, 1987. The Inspector, Major Peter Olver, had been concerned about the large amount of work still to be completed at the time of his visit, although he believed that the extra time would allow the works to be finished.

While the new railway would be staffed and operated by the ELR, the reopening would not have been possible without the support of Bury and Rossendale Councils, along with Lancashire County Council and the erstwhile Greater Manchester Council. The successful purchase of the line and transfer from BR to the preservationists had been a real team effort from all parties and the councils could all see the potential benefits of having a preserved heritage railway running through their communities.

While it had been a long 15 years since they had arrived at Castlecroft, the volunteers of the ELRPS had finally achieved their aim of preserving a section of railway and very soon they would be running passenger trains of their own between Bury and Ramsbottom.

In April 1987, 40145 stands in the platform at Ramsbottom station while volunteers work on the installation of a run-round loop, in preparation for the reopening of the line three months later. THE LATE DAVE DYSON, COURTESY OF TIM GRIMSHAW

On a sunny day in early 1987, the Sentinel diesel shunter hauls a brake van over Brooksbottom Viaduct during a training run along the line to the limit of operations just before Ramsbottom station. PETER M DUNCAN

Open for business: the first five years

The East Lancashire Railway that reopened between Bury and Ramsbottom in July 1987 was a vastly different railway to that which can be seen today. However, during the first five years the railway underwent a startling transformation as it worked to extend the line towards Rawtenstall and adopted a big engine policy, which saw the industrial steam locomotives that were initially the mainstay of services relegated in favour of larger ex-British Railways locomotives.

With approval for the reopening between Bury and Ramsbottom granted by Her Majesty's Railway Inspector, Major Peter Olver, the preservationists who had spent the past 15 years at Bury patiently waiting to operate passenger services finalised plans for the reopening of the line.

In the lead up to the reopening, volunteers worked tirelessly on the preparations. The first train would be formed of six Mark 1 coaches and these would all be painted in matching British Railways maroon livery, with all finished to a very high standard. The 1987 locomotive fleet for the rejuvenated line would involve two steam locomotives, Hudswell Clarke ex-Manchester Ship Canal 0-6-0T No. 32 *Gothenburg* and RSH ex-Meaford Power Station 0-6-0T ELR No. 1, along with Class 40, 40145, and ex-Western Region diesel-hydraulic Class 42 'Warship', D832 *Onslaught*, managing diesel-hauled services.

Due to the poor condition of the platform buildings at Bury Bolton Street

1987 reopening timetable leaflet (left) and reopening information leaflet (right)

most were demolished, although the toilet block was refurbished and clad in yellow brick. The station was repainted and the shop, information office and booking office at street level were all prepared for their new roles.

At Summerseat the platform was cleared of vegetation and a basic bus stop-style waiting shelter was provided on the platform by the Miller Street entrance, while at Ramsbottom the surviving platform was refurbished, a run-round loop was laid, and a temporary portable building was installed containing a booking office, waiting room and toilets.

The new station building was rather basic, but would serve its purpose until a permanent station building could be constructed. The signalbox, which would not be required until the line to Rawtenstall was opened in the future, received a coat of paint on the Bridge Street side to smarten up its appearance.

On July 25, 1987, the reopening day finally arrived and as 11am approached the special VIP train pulled into Platform 3 at Bury Bolton Street, breaking a commemorative banner as it drew into the platform. The Irwell Forge Band played 'See the conquering hero come', which had reputedly been played

Just over 15 years since the last BR passenger train had run along the Bury to Rawtenstall line, the new preservation era begins, as ex-Manchester Ship Canal 0-6-0T No. 32 *Gothenburg* and RSH 0-6-0T ELR No. 1 pull into Platform 3 at Bury Bolton Street ready to break the celebratory reopening banner on Saturday, July 25, 1987. PETER M DUNCAN

EAST LANCASHIRE RAILWAY RE-OPENING 25TH JULY 1987 FIRST TRAIN FROM BURY

For the 1987 season, steam services were operated by ex-Manchester Ship Canal 0-6-0T No. 32 *Gothenburg* and RSH 0-6-0T ELR No. 1, while diesel services were hauled by D832 *Onslaught* and 40145. ELR No. 1 emerges from Nuttall tunnel with a Bury to Ramsbottom service in August 1987. THE LATE MALCOLM ORRETT, COURTESY PETER M DUNCAN

With the former Hoyles Cotton Mill and canteen in the background, which had since been converted into luxury apartments and The Waterside pub, RSH ELR No. 1 hauls a Bury to Ramsbottom service over Brooksbottom Viaduct at Summerseat on August 2, 1987. NEIL HARVEY

when the original ELR route first opened in September 1846 and at 11am the train was ceremoniously waved out of the station by Bury Mayor, Coun Jackie Adler. Upon arrival at Ramsbottom crowds of onlookers had gathered to witness the arrival of the first passenger train to be operated by the ELR.

Following a successful first day, a special evening train was operated for ELRPS volunteers, where they travelled to Summerseat for an evening reception and celebration event at The Waterside, which was a public house and restaurant located in what was the canteen building for the former Hoyles Cotton Mill, the mill itself having since been converted into luxury apartments. The Waterside pub made national news headlines many years later, when it dramatically collapsed into the raging River Irwell below it during the Boxing Day storms of 2015, although by this stage it had been closed for a number of years.

Over the first four weeks of public trains, more than 10,000 passengers travelled on the trains, proving that the preservationists and supporters of the scheme had been vindicated in their efforts to reopen the line.

Another clear sign of the success of the new line was that it quickly became apparent that a number of local residents were using the train to get them into Bury to do their shopping. The time taken by the train to reach Bury was similar to the bus, but the railway's fares were cheaper than the bus company and a few weeks after the line was reopened, the local bus operator reduced its fares between Ramsbottom and Bury to compete with the trains. While it was always envisaged that the majority of users of the line would be tourists, families and enthusiasts, the railway had always been keen to be a part of the community it served. The willingness of local residents to use the train as a viable alternative to the bus so soon after services on the line were launched was a welcome development.

Another noticeable improvement following the reopening was that a

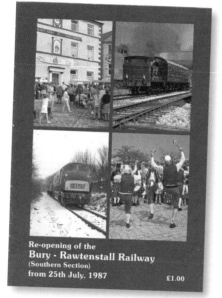

Bury to Ramsbottom Reopening 1987 Souvenir Guide.

number of new businesses were opening in Ramsbottom. The town centre of Ramsbottom had for a number of years presented a rather run-down appearance with numerous empty shop units, but the arrival of the trains had brought a ready supply of tourists and visitors into the town for the first time in many years. Local entrepreneurs realised that the visitors coming to the town by train would have money to spend, leading to a

spike in the number of new shops being opened around the town.

Bury Council had recognised the potential boost to the local economy the railway could bring, but the speed with which Ramsbottom was becoming a popular place for new local businesses was an early and pleasing success for the local authority that had backed the preservation scheme since it first arrived in Bury back in 1972.

A SUCCESSFUL FIRST SEASON

On November 7, 1987, the railway welcomed the first incoming railtour from the BR network when the Southern Electric Group operated its 'East Lancashire Executive' tour from London Euston to Ramsbottom. The train had been hauled from London to Warrington by 86101, before 47452 took over and hauled the train to Bury.

Upon arrival at Bury the Class 47 was removed from the train and D832 *Onslaught* and 40145 then top-and-tailed the 10-coach train through to Ramsbottom and back, before 47452 was once again put in charge to begin the return journey from Bury to London Euston. This would be the first of several railtours to operate on and off the ELR during its formative years.

In December 1987, the ELR operated its first season of Santa Special trains

Ex-BR Western Region Class 42 diesel-hydraulic D832 *Onslaught* works a Ramsbottom to Bury service, approaching Nuttall Tunnel shortly after departing from Ramsbottom on October 24, 1987. TERRY EYRES

Ex-Manchester Ship Canal 0-6-0T No. 32 *Gothenburg* departs from Summerseat with a Bury to Ramsbottom service in March 1988. THE LATE DAVE DYSON, COURTESY OF TIM GRIMSHAW

1988 Diesel Weekend flyer.

along the Bury to Ramsbottom line with more than 8000 passengers carried on the trains during December, bringing down the curtain on a very successful first season. Since reopening at the end of July, more than 35,000 passengers had travelled on the rejuvenated ELR up to the end of 1987.

The 1988 season for the ELR did not start until March with the railway closed in January and February, although in subsequent years the ELR has remained open every weekend.

However, the ELRPS volunteers had cause for celebration when the railway won the 1987 Association of Railway Preservation Societies' Annual Award in recognition of the efforts made by the ELRPS to reopen the line between Bury and Ramsbottom. The award was presented to volunteers at the end of

January 1988 to coincide with the ARPS annual general meeting which was taking place in nearby Manchester.

Two new steam locomotives entered service on the ELR during the 1988 season, relieving some pressure on No. 32 *Gothenburg* and ELR No. 1, which had been the mainstay of services throughout the 1987 operating season. Restoration work was completed on ex-Bickershaw Colliery Hunslet Austerity 0-6-0ST No. 8, which was named *Sir Robert Peel* in recognition of the former British Prime Minister and founder of the modern police force, who was born in Bury. The locomotive, painted in an attractive lined maroon colour scheme, was available for service from the start of the 1988 operating season in March.

The second steam locomotive to debut on the line in 1988 was ex-LMS

3F 'Jinty' 0-6-0T No. 7298 which moved to the line in April from the Llangollen Railway on a two-year hire deal. This was the first ex-British Railways steam locomotive to see use on the reopened ELR line.

DIESEL WEEKEND LAUNCHED

On October 1-2, 1988, the railway held its first ever diesel weekend with seven locomotives in use throughout the weekend, five of them making their passenger debuts on ELR services. The event saw the diesel fleet bolstered with the return to service of Class 14 D9531, Class 24 D5054, Class 25 25909 and Class 35 D7076, along with North British shunting locomotive D2767. The event proved very popular with services operating out of Platform 2 at Bury, while the locomotives not in use on

In May 1989, the ELR, together with Bury and Rossendale Councils, launched a new tourism initiative for the attractions that are closely located to the Bury to Rawtenstall line. Derek Foster's LMS 3F 'Jinty' 0-6-0T No. 7298 runs round its train at Bury Bolton Street, pictured emerging from Bury EL Tunnel carrying the 'Irwell Valley Express' headboard on May 1, 1989. THE LATE DAVE DYSON, COURTESY OF TIM GRIMSHAW

In October 1989, the immaculately restored ex-Western Region Class 35 'Hymek' diesel-hydraulic D7076 stands at Ramsbottom, ready to work its train back to Bury. This locomotive had been restored at Bury from scrap condition over a five-year period, with it returning to service in October 1988. THE LATE DAVE DYSON, COURTESY OF TIM GRIMSHAW

service trains were displayed on Platform 3 for photographers and enthusiasts.

With work on restoring the section of line between Ramsbottom and Rawtenstall advancing, a lot of work was required at Ramsbottom station to prepare it for its forthcoming role as a passing place for services on the extended railway. One of the more noticeable additions to the station during 1988 was a new 2500-gallon capacity water tower, which had been fabricated by ELR volunteers.

Track alterations would need to be made at the station, as a second platform was also to be constructed, which would be linked by a footbridge recovered from Dinting station. Additionally the signalbox and level crossing would need to be completely recommissioned and a full signalling installation would allow trains to safely pass through the station.

Towards the end of the year, work began on the construction of a new £100,000 station building, which had been designed by architect Steven Lever from Bury Council in the style of the original East Lancashire Railway station buildings, complete with arched windows and main entrance doors.

The new station would contain a booking hall, ticket office, gift shop, waiting room and toilet facilities and while it would be much smaller than the buildings that had once adorned Ramsbottom station, it would be a marked improvement on the temporary station building that had been provided since the line had reopened.

Work on the new station building was completed in summer 1989, when the temporary building was taken out of use and moved to Rawtenstall to serve the same purpose.

The ELR made one of the most important decisions that would be made about its future in 1989. Transport

Over the weekend of October 28-29, 1989, members of the Territorial Army joined ELR volunteers to reinstate the final missing section of trackwork after repairs to a damaged culvert, as part of a training exercise. The works train is pictured unloading rails and materials ahead of reinstating the missing link at the site of the former Ewood Bridge station on October 28, 1989. THE LATE DAVE DYSON, COURTESY OF TIM GRIMSHAW

planners in Manchester had been championing the development of a modern light rail system for the city, with railway lines converted for use by light rail vehicles, which would then run on-street through the city in much the way of continental tramways.

One of the railway lines that had been identified for the first phase of the system, to be known as Metrolink, was the Bury to Manchester line. Operating with a unique and rather outdated electrification system and an increasingly elderly train fleet, the line would require significant investment if it remained part of the BR network, so the chance to convert it to become part of the Metrolink system would effectively place the line into private operation.

However, the Bury to Manchester line also provided a main line link between

BR and the ELR, with the line being used to bring items of rolling stock and various railtours on and off the railway from the national network.

If the Bury to Manchester line was to be converted into part of the new Metrolink system, then the ELR would potentially become land-locked, with rolling stock having to be delivered and removed by road transport.

The answer to the problem was to investigate the possibility of reinstating one of the other railway lines that had once served Bury prior to the closures implemented following the publication of the Beeching report. The easiest section to restore would be the line between Bury and Heywood, which was closed to passengers as part of the Bolton to Rochdale line in October 1970, but had been in use regularly until

On November 5, 1989, ex-North Western Gas Board Andrew Barclay 0-4-0T No. 1 crosses over Townsend Fold level crossing with a works train to Rawtenstall, with ex-Bickershaw Colliery Hunslet Austerity 0-6-0ST No. 8 *Sir Robert Peel* providing assistance behind the brake vans. THE LATE DAVE DYSON, COURTESY OF TIM GRIMSHAW

Ex-BR Standard 4, 4-6-0 No. 75078 stands at Rawtenstall station, having carried out a gauging run along the soon-to-be-opened line on November 4, 1990, almost a year to the day after the first works train had operated through to the terminus. THE LATE DAVE DYSON, COURTESY OF TIM GRIMSHAW

An absolutely stunning composition as BR Standard 4, 4-6-0 No. 75078 visiting from the Keighley and Worth Valley Railway, leads ELR resident Standard 4 No. 76079 over Brooksbottom Viaduct in Summerseat on November 4, 1990. No. 75078 had become the first ex-BR steam locomotive to operate through to Rawtenstall on test earlier in the day. MIKE TAYLOR

December 1980 by the coal services travelling through to Rawtenstall.

The section between Heywood and Castleton was still in use for trains coming to and from the Standard Wagon Works at Heywood, with the line joining the Manchester to Leeds Calder Valley Line at Castleton Junction.

MAINTAINING CONNECTIONS

However, between Bury and Heywood the line had not seen a train on it since the passage of the DMUs used on the ELR Phoenix tours in March 1982 and there would be several engineering challenges to overcome before trains could be returned to the route.

While most of the track was still in place, it was in poor condition and large sections of it had been cut up by scrap metal thieves.

BR had also removed a bridge over Pilsworth Road at Broadfield after the line had been taken out of use which would need to be replaced, while at Bury the flat rail crossing on the site of the former Bury Knowsley Street station had been removed and thousands of tonnes of earth had been used to fill in the section of curved trackbed between Bury Bolton Street and Bury Knowsley Street, which would all need to be excavated if the line was to be restored.

Reinstatement of the line between

Bury and Heywood would also need the support of Rochdale Council, which was consulted about the proposals and subsequently joined Bury and Rossendale Councils as partner organisations of the ELR through the supporting ELR Trust.

Rochdale Council joined Bury Council in backing the proposals in December 1989, paving the way for the line to be restored, subject to the necessary funding being secured.

In April 1989 the railway played host to Minister for Tourism, John Lee MP, where the Minister was shown presentations about the railway and its plans for the future. The visit allowed officials to campaign for grant funding to allow the completion of the Ramsbottom and Rawtenstall line, as well as for the possible reinstatement of the Bury to Heywood line.

It was estimated in 1989 that the cost of restoring the Heywood section of line would be in excess of £1 million and further representations were also subsequently made to the European Economic Community for grant aid funding.

A significant visitor to the railway in May 1989 was former Minister of Transport, Barbara Castle, who had originally sanctioned the closure of much of the Bury and Rossendale rail network in the 1960s and early 1970s. By this time Mrs Castle was a European MP and she was given a presentation about the railway as the ELR and its supporting councils campaigned for funding support to achieve their aims of restoring the Heywood line.

With work on the restoration of the Rawtenstall section taking longer than had originally been anticipated, the ELR was forced to postpone the opening date of the railway, which it had already moved from May 1989 to August 1989. This time officials said they were aiming to reopen the four-mile extension of the line in time for Easter 1990, although this date too eventually proved to be too

In 1989, a new station building was built at Ramsbottom, based on original ELR station designs, to replace the original station which was demolished in 1970. The station has since had a canopy added on the platform side, but the construction of a new station building was the start of a comprehensive expansion of the station ready for the opening of the line through to Rawtenstall. DAVID A INGHAM

The arrival of BR Standard 4 2-6-0 No. 76079 in August 1989 created a lot of interest and brought the first ex-BR tender locomotive to the ELR. The popular locomotive remained on the railway until moving to the Llangollen Railway in early 1992. No. 76079 heads through Burrs Cutting on a snowy February 10, 1991. TERRY EYRES

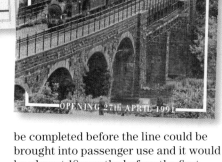

Recreating the scene from four years earlier, ex-Manchester Ship Canal 0-6-0T No. 32 *Gothenburg* and RSH 0-6-0T ELR No. 1 pull into Platform 3 at Bury Bolton Street, breaking a banner as the pair prepare to haul the inaugural VIP train from Bury to Rawtenstall on April 27, 1991, just under 19 years after passenger services to Rawtenstall ended. MIKE TAYLOR

CLOCKWISE: Ramsbottom to Rawtenstall 1991 reopening train pass, souvenir guide and reopening VIP ticket.

optimistic. Another welcome addition to the steam fleet arrived on the line in August 1989 in the shape of British Railways Standard 4, 2-6-0 No. 76079, which had been newly restored from scrap condition by Derek Foster, the owner of LMS 3F No. 7298 which was also based on the line. This was the first tender steam locomotive to operate on the preserved ELR and it operated on the line generally one weekend a month, along with various special events.

Restoration of the Ramsbottom to Rawtenstall line was always going to be the hardest section of the route to reinstate, with three river bridges and one road bridge to be replaced with new structures, along with the repairs to a damaged culvert at the site of the former Ewood Bridge and Edenfield station, and the complete rebuilding of Rawtenstall station platforms on a level graded trackbed.

With all the new infrastructure in place, the final missing piece of trackwork was installed at Ewood Bridge over the weekend of October 28-29, 1989, with the assistance of the Territorial Army from 202 Field Squadron, who reinstated the missing section of track over a 36-hour period as part of a training exercise for the soldiers. An ELR works train was provided throughout the weekend, which was used for carrying materials to the worksite, as well as providing rest and refreshment facilities for the soldiers and railway volunteers working on the project.

With the full line from Bury to Rawtenstall now complete, the ELR decided to operate two steam-hauled works trains through to Rawtenstall on November 5, 1989. Having become the first steam locomotive to be delivered to the railway, the honour of hauling the first train fell on ex-Burnley Gas Works Andrew Barclay 0-4-0ST No. 1, which had been part of the ELR collection since the preservationists had been based at Helmshore.

RETURN TO RAWTENSTALL

The first train worked through to Rawtenstall early in the morning, with ex-Manchester Ship Canal 0-6-0T No. 32 *Gothenburg* assisting the smaller locomotive. The arrival of the train was greeted by crowds of well-wishers and local politicians who came to witness the historic return of trains to the town. Later in the day No. 1 returned to Rawtenstall on a second trip, this time with Hunslet Austerity 0-6-0ST ELR No. 8 *Sir Robert Peel* lending a hand in the proceedings.

Although the arrival of the first train was a significant moment for the ELR, there was still a lot of work to

be completed before the line could be brought into passenger use and it would be almost 18 months before the first passenger train arrived in the town.

Over the Christmas break in 1989, further evidence of the transformation of Ramsbottom station was witnessed with the installation of an LMS lattice steel footbridge which would link the existing platform with a new second platform that was under construction. The structure had previously been located at Dinting station in Derbyshire and was placed roughly where the former footbridge had been during the BR reign on the station, prior to it being dismantled in 1970.

While plans were progressing well with regards to restoring the derelict Bury to Heywood line, an unwelcome development came when BR announced that incoming passenger charter trains on to the ELR would have to cease as work was to get under way on a new Metrolink depot complex on the site of Queens Road Carriage Sidings.

The signalling that allowed passenger trains to access the Bury to Manchester line at Queens Road Junction would be disconnected while the work was being

Class 24, D5054 hauls its train of BR carmine and cream coaches over Rawtenstall West Level Crossing in May 1991, shortly after the line through to Rawtenstall had been brought into use. THE LATE DAVE DYSON, COURTESY OF TIM GRIMSHAW

A timeless scene, as newly restored LMS 4F 0-6-0 No. 4422 works a train of carmine and cream Mark 1 coaches over Brooksbottom Viaduct in an undated view from summer 1992. THE LATE DAVE DYSON, COURTESY OF TIM GRIMSHAW

The new station building at Rawtenstall was opened in April 1992, with a replica clock tower dominating the new structure. The building was constructed in an 'L' shape, covering the former trackbed, which once took the railway on towards Bacup. Too much redevelopment work had been done beyond Rawtenstall to allow any more of the former line to be restored. THE LATE MALCOLM ORRETT, COURTESY OF PETER M DUNCAN

carried out, although the movement of locomotives and rolling stock on to the railway could still take place. The ELR knew that the incoming charters would be affected by the Metrolink works, but they hadn't anticipated it being so soon, with BR services on the line not expected to cease until the latter half of 1991.

While the ELR had loaned some of its diesel locomotives to other railways for special events and hire, a good relationship between the railway and the neighbouring Keighley and Worth Valley Railway (KWVR) saw US-built ex-Southern Region 0-6-0T steam locomotive No. 30072 arrive on the railway in April for a four-month hire.

This was the first of three KWVR-based steam locomotives to visit the ELR over the following months, with BR Standard 4 4-6-0 No. 75078 arriving on the railway in October 1990 for another four-month visit, to assist with Santa

Special trains and for steam events taking place at the end of January and February 1991. The third KWVR visitor was former US Transportation Corps S160 2-8-0 No. 5820, which spent two months on the railway in early 1992.

Almost a year to the day since the first works train had ventured to Rawtenstall, steam returned to the town again. While the ELR had originally hoped to have completed the extension in time to open it during 1990 this had not proved possible due to the amount of outstanding works to be completed.

However, on November 4, 1990, visiting BR Standard 4, 4-6-0 No. 75078 became the first ex-BR steam locomotive to travel through to the northern terminus of the line as part of a gauging run on the line. The station platforms were now nearly complete and the temporary station building that had previously been at Ramsbottom was now installed ready for the day when

it would be required for passengers at Rawtenstall.

Later the same day the opportunity was taken for No. 75078 to be paired with ELR resident No. 76079, providing a stunning BR Standard 4 double-header between Bury and Ramsbottom.

In early 1991, work was completed in the commissioning of the new track and signalling arrangements at Ramsbottom. The ELR's signal engineering department had worked hard over the past two years refurbishing the previously derelict signalbox at Ramsbottom, as well as installing semaphore signals around the station and recommissioning the level crossing.

With work now nearing completion on the extension to Rawtenstall it would not be long before trains continued on towards Rawtenstall, with Ramsbottom used as a passing point for a two-train service.

The arrival of Great Western 2-6-0 'Manor' No. 7828 *Odney Manor* to the line in early 1991 was part of the railway's preparations for running through to Rawtenstall, with regular two-train running meaning that the operational steam fleet needed to be bolstered. This was to be the start of a number of locomotive hire agreements between the ELR and private locomotive owners, with the railway keen to operate mainly ex-BR locomotives as part of its new big engine policy.

After several proposed opening dates for the Rawtenstall reopening had been postponed for various reasons, it was announced the four-mile northern extension from Ramsbottom to Rawtenstall would reopen on April 27, 1991.

As the opening date approached, volunteer familiarisation on the new section began, with locomotive crews and guards terminating their passenger trains at Ramsbottom and then continuing out of service up the line to Rawtenstall. Volunteers of the signalling operations department also got the chance to make themselves familiar

On January 10, 1992, BR Standard 4, 2-6-0 No. 76079 hauls a demonstration freight train through Burrs, as the sun rises for the day at the start of a photographic charter. BOB GREEN

with the operation of Ramsbottom signalbox, while the hand-operated level crossing and signalboxes at Townsend Fold and Rawtenstall West were also brought back into use.

As April 27, 1991, arrived the railway held a recreation of the original reopening train from 1987, when No. 32 *Gothenburg* and ELR No. 1 were charged with hauling the six-coach inaugural passenger service from Bury to Rawtenstall. The train was waved out of Bury by the town's Mayor, Coun Monty Adler, whose wife Jackie had presided over the original reopening ceremony almost four years earlier. The Mayor of Rossendale, Coun Phillip Dunne, unveiled a plaque at Ramsbottom station before the train continued on to Rawtenstall.

In June 1991, a derelict Class 45 'Peak' diesel locomotive, 45112, was delivered to Bury by rail for restoration. This would be the final locomotive delivered to the ELR using the Bury to Manchester line, which was closed by BR in August 1991 when the line was handed over to the operator of the new Metrolink light rail system. Until the Heywood line was reinstated there would be no further rail deliveries to and from the ELR, with all movements having to use low loaders by road.

NEW OPPORTUNITIES

The end of services on the Bury line by BR also saw the closure of the electric train depot at Bury in September, which the ELR and Bury Council were interested in acquiring for the railway's use. However, BR saw the land it owned as being commercially valuable and the price they wanted for the redundant depot and surrounding land was too high. Bury Council also carried out platform lengthening at Summerseat during 1991 to improve the unstaffed station, with a new wheelchair accessible entrance provided and platform lighting on the previously unlit station. The funds for the works were raised through the sale of Brooksbottom Goods Warehouse at Summerseat, which was to be converted into luxury apartments and housing.

By the end of the year, the opening to Rawtenstall had proved to be extremely popular, with an 85% increase in passengers travelling on the railway in 1991 compared to the previous year.

In 1992 planning approval was granted for the Heywood extension, paving the way for the route to be restored and reopened. While the Bury to Manchester line was closed for conversion works to be carried out for Metrolink the opportunity had been taken to build a new bridge over the Metrolink line, as the previous flat crossing at this location would not be suitable and ELR services would need to pass over the Metrolink system by

Visiting the ELR from its usual home on the Swanage Railway, ex-Southern Region 'Battle of Britain' 4-6-2 No. 34092 *257 Squadron* passes the Drum Works on the outskirts of Bury as it works a Bury to Rawtenstall service on September 5, 1992. TERRY EYRES

means of the new bridge.

The bridge, which became known as the ski-jump, featured steep gradients on either side due to the geography of the area. Earth which had been used to fill in bridges around Bury was also excavated in preparation for the tracks being replaced.

Additionally, several other bridges would need to be refurbished and a missing bridge at Pilsworth Road in Broadfield would need to be replaced. There was much work to be done, but the reinstatement of the line between Bury and Heywood would provide the ELR with a vital link to the main line rail network once more via the Calder Valley Line at Castleton Junction.

In February 1992 the ELR also played host to a visit by British Prime Minister, John Major, who was showing his support for Bury North MP, Alistair Burt, with Mr Major taking a short trip along the railway between Bury and

Burrs. During his visit he also drove one of the new Metrolink trams on part of the soon-to-be-reopened Bury to Manchester line.

Just 12 months after the line through to Rawtenstall had been reopened, a brand new station building was opened on April 16, 1992. Built to an ELR design, the new building was larger than the one provided at Ramsbottom and also featured a clock tower similar in design to that which had once adorned the Bury Bolton Street station entrance hall before being destroyed by fire in 1947.

In the five years since the railway had first reopened to Ramsbottom, much had been achieved by the ELRPS volunteers and the ELR was vastly different to how it had been in those early operating days. However, 1993 would be probably the most significant year for the railway and was the catalyst to the railway joining the premier league of UK heritage railways.

Large Great Western Railway Tank 2-8-0 No. 5224 approaches the site of Ewood Bridge and Edenfield station, heading towards Rawtenstall with a Santa shuttle service on a cold and frosty December 20, 1992. For many years the ELR operated Santa Special services between Bury and Ramsbottom, with a separate Ramsbottom to Rawtenstall shuttle service operating to link with the Santa trains on the southern section of the line. MIKE TAYLOR

GROWTH AND DEVELOPMENT

Since reopening in July 1987, the East Lancashire Railway has changed beyond all recognition. While the railway underwent significant changes during its formative operating years, 1993 proved to be something of a pivotal year for the ELR and since then the railway has gone from strength to strength.

Showing the task ahead, this is the view of Heywood station in March 1993, more than 22 years since a passenger train last called at the station. While the extension was re-connected at the end of 1993, it would be a further 10 years before the station reopened to passengers once more. MIKE TAYLOR

The ELR had forged a good working relationship with Pete Waterman, who had been a long-term supporter of the line and was part-owner, along with Sir William McAlpine, of legendary LNER A3 4-6-2 No. 4472 *Flying Scotsman*. Following the expiry of the locomotive's main line running certificate, it had been decided that *Flying Scotsman* would undertake a working tour of several heritage railways, prior to it being withdrawn for major overhaul.

The ELR was offered No. 4472 throughout the month of February 1993, with it working passenger services each weekend and throughout the week during its final week on the line. The locomotive attracted thousands of visitors to the line throughout its stay, although nothing on the scale of what would be witnessed when it next ventured along the ELR line almost 23 years later.

A few months later, in late spring, Bury Council confirmed that it had been successful in purchasing the former Bury Traction Maintenance Depot from BR, with the ELR granted permission almost immediately to access the building and yard to carry out the necessary works to make it fit for use by the railway. The depot building had been kept in relatively good condition and had not suffered too much from vandalism since it had been vacated by GEC Alsthom the previous summer following commissioning of the Metrolink fleet. However, the yard required some

attention to the trackwork before it could be brought into use.

The railway's chief mechanical engineer, Ian Riley, was responsible for organising an ambitious Festival of Steam in August 1993 to mark the 25th anniversary of the end of steam on BR. However, the number of locomotives invited to attend was dependent on two things, these being the successful occupation of the former BR depot premises and the completion of the Heywood line extension to allow light engine movements to come in off the main line, via the railway's new main line connection at Hopwood Junction, a few hundred yards beyond Green Lane Level Crossing on the Castleton side of Heywood station.

Work on the completion of the Heywood line suffered a setback in June 1993, when problems were experienced with the foundations of the new bridge which was being installed at Pilsworth Road, next to the site of the former Broadfield station.

The problem meant that the line would not be completed in time for the August 1993 festival and this in turn precluded the planned appearances of star attractions LNER A4 4-6-2 No. 4498 *Sir Nigel Gresley* and BR Standard 8 4-6-2 No. 71000 *Duke of Gloucester*. The owners of both locomotives were unwilling to allow their engines to be brought in by road, but did promise that they would visit the railway over the coming months once the main line link was reinstated.

LEFT: In April 1993, members of the ELR Permanent Way volunteer gang work on the installation of trackwork on the approach to the Metrolink Bridge at Bury. The bridge was built in 1992 to carry the Heywood line over the Metrolink lines, as the previous flat crossing was no longer an acceptable way for the two lines to cross each other. MIKE TAYLOR

RIGHT: Once the ELR was re-connected to the national rail network at Heywood, some of the larger prestigious locomotives that had been due to visit the line for the August 1993 Festival of Steam were finally brought on to the railway. One such locomotive was BR Standard 8 4-6-2 No. 71000 *Duke of Gloucester,* which subsequently spent many years based on the ELR. No. 71000 stands in the Locomotive Works yard alongside No. 6233 *Duchess of Sutherland,* which is appropriately disguised as 46225 *Duchess of Gloucester* on March 26, 1994. MIKE TAYLOR

Despite the disappointment of the main line connection not being reinstated in time for the event, the August 1993 steam festival firmly put the ELR on the map as a major player in the heritage railway sector and the event was arguably the most ambitious steam event ever organised in preservation history. While the event proved to be very popular with enthusiasts, the huge costs of transporting the locomotives to the ELR and other ancillary costs meant that the event sadly made a substantial financial loss.

With the former Bury Depot now in use by the ELR, the building became the ELR Locomotive Works and agreement was reached between the ELR, Bury Council and Ian Riley for him to relocate his locomotive engineering company to the building, with the ELR and Riley & Son (E) Ltd sharing the facility and working together for the mutual benefit of both Riley & Son and the ELR.

There was a positive end to 1993 with the newly completed Pilsworth Road bridge completed and a short ceremony was held on December 20 to mark

the completion of the reinstatement of the final missing piece of the route between Bury and Heywood, meaning the ELR now had access to the national rail network once more. Betty Beet's Ivatt 2MT 2-6-0 No. 46441 was used to commission the new bridge and declare the line completed, although there was still a long way to go before passengers could be carried along the line.

The first locomotive to use the reinstated route between Heywood and Bury was No. 71000 *Duke of Gloucester,* which arrived on the railway on February 5, 1994, some six months after it had originally planned to attend. The arrival of a locomotive from the BR network via the Heywood line was a real boost to the ELR, whose volunteers had worked very hard to reinstate the line over the previous two years.

Since then, hundreds of locomotive movements have made use of the main line connection at Hopwood Junction and the ELR now plans to extend the limit of its passenger operations to Castleton at some point in the future, where the heritage railway will hopefully

have an interchange with the Network Rail station in the town.

In 1994 a potential deal between the ELR and Bressingham Steam Museum to restore Stanier 'Duchess' 4-6-2 No. 6233 *Duchess of Sutherland* collapsed and the locomotive left the railway after spending six months at Bury. The locomotive has since been sold to the Princess Royal Class Locomotive Trust and returned to main line action, and has also returned to the ELR for a working visit, with the railway enjoying a good relationship with the PRCLT, which also owns ELR stalwart BR Standard 4 2-6-4 No. 80080.

No. 6233 had been brought to the ELR for the August 1993 Steam Railway Festival and while the event had proved costly for the railway in terms of the financial hit it took, the event had generated a lot of good relationships between the railway and other locomotive owners. The railway also won the Association of Railway Preservation Society's annual award for 1993 in recognition for its efforts in organising the ground-breaking month

On September 26, 1993, Stanier 5MT 4-6-0 No. 5407 and Western Region diesel-hydraulic Class 42 'Warship' D832 *Onslaught* top-and-tail a special volunteers' special train along the Heywood line as far as Pilsworth Road bridge, which was the limit of operations at the time. While trackwork was nearing completion, a lot remained to be done before it would be suitable for passenger services. MIKE TAYLOR

LNER A4 4-6-2 No. 60007 *Sir Nigel Gresley* first visited the ELR in 1994 before returning to the line in 1995, becoming part of the home-based fleet for a number of years. Hauling a Santa Special service from Bury to Ramsbottom on December 10, 1995, No. 60007 makes its way through Burrs. MIKE TAYLOR

During the 1997 January Steam Weekend, the presence of three operational Stanier 5MT 4-6-0 locomotives led to an impressive triple headed trip between Bury and Ramsbottom. No. 5407 leads M5337 and 44767 *George Stephenson* through Burrs on January 26, 1997, with the powerful trio in charge of a modest five-coach rake of stock. MIKE TAYLOR

On September 2, 1998, newly restored LNER V2 2-6-2 No. 60800 *Green Arrow* passes over Brooksbottom Viaduct during a photographic charter. The National Railway Museum-owned locomotive was on the ELR for running-in trials, but its return was plagued with boiler leaks and other teething problems. MIKE TAYLOR

of steam. At Bury a new cafe was built on Platform 2 which came into use in 1994. The building was constructed at a cost of £150,000 on the site of the former ELR headquarters, which in recent years had been used for volunteer car parking. The new facility was a massive improvement on the previous Mark 1 RBR kitchen car restaurant and provided capacity for 80 seated customers, along with a large kitchen, volunteer dining area and toilets.

A new arrival to the railway in January 1995 was LMS 4-6-0 'Jubilee' No. 5690 *Leander*, which had been purchased from the Severn Valley Railway by Dr Peter Beet. The locomotive was moved to the Locomotive Works and underwent an overhaul to return it to service, which was completed towards the end of 2002.

A £200,000 project was also carried out to refurbish the station building at Bury Bolton Street, which saw much of the building re-plastered and re-wired, with the building's flat roof also treated to prevent water ingress. Additionally,

a new brick clock tower was built to the front of the station and modifications were carried out to a bridge alongside the building which had been suffering from concrete cancer.

Summer 1995 saw the return to service of Stanier 5MT 4-6-0 No. 45337, which was the first former Barry scrapyard locomotive to be restored entirely on the ELR, with it having arrived at Castlecroft just over a decade earlier. Owned by the 26B Locomotive Company, the locomotive went on to become a regular on the ELR steam roster, as well as making visits to a number of other heritage lines.

In 1996, a long-running legal dispute over the ownership of Hughes Fowler 2-6-0 'Crab' No. 42765 was resolved, with the locomotive being purchased outright by the ELR from its former owner. The dispute arose shortly after No 42765 entered service in the autumn of 1993, as the railway had financed part of the locomotive's overhaul in exchange for a share in the engine. However, the proportion of the ownership was

disputed between the two parties and a court hearing in 1994 had permitted the ELR to use the locomotive until the situation was resolved.

September 1996 saw the railway celebrate the 150th anniversary of the opening of the Bury to Rawtenstall line by the original East Lancashire Railway. A series of special events was organised to celebrate the milestone, while the NRM's pioneer Hughes Fowler 'Crab' No. 2700 was loaned to the railway. Having spent a number of years based at Bury prior to its withdrawal by BR, No. 2700 was assessed for a possible return to service, but it was subsequently found that the costs involved in the work were too high and it moved to Barrow Hill two years later.

A change of ownership took place in 1997 for Stanier 5MT 4-6-0 No. 5407, which was sold to Ian Riley by its former owner, Paddy Smith. The locomotive, which had been a long-term favourite on the main line, had been based on the ELR for the past four years. No. 5407 was immediately withdrawn from

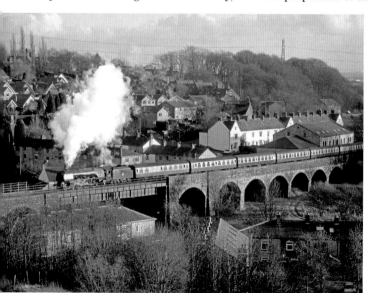

In February 1998, the National Railway Museum's Stanier 'Duchess' 4-6-2 No. 46229 *Duchess of Hamilton* heads a photographic charter over Brooksbottom Viaduct. The locomotive was repainted into BR green for the final three months of its boiler certificate before bowing out the following month. TERRY EYRES

Exactly 30 years to the day since British Railways operated its final steam locomotives on the celebrated '15 Guinea Special', ELR Stanier 5MTs No. 45407 and No. 45337 head a recreation of the famous train through Burrs on August 11, 1998. This was the first day back in service for No. 45407 following overhaul and No. 45337 was disguised as No. 45156 *Ayrshire Yeomanry* for the event. MIKE TAYLOR

In October 1998 two newly overhauled Class 20s were tested on the ELR on behalf of freight operator Direct Rail Services. 20312 was the first to be tested, followed by 20313 a couple of weeks later. 20313 is shown at Ramsbottom with a heavy load of D1041 *Western Prince*, the ELR's 75 tonne diesel crane and a DRS Class 37. THE LATE MALCOLM ORRETT, COURTESY OF PETER M DUNCAN

RIGHT: The damage suffered to Ashenbottom Bridge is clear to see following the devastating flood which took place on June 14, 2002, when a fallen tree was washed down the River Irwell, causing extensive damage to the supporting central pier of the bridge. THE LATE MALCOLM ORRETT, COURTESY OF PETER M DUNCAN

service and overhauled, with Mr Riley confirming that it should return to service during summer 1998 and would be repainted into BR lined black as No. 45407.

Over the late May bank holiday weekend in 1998, the ELR hosted its first 'Warring 40s' event, featuring battle re-enactments, re-enactors in wartime costumes and period entertainment. The 1940s themed event proved to be incredibly successful and has gone on to be one of the main events of the annual calendar, with the ever-popular event achieving record visitor numbers each year, with 2018 being the most successful year to date.

True to his word, the return of No 45407 took place in time for the ELR to celebrate the 30th anniversary of the end of BR steam in August 1998, with the locomotive resplendent in BR black and paired with ELR resident No. 45337 (disguised as long-scrapped No. 45156 *Ayrshire Yeomanry*) for a recreation of the '15 Guinea Special' railtour from August 11, 1968.

In November 1998, Ian Riley acquired a second locomotive when he purchased former ELR resident BR Standard 2-6-0 No. 76079. The locomotive returned to Bury once again, before moving on hire to the West Somerset Railway for a few months ahead of it being retired for a major overhaul, which would see it return to service with a main line running certificate.

Freight operator Direct Rail Services chose the ELR as the location to test and commission two newly refurbished Class 20 diesel locomotives, 20312 and 20313, which had been overhauled for use by the company. Originally, it had been planned that four locomotives would be tested on the railway, but delays with the completion of the final two meant that by the time they were ready for testing it coincided with the ELR's Santa Special services and the railway could not accommodate the testing at such a busy time in its schedule.

In September 1999, the ELR hosted the EWS Classic Traction weekend. The event saw a number of historic main line diesel locomotives hired by the railway from freight operator English Welsh & Scottish Railways.

Visiting the line were 31110 *Traction Magazine*, 33202 *The Burma Star*, 37351, 37906 *Star of the East*, 47306 *The Sapper*, 56006, 73129 *City of Winchester*, 73133 *The Bluebell Railway* and a rake of Mark 1 air-braked coaches, which operated services over three days from September 10-12, 1999. As with the steam festival of August 1993, the EWS Classic Traction event was a ground-breaking event which proved to be very popular, but the high costs of staging the event saw any profits from fares wiped out and the event made a significant financial loss.

The unique Battery Electric Multiple Unit that had been based on the railway since 1988 left the ELR in 2001, after its owning museum was liquidated and the BEMU was sold to the Royal Deeside Railway, which had preserved part of the line where the unit had been based during its BR career before it had become part of the Research Department at Derby.

Ferocious storms hit the area on the evening of June 14, 2002, with the River Irwell bursting its banks at various locations and bringing flooding to several parts of the railway. However, when an inspection of the line was carried out it was found that a large tree had been washed down the river and had collided with the central support pier of Ashenbottom Bridge, close to Irwell Vale station and one of the bridges that had been replaced prior to the reopening of the railway to Rawtenstall. Such was the damage to the bridge that the pier was no longer supporting the bridge span and the ELR was forced to withdraw all services to Rawtenstall until the pier could be rebuilt.

Thankfully, the ELR Trust arrangements for managing the railway's structures ensured that the necessary repairs could be carried out reasonably quickly, but it would be January 2003 before trains could return to Rawtenstall following repairs. In the interim period some services were operated in a top-and-tail format with a locomotive at each end of the train, terminating at Irwell Vale, while on off-peak services they terminated at Ramsbottom.

In October 2002, the ELR-based Class 40 Preservation Society successfully re-certified its flagship locomotive D345 for main line running, becoming the first preserved Class 40 to run on the main line again since the withdrawal of fleet pioneer D200 back in April 1988. Its first inaugural tour saw the locomotive work a railtour to Holyhead on November 30, 2002.

In 2003 the directors of the railway reluctantly took the decision to close

The momentous day when passenger services finally returned to the Bury to Heywood line, when on September 6, 2003, Stanier 'Jubilee' 4-6-0 No. 5690 *Leander* hauled the reopening VIP special to the new eastern terminus. NIGEL VALENTINE

During 2007, the ELR's yard alongside the Locomotive Works was used as a works depot for a major track relaying project on Metrolink, with the ELR Heywood line and yard being used to store materials which were then transported along the Bury to Manchester line by a fleet of shunters. Materials trains were often worked by Class 60s, with a Class 60 also used as a super shunter at Buckley Wells. 60083 *Mountsorrel* runs through Bury Bolton Street station on May 27, 2007. NIGEL VALENTINE

LEFT: During its second working spell on the ELR Midland Railway 4F 0-6-0 No. 44422 hauls a demonstration freight photographic charter through Burrs on January 29, 2006, with the exhaust beautifully highlighted by the rising sun. NIGEL VALENTINE

Bury Transport Museum to visitors, due to the deteriorating condition of the Grade II listed building's roof which was making the building unsafe. Although volunteer efforts were mainly concentrated on operating the building, the directors wanted Bury Transport Museum to have a future as part of the railway and the company and Bury Council began working on proposals to get the building repaired and restored to its former glory.

After years of planning and upgrading works, the line from Bury to Heywood was officially reopened by Pete Waterman on September 6, 2003, with Stanier 4-6-0 'Jubilee' No. 5690 *Leander* charged with hauling the inaugural VIP passenger service. It had been almost 10 year since the line was reinstated for light engine movements, but a huge amount of money had been spent bringing the line up to a suitable standard where regular passenger trains could run along the line again. The restoration of the route had seen Rochdale join Bury and Rossendale

Councils in supporting the railway.

After operating with an interim temporary signalling scheme since the Heywood line had opened the previous year, such progress had been made on the Bury re-signalling scheme that Bury South signalbox was formally brought back into use on July 6, 2004. The scale of the project to fully re-signal the station and its approaches was huge, with the work being done in stages. It would be a further 10 years before the full re-signalling scheme was finally completed, with the whole project taking 15 years from start to finish.

On November 30, 2006, the Heritage Lottery Fund announced that it had approved the railway's application for Stage 1 funding of £1.5million towards the refurbishment of Bury Transport Museum, which had been closed to the public due to the perilous state of the roof. The company, along with Bury Council, was keen to get the Grade II listed building refurbished and restored as a visitor attraction to complement the railway. The overall cost of the project

was estimated at around £2.5 million and funding for the remainder of the required finance had to be sourced from various other funding agencies.

The celebrations about the railway's successful Heritage Lottery Fund application for the refurbishment of Bury Transport Museum was overshadowed by the news that long-standing former ELR chairman, Trevor Jones, had passed away on the same day the announcement about the museum was made. Trevor had served as chairman of the operating company for almost 30 years prior to his retirement from the role in 2001, but he remained a director until his passing following a battle with cancer.

During the summer of 2007, a major track renewal and refurbishment project was carried out by Greater Manchester Passenger Transport Executive (now Transport for Greater Manchester) on the original Metrolink lines, which included the former Lancashire & Yorkshire Railway Bury to Manchester route. Large parts of the line were to have the trackwork completely replaced, with stations also receiving significant attention.

The ELR was crucial to the project, as the railway still had a connection to the Bury to Manchester line at Bury Loco Junction, which had been the former BR connection until the line was closed to BR services in August 1991. The scale of the project would see ballast, sleepers, rails and all other equipment delivered to Bury by rail, using freight operator English Welsh & Scottish Railway locomotives and wagons. A materials depot was established on the ELR's Baron Street site, close to the Locomotive Works and a number of sidings were laid to assist with the project.

Most of the incoming materials trains would be hauled by Class 60s and 66s,

Ten years after it first arrived on the ELR and fresh from a major overhaul unique BR Standard 8 4-6-2 No. 71000 *Duke of Gloucester* hauls a test train along the Heywood line on March 14, 2004. Following successful trail running, the locomotive was repainted into its BR lined green livery before re-entering service on the ELR and on main line tours. NIGEL VALENTINE

On July 10, 2008, Direct Rail Services 57012 hauls one of Network Rail's Railhead Treatment Trains towards Alfred Street Bridge during railhead treatment and adhesion tests which took place on the ELR during 2008. TOM MCATEE

With both of the original ELR re-opening train locomotives out of service, the railway hired in two replacements for its opening train recreation on July 25, 2007. Former ELR resident ex-Manchester Ship Canal 0-6-0T No. 70 was brought in alongside ex-National Coal Board 0-6-0T No. 140 from the Embsay & Bolton Abbey Railway. The pair are seen hauling the recreation through Burrs. NIGEL VALENTINE

while EW&S was also supplying three Class 08/9 which had lower cabs than a standard Class 08 for working trains down the Metrolink line to Manchester, as the height of the overhead wires meant that standard height locomotives could only get as far as Whitefield. Additionally, other Class 08 locomotives based on the ELR were also used on the project.

To accommodate this major contract, a number of ELR volunteers were employed to manage the movements of the trains on and off the railway, as well as coordinating the movements around the Baron Street yard materials depot.

The project was successfully completed in the autumn of 2007 and had been operated seamlessly from the ELR's point of view, while the money raised by the contract was used to finance various improvements on the railway, such as additional lighting and security fencing around the Locomotive Works site.

During July 2007 the railway hosted a number of special events to celebrate the 20th anniversary of the reopening of the railway between Bury and Ramsbottom. With both original reopening locomotives unavailable, two replacement industrial locomotives were hired to haul a recreation of the reopening train. Additionally, GWR 4-4-0 No. 3440 *City of Truro* was brought in from the ELR to haul services on the line.

As part of the 20th anniversary celebrations, ELR resident diesel locomotive D5054 was named *Phil Southern* and 40145 was named *East Lancashire Railway* and dedicated to the memory of Trevor Jones. Both Phil Southern and Trevor Jones had been dedicated volunteers and directors of the railway for many years, but both had passed away in 2004 and 2006 respectively, with their names being bestowed on the locomotives in tribute to them.

During 2008, the ELR hosted trials on the Heywood line of one of Network Rail's new Railhead Treatment Trains. The RHTT was designed to clean rails during the leaf fall autumn season, when trains have traditionally suffered from poor adhesion due to the mulch that is created on the railhead by crushed leaves. For the trials the train was run at speeds of up to 60mph, under the authority of the Railway Inspectorate, with a Class 158 DMU also provided to test the differences in braking performance between untreated and treated rail surfaces.

A major improvement to the station at Ramsbottom took place during 2008 with the completion of a new station canopy on the Rawtenstall-bound Platform 2 alongside the station building. The canopy, the framework of which had been recovered from Atherton station in the early 1980s, was financed by an anonymous donor and was the first replacement canopy installed by the ELR since it had reopened the route, although another canopy on Platform 2 at Bury Bolton Street was installed during 2015 using part of the canopy recovered from Oldham Mumps, with the remainder due to be installed at Rawtenstall in early 2019.

A new special event for 2009 was the operation of a Halloween Ghost Train on the evening of October 31. The event was a new one for the ELR, although other heritage lines had successfully organised such events. The railway offered free travel for any children attending wearing suitably spooky outfits, while adults were charged a flat £10 return fare from Bury to Rawtenstall.

However, despite some publicity locally, the response from people wanting to travel on the train caught the railway out somewhat, with hundreds of passengers coming to Bury Bolton Street, with queues stretching all the way down Bolton Street and forcing the railway to operate a second train later in the evening to satisfy demand and prevent upsetting the families who had come out to travel on the train. The Halloween Ghost Trains have since become a popular addition to the ELR events calendar, although places on the trains are now only available if pre-booked in advance.

In February 2010, another track renewals project on Metrolink, this time between Radcliffe and Whitefield, saw another series of materials trains being brought on to the railway, with the ELR's connection on to Metrolink at Bury Loco Junction being used once again to accommodate the works trains.

Although materials were brought on to the railway over a period of weeks leading up to the main engineering possession, the main difference from the 2007 contract was that the actual track relaying works would only take three days to complete with the ELR supplying three Class 37s, 37109, 37418 *Pectinidae* and 37901 *Mirrlees Pioneer* to haul the engineering trains between Bury and Whitefield, along with 33109 *Captain Bill Smith RNR* as a backup locomotive.

With the ELR having taken delivery of the canopy frame and supports from Oldham Mumps in 2010, the railway held its first 'Raise the Roof' music event at Bury Bolton Street in July 2012, with profits to be donated towards the restoration of part of the Oldham Mumps canopy over Platform 2 at Bury. The event featured a wide range of music acts performing from beneath the canopy on Platform 3, with the audience watching from Platform 2. The event raised more than £8000 towards the canopy appeal and a further four 'Raise

Receiving attention by Riley & Son (E) Ltd at the Locomotive Works, LNER A4 4-6-2 No. 60009 *Union of South Africa* stands in steam in the yard on July 29, 2007, with GWR 4-4-0 No. 3440 City of Truro and S15 4-6-0 No. 825 keeping it company. NIGEL VALENTINE

the Roof' events were organised over the following years.

The following year the canopy over Platforms 3 and 4 at Bury Bolton Street station had its wooden roof boarding and felt removed, with new glazed panels installed, providing a much brighter and airy atmosphere for waiting passengers. The improvement also meant that the railway could now promote the platform as a space that could be used to hold events and special occasions. The ELR now has a licence to hold wedding ceremonies on the platform beneath this canopy.

Storms once again wreaked havoc on the Irwell Valley on Boxing Day 2015, when heavy rain battered the country, with the local area also suffering. While the ELR suffered some damage to the track around Summerseat and the banks of the River Irwell were washed away close to the railway's boundary at Horncliffe, near Edenfield, necessitating a temporary speed restriction through the area until the banks could be rebuilt, the railway mainly escaped any serious damage.

However, it was a building that had past links to the ELR which made the news headlines. The Waterside public house and restaurant at Brooksbottom, which had provided the backdrop to so many photographs taken of trains crossing Brooksbottom Viaduct and also hosted the ELRPS annual general meeting for many years, substantially collapsed into the raging river during the fierce storms, with the remainder of the building demolished over the following weeks.

Thankfully, the building had been closed for three years at the time of its collapse and no one was inside, but as the former canteen of Hoyles Mill in the village, The Waterside had been part of Summerseat for more than 200 years and its loss dramatically changed the landscape around where it once stood.

Two weeks later the area was in the news again, but this time for more positive reasons. The eagerly awaited return to service of LNER A3 4-6-2 No. 60103 *Flying Scotsman* saw crowds descend on the ELR, where the locomotive took part in two weekends of public running-in trials along the

railway. Thousands of people came to travel behind, or just to see, the iconic locomotive providing a much-needed morale and financial boost to the railway and the local towns, who were still reeling from the floods just two weeks previously.

Those public trips by *Flying Scotsman* heralded the start of what was to become the ELR's most successful year to date, with the railway achieving its long-awaited target of attracting more than 200,000 visitors during the course of the year.

Another significant achievement during 2016 that recognised the efforts of the railway's volunteers was the announcement that the ELR had been awarded the Queen's Award for Voluntary Service, which is the highest award that can be given to a voluntary organisation in the UK. Recently retired ELR company chairman, Peter Duncan, attended a garden party at Buckingham Palace to celebrate the honour, while ELRPS society chairman, David Wright, was invited to attend a street party of other winners of the prestigious award.

In October 2016 a new station halt was opened at Burrs Country Park to serve the adjacent leisure facility and caravan site, which had been planned

BR Standard 4, 2-6-0 No. 76084 arrives at Platform 4 ready to work to Rawtenstall on January 8, 2017. This locomotive spent much of its working life on BR at the nearby Lower Darwen shed, but now normally works on the North Norfolk Railway. LIAM BARNES

for many years. The five-coach platform and waiting shelter was officially opened by the then-Mayor of Bury, Coun Mike Connolly, but was not brought into permanent use by the ELR until the start of the 2017 timetable the following January.

In 2017 the ELR's 'Dining with Distinction' product was voted the No. 1 restaurant experience in Greater Manchester on review website Trip Advisor, out of more than 3000 competing restaurants. The food quality and service from staff were highlighted among the many glowing reviews and the railway's dining train has remained consistently at or near the top of the Trip Advisor reviews.

Arriving on the ELR in July 2017 was Tracey Parkinson, who was appointed the railway's general manager, having held the same position on the Talyllyn Railway prior to her appointment.

The 2017 Santa Special season saw the railway carry more than 40,000 passengers between Bury and Rawtenstall, with Father Christmas handing out more presents to children on the railway than he ever had in previous years.

Which brings us to 2018. The ELR has enjoyed a busy year to date, with passenger numbers ahead of where they were at this stage last year and working visits by prestigious locomotives such as *Flying Scotsman*, *Tornado* and *Union of South Africa* have seen crowds throng to the railway once again. With a strong programme of events and increases in the number of passengers wishing to travel on the dining trains, indications are that 2018 could indeed become a record-breaking year for the railway.

It hasn't all been good news though. Problems discovered with the boiler of Hughes Fowler 2-6-0 'Crab' No. 13065 have caused its premature withdrawal from service, with the boiler now being overhauled by Riley & Son (E) Ltd at its Heywood base. It is expected that the locomotive will re-enter service in early 2019 should no further problems be found.

The loss of No. 13065 and the delayed return to service of BR Standard 4 locomotive Nos. 80080 and 80097 caused a temporary shortage of steam locomotives during the summer months, although this was alleviated somewhat in July when steam locomotives were removed from service for three weeks due to fire risk during the 2018 summer heatwave.

With the railway continuing to experience growth in most of its areas, it is clear that over the coming years the ELR will continue to make the headlines and the hard work of the railway's team of staff and volunteers has turned the ELR into one of the UK's leading heritage railways.

PEOPLE PROFILE

ANDI MOYES

STEAM DRIVER AND STEAM EVENT ORGANISER

How did you get interested in railways?
"I've always had an interest in steam railways for as long as I can remember. We lived in Goole in East Yorkshire and my dad was always interested in railways and he used to tell me about the fish train that used to pass through Goole every day, hauled by a 'Black 5' and those stories by my dad helped grow my interest. He also used to take me with him to various railway events as a child and passed down his enthusiasm for trains and railways to me too."

When did you get involved in volunteering at the ELR?
"For my 21st birthday my parents bought me a footplate experience course on the ELR, which I did in May 2000 and thoroughly enjoyed every minute of it. Even though the footplate experience courses only give you a very small taste of what it is like to be on the footplate of a steam locomotive, I decided there and then that I wanted to become a volunteer on the ELR and preferably in the steam department.

"I started as a cleaner on the railway the following weekend and it's the job of the cleaner to come in at 6am and clean the engines ready for the day's service. It's also a crucial way of learning how locomotives work and what the various components do. As a cleaner, you also go out with the locomotives as a riding turn and it is during these turns that you get the chance to fire the locomotives and learn about operating a steam engine while it is hauling a train. The majority of our drivers and firemen are also more than happy to impart their knowledge and experience to cleaners, as these volunteers are going to be the drivers and firemen of the future.

"After four years as a volunteer cleaner, I took my fireman's exam and became a passed cleaner, where to all intents and purposes you are a fireman, but you remain on the cleaning roster until you get a bit more experience. After a couple of years as a passed cleaner I progressed on to the fireman's roster.

"Then, much like the progression from being a cleaner to passed cleaner, I got the opportunity to learn about the driving of locomotives and the duties of a driver,

The locomotive that Andi Moyes passed his driver's exam on was BR Standard 5 4-6-0 No. 73129, which was visiting from its home on the Midland Railway Butterley. No. 73129 heads a Heywood to Rawtenstall service through Burrs on January 29, 2011. TERRY EYRES

such as route knowledge and the location of signals, stations and other things that the drivers need to be aware of. After a while you then progress on to the driver training link and after a certain amount of training days you have a driving exam with one of our traction inspectors. I did my driving exam on visiting BR Standard 5 No. 73129 during the summer of 2010 and after a good day on the footplate I passed my exam and became a passed fireman, before progressing on to the drivers' roster.

"The other role I have got actively involved in is as organiser of our steam events, which is something I really enjoy, although it can get stressful at times, and I have on occasions had to rewrite event plans at very short notice when a locomotive suddenly becomes unavailable, or something else happens that means a rewrite is required. However, by the end of the event there is a great sense of relief and most of the time our events run well, although like any other railway we are not immune from problems.

"I'm also trained as a responsible officer, who is nominally the person in charge of the operational railway when they are on duty and have to deal with any incidents that may occur."

What are some of the highlights of your time on the ELR?
"I love organising the steam events and try to avoid things like tender-to-tender running and unauthentic double-headers, but you can't please everyone and it's a challenge coming up with something that is interesting for our visitors, but isn't too complicated. While it can be tempting to try and organise a 'busy' event with an intensive timetable and multiple locomotive changes, we have to be careful not to be too ambitious, as the more complex the event plan is, the more likely it is that the timetable will start to suffer and we'll lose time. That's not to say we don't do our best to put on a good show for the people who come to visit the event.

"The March steam event in 2018 was a particularly difficult one, as we suffered from a heavy snowfall brought in by 'the beast from the east', where we experienced engines that were shunted out of the shed into the yard with frozen rods and motion after less than an hour. However, the extreme conditions and the problems that caused brought out the best in the department and all the lads in the steam department worked together to keep the show on the road. We did lose a bit of time and did suffer various operational problems throughout the day due to the weather, but we kept on running when many other railways had to give up their services and I think we still managed to put on a good event.

"I'm passionate about the ELR and I love it there. Like everything it can be frustrating at times, but the ELR is in my blood and I've made so many friends at the railway over the years.

"Another highlight for me was being given the opportunity to drive LNER A3 'Pacific' No. 60103 *Flying Scotsman* while it was on the railway. The locomotive still draws in the crowds wherever it goes and to be entrusted with it by Ian Riley and his representatives has been a real honour for me. *Flying Scotsman* is without a doubt my favourite engine for driving out of all the locomotives I've driven on the ELR so far. I've also learnt a lot from Ian Riley over the years and he is someone who I have great deal of respect for. While it's great to drive the big engines, it is sometimes more enjoyable spending time on the smaller locomotives that occasionally run on the railway. With a good fireman at your side, getting a great performance out of a smaller locomotive can ultimately be more satisfying than driving some of the larger locomotives."

What can be done to encourage a younger generation to get involved?
"We actually do have quite a few younger volunteers coming through into our department now, but we need more. We need to get them interested while they are still young and before they find other things to occupy their time.

"Most of our younger volunteers start working as station staff before moving to the steam or diesel department when they reach 18, but for some of them this doesn't suit them and that's when we lose them. It would be good for us to come up with a way where they can come into the departments at a younger age, under suitable supervision, to ensure they can come to the section they want to volunteer in as soon as possible after they start volunteering."

Which locomotive would you like to see on the ELR in the future?
"For me that's quite an easy choice, although whether it could ever happen I'm not sure. I'd love to see the National Railway Museum's Lancashire & Yorkshire Railway 'Radial' 2-4-2 Tank No. 1008. To see this locomotive working on the ELR through firm L&YR territory would be a dream come true and it would be perfect for hauling dining trains and some of our low-peak services."

MIKE KELLY

THE VIEW FROM THE CHAIR

Andy Coward speaks to East Lancashire Light Railway Company chairman, Mike Kelly, about how and why he got involved in the railway following a successful career in local government, including some of the highlights and challenges of his time in office and what his vision is for the future of the East Lancashire Railway in an ever-changing social and economic climate.

MIKE KELLY COLLECTION

Mike Kelly is a man with a vision and a passion for the East Lancashire Railway. He wants to see the ELR become even more successful at a time when the railway is arguably the most successful it has ever been. A friendly and engaging man with a soft North Eastern lilt in his voice, Mike Kelly has been chairman of the East Lancashire Light Railway Company Ltd, the operating company of the ELR, for the past two-and-a-half years, having joined the Board as a director just a few months earlier.

Unlike many of his colleagues on the Board, he had previously only a passing interest in railways for many years until his job brought the ELR to his attention. Having worked in local government for many years, Mike got his grounding on the ELR through his role of deputy chief executive of Bury Council, and then went on to become chief executive and, by default, became company secretary of the East Lancashire Railway Trust, which is the organisation that oversees the railway's infrastructure on behalf of the three supporting local authorities of Bury, Rossendale and Rochdale, along with representation from the ELR's operating company.

Mike explains: "I have to say, Bury Council has always been very supportive of the East Lancashire Railway stretching way back from before the reopening of the railway from Bury to Ramsbottom in 1987 and continues to support it actively. Through my role as company secretary I wanted to understand all about the railway and, as such, I got more and more involved in meetings as time went by and I helped with some of the various developments that take place on the railway, such as the construction of the new station halt at Burrs Country Park and ambitious plans for developing Rawtenstall Station. The heritage railway is a great leisure attraction for the local area and I was very happy to be involved in what is very much a community asset for local people."

Very much a people person, Mike retired from his position with Bury Council in 2015 after a career spanning 50 years. However, he readily admits that he found it hard to adjust to life after retirement and found himself struggling for things to do with his new-found spare time, having had such an active and varied life while he was working, as he explains: "I loved my job and the people I worked with. I was given a wonderful leaving party by the council, but the next morning I woke up and realised that for the first time in many years I had nothing to do. I had five very bad months at the start of my retirement, where I went from being very active in my job to having no focus at all. After all you can only do so much decorating and gardening and it's quite a challenge to fill those missed busy days. However, I knew that I didn't want to be one of those people who retire and then sit around doing nothing and simply fade away.

I needed something to occupy my time again and give me back some sense of purpose."

Thinking back to his involvement with the ELR Trust, Mike approached then-ELLRCo chairman, Peter Duncan, to offer his services, skills and contacts to help benefit the railway. That conversation led to Mike being invited on to the ELLR Board of directors as a guest and he quickly got to learn some of the challenges faced by the railway. Mike comments: "What struck me about the Board was that, with one exception, they were all people with a railway background, mainly in railway engineering. My background was completely different, but I certainly believed that I had skills that I could use to help the railway."

Towards the end of 2015, the chairman's position became vacant when Peter Duncan retired as the chairman and the Board decided that the company needed to make a change with regards to the lead role of the company. The previous chairman, Peter Duncan, had held two roles as he was also director of signal engineering. It was felt the new chairman should not run a specific department or be involved in the railway operationally.

At that point, as Mike said: "If you don't buy a ticket, you can't win the raffle, as it were. I decided to apply for the role and was subsequently successful, even though I had only been attending Board meetings for a short time." Mike explains: "I felt the role of chairman needed focus on strategic and resilience issues; to be high profile; to be an identifiable figurehead if you wish to relate to, the voice of the railway with more engagement with volunteers, staff, visitors, politicians and other key partners."

Mike added: "The work of the Board can feel quite remote, maybe even seen as detached by many. By peeling back the curtains I wanted our staff and volunteers to have an appreciation of the work of the Board, who are also unpaid volunteers.

"I was convinced that our staff, volunteers and people more widely were interested in finding out what issues the Board were talking about and what important decisions were being made about the future of the railway."

On January 10, 2016, newly restored LNER A3 4-6-2 No. 60103 *Flying Scotsman* heads an ELR service train during its running-in trials, seen heading past the former ELR Goods Warehouse at Brooksbottom in Summerseat. The return to service of this locomotive was one of the biggest events ever held on the ELR and was also Mike Kelly's first taste of being the public face of the railway, having been appointed chairman a few days earlier. LIAM BARNES

"As a high-profile ambassador for the railway, you also have to be a good communicator, which I strive to be. One of the first things I set up after being appointed was a dedicated Twitter feed and a chairman's blog on the ELR website, so that I could share some of the news coming from the company with anyone who might be interested.

"This style of management helps to create a more open atmosphere between the company and our most important assets – the volunteers. I've had a lot of positive feedback to both the Twitter feed and the chairman's blog and it's helping not only to promote the railway but also to make the railway more transparent to its members and supporters." A recent blog posting about Hughes Fowler 'Crab' 4-6-0 locomotive No. 13065 being taken out of service had interest generated from a dozen countries.

The monumental rise of the railway into the premier league of heritage lines in a relatively short timescale has been both a blessing and a curse for the ELR. Mike explained: "The problem with the ELR is that in many ways it has grown far too quickly and some of the things the railway could have focused on as it got bigger were not able to be progressed, as people were so busy trying to keep up with the rise in growth of the railway. As a result, we have been playing catch-up for a while now, both operationally and administratively, in this respect, but where it is necessary we are ensuring that we have suitable skilled paid and volunteer resources in place. There is no point the railway chasing more and more visitors if we can't provide the front-line and behind-the-scenes resources to manage those visitors and the money they bring to the ELR."

The ELR, as a not-for-profit organisation, is now the second biggest paid attraction in Greater Manchester with an annual turnover of around £4 million, which has more than doubled in the past 10 years. It impacts positively on tourism, jobs and economic development. This is a fantastic achievement and one the railway can be very proud of. However even with such a significant level of turnover, there is no guarantee the railway can reach break-even or generate surpluses. For example, in 2017 the railway lost more than £100,000.

Nationally, heritage railways are seeing a resurgence in visitors. Heritage offers a unique experience as a 'living history'. The ELR has enjoyed year-on-year increasing levels of revenue and visitor growth. This has been achieved by growing the aspects of the railway which bring in the most revenue, such as dining trains, Santa Specials, Footplate Experience and special events. Mike readily admits that running a passenger train service alone without all the other ancillary products would make the business unsustainable. The ELR has developed into an award-winning major leisure destination operating passenger services alongside hosting more than 50 events annually. This business model ensures the railway can continue to host several steam and diesel galas each year for enthusiasts.

Following his appointment in January

As one of the main public faces of the railway, Mike Kelly is often called on for various publicity purposes, such as this one where he accepts a defibrillator from the North West Ambulance Service, with No. 13065 providing the backdrop.
KATE WALKER/EAST LANCASHIRE RAILWAY

2016, Mike found himself somewhat thrust into the limelight at one of the ELR's most high-profile events for many years, as he explains: "The first event following my appointment as chairman was the relaunch of the National Railway Museum's flagship locomotive, No. 60103 *Flying Scotsman*, which was undertaking 'running-in' trials on passenger services along the railway following its protracted major overhaul. The relaunch of the iconic locomotive brought thousands of people to the ELR to witness *Flying Scotsman* hauling trains again for the first time in more than a decade. It also saw the railway swamped with scores of

TV crews and journalists, giving us a great opportunity to showcase the railway and facilities. It was an exhausting few days, but I really loved it and the railway put on a very good show for everyone. I felt extremely proud to be leading the ELR at such an exciting time."

In June 2009, the ELR Trust published a development strategy about how the railway could grow over the following decade. Compiled by Locum Consulting, the strategy looked at all aspects of the railway and some of the initiatives that could be looked at to try and increase visitor numbers, which had remained fairly static for a number of years at between 100,000 and 110,000 visitors per year.

The Locum development strategy identified a target of 200,000 visitors per year by 2020, which seemed achievable, but was still optimistic at the time the report was published and a lot of work would have to be done if the target was to be achieved. Following the publication of the report, the ELR invested heavily in its staffing, both paid and volunteer roles, and has also taken on board a number of suggestions that were contained in the original report.

However, following impressive increases in visitor numbers year on year, thanks in part to improved promotion of more commercially successful events, the target number of 200,000 was actually achieved during 2016, helped by two working appearances of LNER A3 4-6-2 'Pacific' No. 60103 *Flying Scotsman.*

Inevitably there was a dip in numbers in 2017. On the plus side, for 2018, the ELR welcomed back not only *Flying Scotsman* but also celebrated new-build LNER 4-6-2 A1 'Pacific' A1 No. 60163 *Tornado*. However, a cautious Mike says the ELR needs to ensure it focuses on providing a quality day out for the visitors that come to the railway rather than continually chase higher and higher visitor numbers: "My view is so what? The arbitrary figure of 200,000 doesn't look

Mike Kelly and then-Mayor of Bury, Coun Mike Connolly, pose on the footplate of BR Standard 4 No. 80080 on May 26, 2016, to celebrate the start of construction work on Burrs Country Park station halt.
RORY LUSHMAN/EAST LANCASHIRE RAILWAY

at the yield generated by those visitors, or the quality of what we are offering and, while we all want the railway to grow, we have to ensure that we don't let quality slip or overwhelm our volunteers and infrastructure in the quest for ever higher visitor numbers. That said, we don't intend to stop trying to attract more people, we just need to make sure we get it right."

"Our railway is now very much events-focused and we run some fantastic events which are extremely popular. Events generate the bulk of our revenue and with the support of great staff and volunteers we have become very good at managing a varied programme throughout the year. We are always happy to try out new events and some of these have been very successful and others less so. We also have to ensure that we put on the best possible events for our visitors to ensure they go home happy and entertained and to ensure that they will hopefully come and visit us again. While attracting more visitors each year is fantastic we need to ensure that we give them value for money, as well as listening and reacting to feedback, both positive and negative. An example of this was the introduction of accessible carriages for wheelchair users."

Another thing that Mike is passionate about is acknowledging the work of nearly 800 volunteers who give up their spare time for the benefit of the ELR and he recognises just how important it is that those volunteers come to the railway for enjoyment, but also go home feeling appreciated by the company. He explains: "It's very easy to forget the contribution made to the railway by the volunteers who turn up each week, but without them the railway wouldn't survive. We have a small, dedicated team of paid staff who do a tremendous job behind the scenes, but the volunteers will always be the lifeblood of the ELR. As such, the Board have developed a Volunteers Charter, which

The ELR experienced one of its most successful years in 2018, thanks to a number of very successful events and growth in many key areas of the railway's business. One successful event was held over the Easter weekend, when Peppercorn A1 4-6-2 No. 60163 *Tornado* paid a working visit to the railway. On March 31, 2018, No. 60163 departs from Summerseat. LIAM BARNES

sets out what we as a company expect from our volunteers and what they can expect in return from us. Personally, volunteering has been my salvation and I want our volunteers to know how much they are appreciated and valued."

He believes that volunteering can be the key to unlocking some of the social isolation felt by retired people and explains that many of the volunteers form close friendships from their volunteering which they would not have done without it. At the other end of the scale, Mike would also like a sharper focus to be placed on attracting new younger volunteers, as a new generation of volunteers will be needed to run the railway in the future as the average age of the railway's volunteers continues to increase each year.

So what does he see as being the other priorities for the company at the moment? "We need to do the boring bits better by dealing with the rapid growth of the business, improve the corporate governance of the railway and implement more budgetary controls, which will help to make the railway more financially and operationally sustainable. Our Board are very committed in developing the railway for the future and allow the full-time staff and volunteer heads of departments, led by our general manager Tracey Parkinson, to run the railway. This has been a fundamental change for the Board, but they have embraced these challenges and we know we must also do better at the wider safety, strategic, and development aspects of the ELR.

"Another change we have made is to move to a single company structure and once accepted by the Charity Commission, directors will only serve a three-year term and then have to seek re-election. Previously, the directors could remain on the Board until they chose to leave and no one could be removed from the Board unless a vote of no confidence was passed. Now all directors' posts carry job descriptions for their roles and they are accountable for their own performance and success.

"To promote this change, I put myself up as the guinea pig for this style of appointment and in January 2019 I will have to state what I have done during my present term, prior to seeking re-election, and it will be up to the other directors whether they want me to continue, or move on."

Another project that Mike was

The opening of Burrs Country Park in October 2016 has been one of Mike Kelly's proudest achievements, with him having been instrumental in the project since its initial planning days when he was still chief executive of Bury Council. Mike poses with the invited officials, following the official opening ceremony. RORY LUSHMAN/ EAST LANCASHIRE RAILWAY

Under Mike Kelly's leadership, the ELR is investing heavily in the longer term planning of the railway locomotive and coaching stock fleets. Recently withdrawn from service for a major overhaul has been LMS Hughes-Fowler 2-6-0 'Crab' No. 13065 after experiencing boiler problems. It is now undergoing repairs and is expected back in traffic in early 2019. No. 13065 heads through Lumb, on the approach to Irwell Vale, on December 4, 2016. LIAM BARNES

instrumental in was the construction of the new £240,000 station halt at Burrs Country Park, which opened in 2016. The five-coach platform was built to serve the adjacent Burrs site, which is popular with visitors and also boasts a very successful caravan park just a stone's throw from the new station halt. Securing the necessary funding for the new station was achieved by Mike while he was still chief executive of Bury Council and he was extremely proud when the new station halt was opened a few months after he had taken over as chairman of the ELR. During 2017, more than 2000 people used the new station halt, which Mike says is a huge success. It has proved to be popular with users of the adjacent Caravan Club Park and also local walkers and families.

What are the company's investment challenges? Mike responded: "As a heritage railway we are rightly proud in maintaining and restoring heritage traction and rolling stock, where regular and planned maintenance is essential. To achieve this we need to urgently and directly improve the resilience of our Traction and Rolling Stock Department, and improve and expand the workshop and storage facilities at Buckley Wells. To date everyone involved is working flat out to simply 'stand still' and on occasions they become overwhelmed.

"The readily available supply of reliable locomotive power and quality rolling stock is a key element to any targeted growth in services and events. The ELR Board quite rightly are cautious when it comes to making big investments as they don't want to burden the railway with large debts. At the current time the ELR is debt free, so there are opportunities to take on a reasonable amount of debt to make targeted investments into improving the Traction and Rolling Stock operation and performance."

However, Mike realises the railway has to come up with more long-term planning when it comes to the provision of traction and rolling stock, in particular relating to steam locomotives: "We have to get more self-sufficient when it comes to the operation of our steam locomotive fleet. At the moment we are actively fundraising to purchase No. 34092 *City of Wells* and more than £200,000 towards the target of £340,000 has already been raised in a relatively short timescale, but we need to build up a fleet of several large steam locomotives which we can use for our core services and events during the summer months, supported by

Mike Kelly helps out as a Christmas Elf during the 2017 Santa Special services and grabs a quick photograph alongside Father Christmas. MIKE KELLY COLLECTION

smaller locomotives for off-peak periods and dining trains.

"We also need to invest in overhauling locomotives that can be used on the railway and to have modern workshop and storage facilities. We already have a fantastic diesel fleet, but we recognise that if people come to travel on our steam service, we must do what we can to ensure a steam locomotive is at the head of that train. Our aim is to have a dedicated fleet which is properly managed, with planned maintenance and overhauls, to ensure that we can fulfil our requirements, with only the occasional need to hire in locomotives for special events or exceptional circumstances."

As part of their long-term planning, the ELR has recently announced it is also investing more than £250,000 in its Traction and Rolling Stock Department to help futureproof this important part of the railway, which manages the railways steam, diesel and carriage departments.

The investment will see eight new skilled positions being advertised. A new departmental head of engineering will be in overall control of the departmental work planning for maintenance and restoration, budgets and operational outputs.

Beneath the new head of engineering will be specific posts of head of carriage and wagon, head of steam and head of diesel, who will be responsible for the performance of the paid and volunteer staff working within their respective sections, as well as trying to promote additional volunteering opportunities. Additionally, a foreman of mechanical engineering will be established to assist in mentoring and transferring skills to staff and volunteers.

A large six-figure financial investment will also be made at Buckley Wells, which will see the expansion of workshops and storage facilities starting with accommodation for housing the railway's 'Dining with Distinction' carriages.

Mike Kelly has led the ELR for the past two-and-a-half years and still has all the enthusiasm and passion for the railway that he has always had, but how would he like to be remembered? He responds: "I hope I can last a bit longer than three years! Under my chairmanship the culture and heritage of the ELR and the appreciation of our volunteer contributions will always be a top priority. As a volunteer myself, I have overseen an interesting but challenging period of change for the ELR, which will ultimately help the railway to be more self-sufficient in the future. When the time comes for me to leave the chairman's role I would like to think that the railway is more well known as a premier leisure destination, to be in a much stronger position than it was when I arrived financially, culturally, operationally and with increased volunteer numbers."

The list of past ELR chairmen may not be long, but all the people who have held the position in the history of the organisation have spearheaded the railway through very different periods of growth. Under Mike Kelly's tenure it is clear that the railway is thriving, but he is determined to keep striving to make it even better. These are interesting times for the ELR.

Steam Locomotives on the ELR

The East Lancashire Railway has become well known for its wide variety of steam locomotives that have operated along the line and while it would be impossible to document every steam locomotive that has graced ELR metals, this chapter sets out to list those locomotives which have spent time based at Bury as part of the ELR steam fleet.

The two locomotives used for the reopening service from Bury to Ramsbottom on July 25, 1987, were ex-Manchester Ship Canal 0-6-0T No. 32 *Gothenburg* and former Meaford Power Station 0-6-0T ELR No. 1. After hauling the first VIP train from Bury to Ramsbottom, the pair run round the train, prior to returning to Bury. PETER M DUNCAN

The ELR has established itself as one of the UK's leading heritage railways, operating a varied fleet of steam and diesel locomotives throughout the last 31 years. During the pre-opening days at Bury Transport Museum, brake van rides and steaming days were the domain of the small collection of ex-industrial steam locomotives based at Bury.

The only ex-BR steam locomotives at Castlecroft prior to the reopening of the line to Ramsbottom in 1987 were unrestored locomotives that had been rescued from Dai Woodham's famous scrapyard in Barry, South Wales.

However, since those early days, the ELR has gone on to operate a huge number of steam locomotives, including many of the high profile prestigious locomotives, such as *Canadian Pacific*, *Duchess of Hamilton*, *Flying Scotsman* and *Tornado*.

While this chapter is not a definitive list of every steam locomotive that has worked over the ELR, it does seek to highlight many of the locomotives that have spent extended periods of time based on the railway.

INDUSTRIAL BEGINNINGS

When the line between Bury and Ramsbottom first opened in July 1987, the railway relied on just two industrial

Ivatt 2MT 2-6-0 No. 46441 spent several years operating on the ELR following its appearance at the August 1993 Steam Railway Festival. The locomotive was popular with crews and more than capable of handling many of the services on the Bury to Rawtenstall line. On December 22, 1996, No. 46441 hauls the Ramsbottom to Rawtenstall shuttle train stock through Burrs as the sun comes up for the day. MIKE TAYLOR

tank locomotives to haul its services, with ex-Manchester Ship Canal 0-6-0T No. 32 *Gothenburg* and ex Meaford Power Station 0-6-0T ELR No. 1. These two locomotives were in charge of services throughout the 1987 season.

The following year, the fleet was boosted with the addition of ex-Bickershaw Colliery Austerity Saddle Tank 0-6-0ST No. 8, which was named *Sir Robert Peel* by the railway in tribute to the former British Prime Minister and founder of the Police Service, who was born in Bury.

The arrival of Derek Foster's ex-LMS Fowler 3F 0-6-0 No. 7298 in 1988 and his newly restored BR Standard 4 2-6-0 No. 76079 brought an end to the exclusive use of former industrial steam locomotives on the railway, although a number of industrial locomotives have worked on the ELR since those early years. 1989 saw the arrival of Hunslet Austerity 0-6-0ST No. 193 *Shropshire*, as the railway

Austerity 0-6-0ST No. 193 *Shropshire* arrived on the railway in 1989 and worked on the railway for a number of years. The locomotive approaches Summerseat with a Bury to Rawtenstall service on May 5, 1991, during the ELR's second weekend of passenger operations through to Rawtenstall. MIKE TAYLOR

It was appropriate that the first steam locomotive to be purchased for the ELR, former North West Gas Board 0-4-0 No. 1, should be charged with hauling the first works trains through to Rawtenstall on November 5, 1989. The locomotive is seen hauling a pair of brake vans and Austerity 0-6-0 No. 8 *Sir Robert Peel* assisting the train over Alderbottom No. 2 Bridge heading towards Rawtenstall with the second train of the day. The photograph has been taken from the adjacent bridge which once carried the Stubbins to Accrington line. THE LATE DAVE DYSON, COURTESY TIM GRIMSHAW

sought to increase its operational steam fleet in preparation for the extension of services towards Rawtenstall.

One of the earliest locomotives to be based on the fledgling ELR was Andrew Barclay 0-4-0ST NWGB No. 1, which came to Helmshore courtesy of North Western Gas Board from Burnley Gas Works. Although too small to work service trains on the railway, the locomotive was used to haul the first works trains through to Rawtenstall on November 5, 1989, working two trains on the line assisted by No. 32 *Gothenburg* on the first train and No. 8 *Sir Robert Peel* on the second. NWGB No. 1 has not steamed for many years and is now on semi-permanent display inside the rejuvenated Bury Transport Museum.

Although the ELR chose to primarily operate former BR steam locomotives on its services following the opening of the line to Rawtenstall in April 1991, there have still been plenty of visits from ex-industrial steam locomotives, primarily to work off-peak season and dining train services. Industrial locomotives that have spent extended periods in use on the railway's services over recent years have mainly been various Hunslet Austerity 0-6-0STs.

LONDON MIDLAND AND SCOTTISH RAILWAY

Being firmly based in the heart of the former British Railways London Midland Region, it is probably unsurprising that so many former LMS steam locomotives have worked on the railway over the years.

The first LMS steam locomotive to operate on the preserved ELR was Derek Foster's Fowler 3F 'Jinty' 0-6-0 No. 7298, which arrived on the ELR in 1988. As the first non-industrial steam locomotive to run on the railway, the 'Jinty' instantly proved to be extremely popular with locomotive crews, passengers and lineside photographers alike. It remained on the ELR for two years before leaving the line for a major

overhaul, returning to its previous home on the Llangollen Railway following the completion of works. No. 7298 returned to Bury in July 1993 for a three-month visit, before returning to North Wales.

However, No. 7298 returned to Bury in 2012 when it was purchased by Ian Riley. It has not yet returned to service, with Ian's main line locomotive fleet and contract work being prioritised, although the 'Jinty' is now nearing the end of its overhaul and it is likely to see use on the ELR following its completion.

Following its purchase from its previous owners on the Avon Valley Railway, several ELR members brought 'Jinty' No. 47324 to Bury in the mid-1990s. No. 47324 had undergone some restoration work, which was not completed, but as had been experienced with No. 7298 these powerful locomotives were more than capable of handling most services on the line.

With much of the funding for its overhaul coming from the ELR, agreement was reached for the ELR to have use of the locomotive throughout

the duration of its 10-year boiler certificate. No.47324 returned to service in 2005 and saw extensive use on the railway, as well as paying working visits to a couple of other heritage lines. Following its withdrawal, work is now under way on another major overhaul, which should hopefully be completed over the next couple of years.

The first LMS tender locomotive to grace ELR metals was 4F 0-6-0 No. 4422 which first arrived on the ELR in late 1992, following its return to service on the North Staffordshire Railway at Cheddleton earlier that year. The locomotive spent a number of months working on hire to the ELR and proved very popular.

Following a major overhaul the locomotive returned to Bury, this time painted in BR livery as No. 44422 and worked on the railway for an extended period between 2005 and 2007. The locomotive was subsequently placed on a long-term hire deal to the West Somerset Railway and is now based at Minehead.

The first former British Railways steam locomotive to be used on the modern-day East Lancashire Railway was LMS 3F 0-6-0 'Jinty' No. 7298, which was owned by Derek Foster. The locomotive ran on the ELR between 1988 and 1990, but returned for another shorter visit in the summer of 1993 and is seen heading through Little Burrs on June 27, 1993. MIKE TAYLOR

On November 4, 1990, ex-British Railways Standard 4 2-6-0 locomotive No. 76079 crosses over Brooksbottom Viaduct with a service from Bury to Ramsbottom. No. 76079 was the first ex-BR tender locomotive to run on the ELR. Behind the viaduct can be seen The Waterside public house, which was famously washed away during the Boxing Day floods of 2015. BOB GREEN

GWR-designed ex-British Rail 4-6-0 'Manor' No. 7828 *Odney Manor* arrived on the ELR in 1991 and remained on the railway until 1995, when it moved to a new home on the West Somerset Railway. The 'Manor' prepares to depart from Ramsbottom on September 1, 1991, heading towards Rawtenstall. KEITH SANDERS

The most common type of steam locomotive to have seen use on the ELR has been the ever-popular Stanier 5MT 4-6-0 'Black 5', with eight preserved members of the type having graced ELR metals. The first 'Black 5' to be hosted by the ELR was No. 44806, which at the time was painted into an attractive lined green livery, when it visited Helmshore station in August 1970 for what was the busiest ever open weekend held at the former preservation centre.

In 1984, the 26B Railway Company purchased No. 45337 from Dai Woodham's scrapyard in Barry. After a restoration spanning just over a decade, No. 45337 returned to service in 1995 and saw use both on the ELR and other heritage lines throughout the duration of its first boiler certificate. After being retired from service in 2005 No. 45337 underwent a major overhaul at the Locomotive Works, before returning to service in 2010. It moved to the Llangollen Railway the following year and is now part of the Llangollen Railway fleet.

The ELR Steam Railway Festival in August 1993 saw the late Paddy Smith move his ever-reliable LMS liveried No. 5407 to Bury to take part in the event. Paddy and his small support crew were instantly made welcome at Bury and following the end of the month-long festival he decided to keep No. 5407 at Bury and it joined the resident steam fleet. With No. 45337 still undergoing restoration at the time, it was No. 5407 which became the first preserved Stanier 5MT to work on the rejuvenated line to Rawtenstall.

In 1997 Paddy Smith sold No. 5407 to Bury-based engineer Ian Riley, who immediately set about overhauling the locomotive at his workshops, before it re-emerged resplendent in lined BR black as No. 45407, in time to work a special commemorative 30th anniversary recreation of the 1T57 '15 Guinea Special' along the ELR in August 1998.

Since then, No. 45407 has been a regular fixture once again on the main line network and at the ELR. It is now named *The Lancashire Fusilier*, but has spent two lengthy periods disguised as long-scrapped sister locomotive No. 45157 *The Glasgow Highlander*, including the 2018 season.

After being moved to Bury for restoration by the late Dr Peter Beet, 1968 End of Steam 1T57 Stanier 5MT No. 44871 was subsequently sold to Ian Riley, who had made no secret of his desire to purchase another 5MT to join No. 45407, in 2006. Ian continued the restoration of the locomotive, which returned to service in late 2009.

As with No. 45407, his second 'Black 5' has been certified for main line running and both locomotives spend a lot of time working on the main line and making occasional visits to other heritage railways, but still call the ELR home. At least one of Ian's locomotives is usually made available to the ELR during the winter months if not undergoing maintenance or overhaul work. A restoration and operating agreement between Ian Riley and the Keighley and Worth Valley Railway in 2013 has seen No. 45212 also join Ian's fleet of main line registered steam locomotives. No. 45212 returned to action during 2016 and, as with his other locomotive, it often spends time at Bury when not in use elsewhere, although it is also expected to pay regular working visits to its owning railway over the Pennines.

The late Bert Hitchen moved his Stanier 5MT No. 45231 *The Sherwood Forester* to Bury in 2007, where it saw regular use on the ELR for five years until 2012, when it moved to Carnforth to join the main line steam fleet used by West Coast Railways. Following the death of Bert Hitchen in 2015 No. 45231 was purchased by Jeremy Hosking and moved to Crewe, where it has been overhauled and returned to action in 2017.

Other Stanier 5MTs that have spent time working at Bury have been Ian

LMS 4F 0-6-0 No. 4422 spent a number of months on hire to the ELR in 1992 and 1993, returning one of these locomotives to Lancashire for the first time in many years. No. 4422 passes over Brooksbottom Viaduct as the sun sets on December 28, 1992. BOB GREEN

In August 1993, the ELR organised its Steam Railway Festival to commemorate the 25th anniversary of the end of steam on British Railways. Among the many visiting locomotives was the Keighley and Worth Valley Railway's Stanier 8F 2-8-0 No. 48431, which for the final day of the festival was renumbered as No. 48278 and adorned with accurate markings, as applied to No. 48278, which was the final Copy Pit banker locomotive at the end of the steam in 1968. The completed locomotive awaits unveiling at the Locomotive Works yard on August 29, 1993. MIKE TAYLOR

Adopting a particularly Great Western Railway feel, the GWR trio of 'Manor' 4-6-0 No. 7828 *Odney Manor*, 'Castle' 4-6-0 No. 5029 *Nunney Castle* and 2-8-0T No. 5224 await their next duties outside the running shed at Castlecroft on the evening of November 13, 1992. MIKE TAYLOR

Storey's No. 44767 *George Stephenson* and the Mid Hants Railway's No. 45379.

Hughes-Fowler 'Crab' 4-6-0 No. 42765 was delivered to Bury in August 1993 following a major overhaul at Ian Riley's former workshops at Kirkby in Merseyside. The engine was owned by a private individual but the ELR had provided a large amount of the money required to overhaul No. 42765 and had a share in the locomotive as a result. Following its delivery to Bury the locomotive was tested and moved around Buckley Wells under its own power before being repainted into BR lined black livery.

However, a legal dispute over the ownership of the locomotive overshadowed its return to service and after working a few services on the railway it was taken out of service, pending the resolution of the legal dispute. After a few months of legal wrangling, agreement was finally reached for the locomotive to be purchased outright by the ELR and, following this, it settled down to become a regular and reliable performer on the railway.

No. 42765 was withdrawn in 2003 for major overhaul, but the return to service was rather protracted. It returned to use in 2013 painted in original LMS crimson as No. 13065 and saw five years' use on the ELR before problems with the boiler tubes caused its premature withdrawal in early 2018. The boiler is now being overhauled by Riley and Son (E) Ltd at its new Heywood facility and it is expected to re-enter service with a new 10-year boiler certificate in early 2019.

In September 1996, the National Railway Museum's Hughes Fowler 'Crab' No. 2700 was delivered to Bury as part of the ELR 150 celebrations to commemorate the 150th anniversary of the opening of the Bury to Rawtenstall line. The locomotive had spent a number of years based at Bury prior to being preserved as part of the National

Collection. Known to be in fairly poor condition, No. 2700 was fully assessed by the ELR with a view to it being returned to service on the railway, subject to a suitable agreement with the NRM. However, when examined it was found that the work to return it to steam would be both extensive and costly, leading to the ELR deciding that it could not restore the locomotive to service. As a result, it moved to Barrow Hill, before then moving to the NRM's Locomotion site at Shildon, where it has since been repainted into original LMS crimson livery and renumbered as No. 13000.

The ELR has also played host to three of the four surviving Stanier 4-6-0 'Jubilee' locomotives. Nos. 5593 *Kolhapur* and 45596 *Bahamas* both visited the railway for the August 1993 Steam Railway Festival, with both paying return visits over the following couple of years. No. 5593 has now not steamed for a number of years and is awaiting an overhaul at Tyseley Locomotive Works, while No. 45596 is also at Tyseley where it is nearing the

end of a major overhaul and should return to service before the end of 2018.

In 1994, the Severn Valley Railway sold 'Jubilee' No. 5690 *Leander* to the late Dr Peter Beet, who moved the locomotive to Bury for restoration. Work was completed towards the end of 2002 and it was repainted into the popular LMS crimson lake colours as No. 5690 before entering regular service on the ELR in 2003. It was also chosen as the locomotive charged with hauling the first passenger train to Heywood when the Bury to Heywood line was officially opened in September 2003.

It had long been the intention of the owners for *Leander* to return to main line action and, therefore, after seeing regular use on the ELR for a number of years Dr Beet's son, Chris Beet, moved the locomotive to Carnforth in 2008 where it joined the main line steam fleet operated by the West Coast Railway Company. However, the locomotive paid a brief but welcome return visit to the ELR in March 2018, now painted in BR lined black livery, to take part in the

The first Southern Region locomotive to visit the ELR was Merchant Navy Class 4-6-2 'Pacific' No. 35005 *Canadian Pacific* which, unusually, faced south for the month of its visit in 1991. The Pacific arrives at Bury Bolton Street station on August 11, 1991, having hauled a service from Rawtenstall. KEITH SANDERS

After the end of the 1993 Steam Railway Festival, two former residents of the now-closed Steamtown in Carnforth relocated to Bury, with Paddy Smith's ever-reliable Stanier 5MT 4-6-0 No. 5407 and Betty Beet's Ivatt 2MT 2-6-0 No. 46441. No 5407 stands at the head of a special train to Pilsworth Road bridge on the Heywood line, which was the limit of operation at the time, on July 25, 1993.
MIKE TAYLOR

Returned to service in September 1993 was Hughes Fowler 'Crab' 2-6-0 No. 42765. The locomotive was eventually purchased by the ELR from its original owner and has remained a valuable part of the steam fleet ever since. During a 26D Charters photographic charter, the 'Crab' hauls a demonstration freight service over Brooksbottom Viaduct in Summerseat on December 16, 1997.
TERRY EYRES

railway's spring steam weekend.

Although none have been based on the railway, three preserved Stanier 8F 2-8-0 locomotives have spent time working on the ELR. First to visit the line was No. 48431 from the Keighley and Worth Valley Railway. The locomotive worked on the railway for a number of months and during the 1993 Steam Railway Festival, No. 48431 was suitably disguised as No. 48278, which had been the last Copy Pit Banker in 1968.

The Severn Valley Railway's No. 48773 also paid a brief working visit to the railway in 2012, while LMS crimson liveried No. 8624 paid a month-long visit to Bury in 2010, before returning again as BR black No. 48624 in 2017 from the Great Central Railway.

Former Somerset and Dorset Railway 7F 2-8-0 No. 53809 spent a number of months based on the ELR between 1993 and 1994, this being the only working appearance on the ELR for one these popular and versatile locomotives.

Another Beet family steam locomotive to call the ELR home for a number of years was Ivatt Class 2MT 2-6-0 No. 46441, which had been another

guest at the August 1993 Steam Railway Festival. The locomotive carried a non-authentic, but attractive, lined BR maroon livery and proved to be ideally suited to hauling ELR services.

The Ivatt remained on the ELR for almost 10 years until the expiry of its boiler certificate in 2002. In 1998 it was repainted into BR black livery, which it retained until after it was withdrawn from service, when it was returned to the owners' preference of BR lined maroon. No. 46441 was subsequently moved to the Ribble Steam Railway for static display, but moved to the Lakeside and Haverthwaite Railway in 2018 for an overhaul to return it to working order.

With work on BR Standard 4 Tank 2-6-4 No. 80097 nearing completion, the Bury Standard 4 Group has now started work on stripping down and overhauling its Ivatt 2MT locomotive, No. 46428, which has been stored on the ELR since arriving at Bury in 1987, although it is likely to be a number of years before its second locomotive enters service on the ELR. Another Ivatt 2MT that has seen use on the ELR was the Severn Valley Railway's No. 46443, which visited

the line in 2011 for three months. This locomotive is now out of service and on display at the SVR's Engine House museum at Highley.

In 1995, former Lancashire and Yorkshire Railway 0-6-0 No. 1300 moved to Bury and brought the locomotive back firmly into its former L&YR territory. The locomotive was subsequently sold to ELR member and volunteer Andy Booth and has seen use on the railway regularly over the years, but is also hired to other heritage railways on occasion. It is currently painted in BR unlined black livery as No. 52322.

One of the preserved LMS 'Pacific' locomotives to call the ELR home was 'Princess Royal Class' 4-6-2 No. 6201 *Princess Elizabeth* which arrived at Bury in 2004. The prestigious locomotive was used at special events on the railway and during its time at Bury it also underwent a major overhaul by Riley and Son (E) Ltd in the Locomotive Works. A regular performer on the main line, No. 6201 left the ELR for a new home at Crewe Heritage Centre in 2009. The locomotive is currently out of service awaiting major repairs and has recently moved to the West Coast Railway Company base at Carnforth.

Two of the three preserved Stanier LMS 'Coronation Class' 4-6-2 locomotives have also operated on the ELR. While owned by Bressingham Steam Museum, No. 6233 *Duchess of Sutherland* was brought to Bury as a static exhibit for the August 1993 Steam Railway Festival and attempts were made by the railway to restore the locomotive, although final agreement could not be reached. Now owned and operated by the Princess Royal Class Locomotive Trust, the locomotive returned to Bury 20 years later painted in BR green livery as No. 46233 for a working visit.

The National Railway Museum's former flagship locomotive No. 46229 *Duchess of Hamilton* first visited the

On April 13, 1993, LMS 4F 0-6-0 No. 4422 was disguised as long-scrapped sister locomotive No. 44525 for a photographic freight charter along the line. In a timeless scene, No. 44525 stands at Ramsbottom station.
KEITH SANDERS

ELR in 1996, returning the following year for another working spell on the railway. During this visit, the locomotive was repainted into BR green livery following an approach by a group of locally based photographers who offered to fund the works and return the locomotive to the NRM's preferred choice of BR maroon after an agreed period.

During this visit it was inspected by a boiler inspector who stated the locomotive must be withdrawn following a limited number of steamings and after carrying BR green for three months, the 'Pacific' was withdrawn after a special event in March 1998. It was then repainted into BR maroon, as promised, and returned to the NRM for static display. It has since had its streamlined outer casing returned to it, but has not yet been returned to steam.

Between 2012 and 2014 the ELR also operated sole-surviving London and North Western Railway 0-8-0 'Super D' No. 49395, which belonged to the National Railway Museum but was being operated by Pete Waterman after he had sponsored the cost of returning the locomotive to service. It was withdrawn from service at the start of 2014 following the discovery of leaking boiler tubes.

GREAT WESTERN RAILWAY

During the early years of the ELR's big engine policy, you could be forgiven for thinking the line was based firmly in Great Western territory, rather than deep in the London Midland Region.

The first ex-GWR designed locomotive to arrive on the ELR was 4-6-0 'Manor' No. 7828 *Odney Manor*, which arrived on the railway in early 1991. Initial gauging trials with the locomotive found that its protruding cylinders fouled the curved platform edges at Ramsbottom station, leading to volunteers having to hastily trim back the platform coping stones before the locomotive could be used on the railway. No. 7828 remained on the railway in regular service

The arrival of ex-Lancashire and Yorkshire 0-6-0 No. 52322 returned the locomotive to the ELR route which passed to the L&YR following that company taking over the original East Lancashire Railway. During a special photographers' freight charter on November 1, 1995, No. 52322 crosses over Brooksbottom Viaduct, looking very much at home. MIKE TAYLOR

until 1995 when it moved to the West Somerset Railway. No. 7822 *Foxcote Manor* also paid a short working visit to the line in June 2003 from the Llangollen Railway.

In 1992, two further GWR visitors arrived on the railway in the shape of Collett 4-6-0 'Castle' No. 5029 *Nunney Castle* and 2-8-0 Tank No. 5224. No. 5029 returned to Bury again in 1994 and 1997, while No. 5224 also came back to the ELR for another working spell in 1994.

Two other 'Castle' Class locomotives have also visited the railway, in the shape of Tyseley's Nos. 5080 *Defiant* and 7029 *Clun Castle*.

Visiting from Didcot Railway Museum, GWR Hawksworth Modified Hall 4-6-0 No. 6998 *Burton Agnes Hall* was the first 'Hall' to grace ELR metals in August 1993. Another Modified Hall, No. 6990 *Witherslack Hall*, visited the railway in the summer of 2017 from the Great Central Railway and returned again for a further hire period in summer 2018. A Collett 4-6-0 Hall, No. 4936 *Kinlet Hall*, also spent a few months on the line between the winter of 2008 and spring of 2009.

Other GWR visitors to the 1993 Steam Railway Festival were Churchward 2-8-0 No. 2857 from the Severn Valley Railway and Collett 2-8-0 No. 3822 from Didcot Railway Centre. During its visit No. 3822 hauled a train of 23 Mark 1 carriages from Bury to Rawtenstall, becoming the heaviest train to be worked by a steam locomotive in preservation history. Another Collett 2-8-0 No. 3802 visited for the autumn 2007 steam gala weekend.

The National Railway Museum's GWR Churchward 4-4-0 No. 3440 *City of Truro* was one of the star attractions at the ELR's 20th anniversary of reopening celebrations in the summer of 2007.

Another GWR that saw use on the railway for a number of months during 2015 was the Furness Railway Trust's 0-6-2T No. 5643. The small but powerful Port Talbot Docks 0-6-0ST locomotive No. 813 visited the ELR from its usual home on the Severn Valley Railway during 2017 and returned to the ELR during summer 2018 for a further period on hire to the railway.

The ELR has two ex-GWR based on the line which are still undergoing restoration to working order. Collett

Unique BR Standard 4-6-2 'Pacific' No. 71000 *Duke of Gloucester* was based on the ELR between 1994 and 2012, operating on the railway when it was not in use on the main line. On April 14, 1995, No. 71000 crosses over Ramsbottom Level Crossing while working a Rawtenstall to Bury service. NEIL HARVEY

Great Western Railway tank locomotive No. 4277 hauls a short train of three Mark 1 coaches away from Irwell Vale, with a service to Rawtenstall on December 27, 1996. MIKE TAYLOR

Brought to the ELR for running-in trials, the National Railway Museum's LNER V2 2-6-2 No. 60800 *Green Arrow* had a rather shaky start to its return to service, due to numerous leaks from the boiler which had to be repaired. On September 2, 1998, No. 60800 heads through Burrs on a photographic charter train. TERRY EYRES

'7200' 2-8-2T locomotive No. 7229 arrived on the railway in 1989 and was quickly stripped down to allow restoration work to start. While a lot of work was completed on the frames and a new bunker was constructed, restoration was not completed and the locomotive was stored as a kit of parts at Bury for many years.

During 2017 it was reassembled to allow a detailed inspection to take place as to the work required to return it to steam and it is now planned that the locomotive will be rebuilt over the next few years, although no completion date has yet been stated.

Also based on the line undergoing restoration is another Collett designed GWR locomotive. 2-8-0 No. 3885 is being restored from scrap condition by Andy Booth, the owner of Lancashire and Yorkshire Railway 'A' Class No. 52322 and converted Austerity 0-6-0 tender locomotive No. 2890, both of which are also nominally based at the ELR. Mr Booth has completed the restoration of the locomotive's tender and is also starting work on the restoration of

the locomotive itself, although with a number of other locomotives in his ownership, its restoration to working order is still some way from completion.

LONDON NORTH EASTERN RAILWAY

The first locomotive classed under the LNER banner to run on the railway was ex-Great Eastern Railway N7 No. 69621, which visited the ELR for four months in the summer of 1991. The locomotive proved to be extremely popular and was a useful addition to the steam fleet for the first few months of two-train running through to Rawtenstall, which had opened shortly before the N7 arrived on the line. No. 69621 is currently out of use awaiting a major overhaul and can be found on display at the East Anglian Railway Museum.

After receiving repairs by Riley & Son (E) Ltd in the Locomotive Works, LNER Holden B12 No. 61572 undertook some test running and use on passenger services in December 2003 and January 2004 before returning to its normal home base on the North Norfolk Railway.

Both preserved LNER Thompson B1 4-6-0 locomotives have visited the ELR, with No. 61264 arriving for a short working visit in 2004, returning again 10 years later in 2014, while No. 61306 *Mayflower*, then owned by Neil Boden, arrived in October 2012 for the annual autumn steam event.

LNER Peppercorn K1 2-6-0 No. 62005 is another locomotive which has appeared at the ELR on two occasions. The locomotive, which is a regular performer on the main line, first appeared on ELR service trains in 1999 and returned to the railway again during 2013, when the opportunity was taken to pair it up with John Cameron's K4 No. 61994 *The Great Marquess*.

In November 2003 North Eastern Railway J27 No.2392 visited the ELR from the North Yorkshire Moors Railway and remained on the line until February 2004.

Another regular visitor to the railway when it was not in main line use was John Cameron's Gresley K4 2-6-0 No. 61994 *The Great Marquess*. The popular locomotive spent a number of periods on hire to the railway, but following the expiry of its boiler certificate the owner now plans to cosmetically restore the locomotive prior to displaying it in a specially built museum facility on his farm in Scotland, along with LNER A4 No. 60009 *Union of South Africa*. There are no plans by the owner for the locomotive to be returned to steam at any point in the future and it is currently in store at the Bo'ness and Kinneil Railway.

The National Railway Museum's ever-popular LNER 2-6-2 V2 No. 60800 *Green Arrow* arrived at Bury in September 1998 for running-in trials, following completion of its restoration at York. However, problems were quickly experienced with the boiler during the trials and it suffered from numerous steam leaks, with repairs having to be carried out before it could be used again.

Green Arrow returned to Bury for

LNER A2 4-6-2 No. 60532 *Blue Peter* spent the winter of 1999/2000 based at Bury, with it seeing use primarily at both the January and February 2000 steam events. Shortly after its arrival in Bury, No. 60532 stands in Platform 3 at Bury Bolton Street for a photographic evening using the locomotive, which was not in steam for the event. TERRY EYRES

Stanier 4-6-0 'Jubilee' No. 45596 *Bahamas* emerges from Bury EL Tunnel with a Bury to Rawtenstall service on July 17, 1994. DAVID A INGHAM

GWR 'Hall' 4-6-0 No. 4936 *Kinlet Hall* visited the ELR in 2008 from its usual base at Tyseley Locomotive Works and is pictured heading through Burrs with a Heywood to Rawtenstall service on February 17, 2008. NIGEL VALENTINE

The appearance of National Railway Museum Stanier 'Duchess' 4-6-2 No. 46229 *Duchess of Hamilton* in BR green livery brought much attention to the ELR and the NRM's flagship locomotive, which was due to be withdrawn following a limited number of steamings. On the evening of January 24, 1998, the locomotive stands in the Locomotive Works yard awaiting its next duties. KEITH SANDERS

another working visit in 2001 and again in 2008 towards the end of its boiler certificate, by which time it had been repainted into LNER apple green livery as No. 4771. Since expiry of its boiler certificate the locomotive is now on display at Locomotion in Shildon and there are no current plans for it to be returned to service.

LNER Gresley N2 0-6-2 Tank locomotive No. 1744 was loaned to the ELR for a six-month period, arriving on the line from its usual home on the Great Central Railway in October 2012.

The ELR is also one of the few heritage lines to have played host to a member of each of the East Coast A1-A4 classes of locomotives. New build Peppercorn A1 4-6-2 No. 60163 *Tornado* first visited the railway in 2010 and returned again during Easter 2018, where its visit also coincided with a static appearance by the National Railway Museum's A3 No. 60103 *Flying Scotsman* at Bury Bolton Street station.

The sole-surviving A2 4-6-2 No. 60532 *Blue Peter* also visited the line in 2000 during its last period of operation. The A2 has now been out of service for a number of years and it is now owned by Jeremy Hosking and undergoing an overhaul at his Crewe Diesel Depot Workshops.

A3 4-6-2 No. 60103 *Flying Scotsman* first spent a month on the ELR in February 1993, when it was still carrying LNER apple green livery as No. 4472, while the world famous locomotive was working a tour of heritage railways under the auspices of then-owners Sir William McAlpine and Pete Waterman.

Following the purchase of the locomotive by the National Railway Museum in 2004, the contract to overhaul the locomotive was awarded to Bury-based engineering company Riley and Son (E) Ltd, with the contract including the first two years of operation and maintenance following the completion of the overhaul.

After a somewhat protracted overhaul where a number of unexpected items were discovered during the works, the locomotive returned to steam in January 2016 and completed its test running at the ELR, attracting attention from the national media and bringing in a huge amount of publicity for the railway.

No. 60103 returned again during 2016 for a short working visit, where it was used on a number of services, with every train hauled by the locomotive being sold out, including premium luxury dining trains.

Although 2017 saw no visits to the railway by the locomotive, it returned to the railway during 2018, where it has been put on static display at Rawtenstall and Bury Bolton Street stations for footplate visits, as well as working trips along the railway. Riley and Son (E) Ltd has since been awarded the operating contract for the locomotive for the next six years and No. 60103 is often stabled at Bury when it is not working on the main line or on display at the National Railway Museum in York.

The ELR has also played host to two LNER Gresley A4 4-6-2 locomotives, with both No. 60007 *Sir Nigel Gresley* and No. 60009 *Union of South Africa* spending periods of time on the railway. No. 60007 was based on the line for a number of years before relocating to the North Yorkshire Moors Railway, which remains its home railway to the present day, although it is currently undergoing a major overhaul.

No. 60009 has also visited on a couple of occasions between main line trips and has also spent a lot of time on the railway during 2017 and 2018 while undergoing various repairs and maintenance work by Riley and Son (E) Ltd engineers.

The most recent trips operated by No. 60009 on the ELR have proved to be particularly popular with enthusiasts

RIGHT: With a hard and severe frost on the ground, BR Standard 4 4-6-0 No. 75014 heads through Walmersley Woods on December 30, 2000. While the conditions were far from ideal for the photographer, the harsh weather ensured some dramatic images were captured. NEIL HARVEY

Some of the most powerful locomotives to run on the ELR have been the BR Standard 2-10-0 9Fs, with No. 92214 pictured passing beneath Market Street Bridge in Bury, about to negotiate the steep climb over the Metrolink Bridge, before arriving at Bury Bolton Street station, on January 29, 2006. NEIL HARVEY

Small but powerful is an apt description for LMS Fowler 3F 0-6-0 No. 47324, which entered service on the ELR in 2005 following restoration from scrap condition. The locomotive is pictured heading up Broadfield Bank between Bury and Heywood on May 30, 2009. NIGEL VALENTINE

following the announcement by its owner, John Cameron, that the locomotive will be permanently retired upon the expiry of its current boiler certificate and placed on display in a specially built museum facility at his farm in Scotland.

SOUTHERN REGION

One of the first Southern Region locomotives to visit the ELR in 1990 was former USA 0-6-0T No. 30072 which visited for four months from the Keighley and Worth Valley Railway. No. 30072 was one of a number of former US War Department locomotives to be taken on by the Southern Railway in 1947 and was bought for preservation on the KWVR in 1967.

The locomotive is now owned by ELR volunteer Andy Booth, but is being overhauled at the Ribble Steam Railway. As one of the locomotives to haul the reopening train on the KWVR in June 1968, it had been hoped that No. 30072 could be returned to service in time for the KWVR's 50th anniversary celebrations in June 2018, but its overhaul has not yet been completed.

The next Southern locomotive to arrive at Bury was somewhat bigger,

in the shape of Merchant Navy 4-6-2 'Pacific' No. 35005 *Canadian Pacific*, which paid a working visit to the ELR in August 1991, becoming the first 'Pacific' to run on the preserved line. *Canadian Pacific* returned to the ELR for the August 1993 Steam Railway Festival, again spending a number of weeks working in Lancashire. No. 35005 is now based on the Mid Hants Railway and undergoing overhaul.

The most numerous Southern Region locomotives to appear at the ELR have been examples of the Bulleid 'Battle of Britain' and 'West Country' 4-6-2s. Rebuilt No. 34027 *Taw Valley* was delivered to Bury Transport Museum during the mid-1980s following its rescue from Woodhams Scrapyard, but left the ELR before its restoration was completed. It subsequently returned to the railway in 1999 for a working visit and spent a number of months based at the Locomotive Works. No. 34027 was eventually sold to a prominent member of the Severn Valley Railway and is now regularly in service on their line.

Jeremy Hosking sent his rebuilt 'West Country' No. 34046 *Braunton* to Bury in 2012 for contract repairs by Riley & Son (E) Ltd and following the completion of

repairs the locomotive saw use on ELR services for a number of weeks.

No. 34072 *257 Squadron* was the first example of the design to see use on the ELR, when it spent six months on hire to the railway in 1992, courtesy of its owner Southern Locomotives Ltd.

No. 34067 *Tangmere* was completely rebuilt at Bury by Ian Riley in the Locomotive Works between 1996 and 2003. Following completion of its restoration the locomotive was owned and operated jointly by Ian Riley and John Bunch, working extensively on the main line network, as well as the occasional working spell on the ELR. No. 34067 was subsequently sold to an individual connected to the West Coast Railway Company and continued to see use on the main line, prior to the expiry of its boiler certificate. It is currently out of service.

Visiting from the Keighley and Worth Valley Railway in 2015 was No. 34092 *City of Wells* (then temporarily named *Wells*), which saw extensive use on the railway. However, a ban on locomotives being delivered to the KWVR due to road damage resulted in No. 34092 staying at Bury beyond its original intended return date.

Facing south, LNER Gresley A4 4-6-2 'Pacific' No. 60009 *Union of South Africa* emerges from Brooksbottom Tunnel, on the approach to Summerseat station, with a train from Rawtenstall to Heywood on April 23, 2017. LIAM BARNES

Bathed in steam at the Locomotive Works, BR Standard 4, 2-6-0 No. 76084 is highlighted by the shed lights during a Lostock Hall themed photographic evening on March 9, 2017. LIAM BARNES

Agreement was subsequently reached for it to remain at Bury on hire throughout 2016 and 2017. In 2017 the three owners of the locomotive agreed to sell the locomotive to the ELR, subject to the purchase price being paid in full by the end of 2018. A major fundraising appeal is now under way to raise £341,000 towards the purchase price, with more than £200,000 having been raised at the time of writing. The purchase of No. 34092 is part of the ELR's aim to become more self-sufficient in relation to available steam locomotives for the line.

Another 'Battle of Britain' to be based on the railway was unrestored No. 34073 *249 Squadron*, which spent a number of years stored in the Locomotive Works yard while No. 34067 was also based on the railway. No restoration work was carried out on this locomotive and it was moved from Bury to Carnforth in 2014.

Other Southern Region locomotives which have run on the railway have been Urie S15 4-6-0 No. 30506 which visited in August 1993 and the NRM's 'King Arthur' 4-6-0 No. 30777 *Sir Lamiel*, courtesy of custodians the 5305 Locomotive Association in February 2010. Maunsell 4-6-0 No. 850 *Lord Nelson* also spent a few weeks at Bury in February and March 2012.

BRITISH RAILWAYS

The first tender locomotive to run on the ELR was BR Standard 4 2-6-0 No. 76079 which arrived on the railway in August 1989 following an overhaul by its then-owner Derek Foster. The locomotive instantly proved to a popular attraction and it operated services on the line on one weekend per month, along with various special events.

It subsequently moved to the Llangollen Railway in 1992 but returned to Bury briefly in August 1993 for the ELR Festival of Steam event, where it was named *Trevor T Jones* in support of the then-ELR chairman.

No. 76079 returned to Bury in late 1998 after it was bought by Ian Riley and following an overhaul it operated on the main line alongside his Stanier 5MT 4-6-0 No. 45407 *The Lancashire Fusilier*. Gaining the nickname 'The Pocket Rocket', No. 76079 operated on the ELR when it was not in main line use and once again proved itself ideal for the line. Ian Riley sold No. 76079 to the North Yorkshire Moors Railway and it moved to its new home in 2009, where it remains.

No. 76084, owned by the 76084 Locomotive Company Ltd, has also paid two working visits to the railway, returning this locomotive to Lancashire for the first time in preservation, with it spending much of its working life on BR based at Lower Darwen, just a few miles away from Bury. The locomotive is usually based on the North Norfolk

During its second working visit to the ELR, new build Peppercorn A1 4-6-2 'Pacific' No. 60163 *Tornado* departs from Irwell Vale with a service to Bury on March 29, 2018. LIAM BARNES

Railway, but is also registered for main line running.

The ELR has also been visited by various BR Standard 4 4-6-0 locomotives, with the Keighley and Worth Valley Railway's No. 75078 becoming the first when it arrived at Bury in 1990 for a three-month visit, with it being paired with No. 76079 at a number of special events. No. 75078 also had the honour of being the first ex-BR steam locomotive to arrive at Rawtenstall in the preservation era, when it took part in a gauging run to the still-to-be-opened Northern terminus on November 4, 1990, a year after the first works train had visited the terminus.

No. 75014 also spent a number of working visits to the ELR while owned by the late Bert Hitchen and Brian Cooke. No. 75014 was another main line registered locomotive, which regularly spent the winter months and periods when it was not in main line use based at the Locomotive Works. No. 75014 was sold to the Paignton and Dartmouth Railway and is regularly in service on the line following a return to steam in December 2016 after a major overhaul.

The third BR Standard 4 4-6-0 to run on the ELR was the North Yorkshire Moors Railway's BR lined green liveried No. 75029 *The Green Knight*, which visited the line along with Stanier 5MT No. 45212 for the October 2002 steam weekend.

Another type of locomotive appropriate for the area are the BR Standard 4 Tank 2-6-4 locomotives, some of which were allocated to Bury Steam Shed during BR days. The ELR has played host to a number of the operational BR Standard 4 Tanks over the past few years, while another, No. 80097, is now in the final stages of reassembly at Bury following a 30-year restoration and it is expected to enter service on the railway during the summer of 2018.

The first operational locomotive of the type to see use on the ELR was newly restored No. 80136, which visited

the railway from its then-home on the North Staffordshire Railway in 1999.

The Princess Royal Class Locomotive Trust's No. 80080 has also spent a number of years on hire to the railway, operating services between 2011 and 2016, but has spent the past two years under overhaul at the owners' Swanwick base. No. 80080 is due to return to the ELR during 2018 for a further hire period, where it will hopefully see use alongside No. 80097. The PRCLT's other Standard 4 Tank, No. 80098, also spent a period on loan to the ELR during 2009, before the expiry of its boiler certificate.

The North Yorkshire Moors Railway's Standard 4 Tank, No. 80135, paid a short working visit to the ELR in October and November 2006, while No. 80072 from the Llangollen Railway was a visitor for the winter steam event in February 2011.

Perhaps one of the most powerful BR Standard locomotive designs was

During the past few years, LNER Gresley A4 4-6-0 No. 60009 *Union of South Africa* has been a regular visitor to the railway, having undergone a series of repairs by Riley & Son (E) Ltd staff at the Locomotive Works. On October 12, 2017, No.60009 stands in Platform 4 at Bury Bolton Street station after arriving on the railway from main line duties. LIAM BARNES

The ELR is currently actively fundraising to purchase Southern Railway 'West Country' 4-6-0 No. 34092 *City of Wells*, which has been based on the railway since 2015. On September 17, 2016, No 34092 approaches Irwell Vale with a service for Rawtenstall. Over £200,000 has been raised towards the £340,000 appeal at the time of writing. LIAM BARNES

For the 2018 season, Ian Riley's Stanier 5MT 4-6-0 locomotive No. 45407 is being disguised as long-scrapped No. 45157 *The Glasgow Highlander* and the locomotive is seen emerging from Ramsbottom sidings with a demonstration good train on March 4, 2018. Shortly afterwards, the locomotive left the ELR for another successful season in Scotland working 'The Jacobite' services on behalf of West Coast Railway Company. NIGEL VALENTINE

the 9F 2-10-0 locomotives and three of the preserved examples have seen use on the ELR. The first 9F to run on the railway was the late David Shepherd's No. 92203 *Black Prince*, which first arrived on the railway in August 1993 and subsequently returned to the line again for a second time in 1995.

No. 92212 arrived on the ELR for the winter in 2001 and saw use on Santa Specials and at the January and February steam events in 2002, while No. 92214 joined the home-based fleet between 2005 and 2008, where it saw extensive use on passenger services, especially during peak season, where it could easily handle the heaviest of trains.

In 1986, the ELR took delivery of No. 92207 from Woodhams scrapyard. The locomotive was named *Morning Star* by its owner and during its time at Bury a large number of parts were acquired for the locomotive by its owner. After 19 years based on the ELR, but still a long way from returning to service, No. 92207 moved to Shillingstone on the former Somerset and Dorset Railway, where restoration work on the locomotive continues.

The ELR was due to be the home base of single-chimney BR Standard 9F 2-10-0 No. 92134, the frames of which arrived at Bury in 2016, with the intention being that restoration of the locomotive was to be completed before the 9F entered service on the ELR. The locomotive does not currently have a tender and the owners planned to hire a tender from an out-of-service locomotive, pending the construction of a new tender for No. 92034. The boiler was steamed for the first time at LNWR Heritage at Crewe in late 2017, before moving to Bury and being placed in the locomotive's frames.

However, in 2018 the ELR announced that it did not have the resources available to complete the reassembly

of the locomotive until 2019 and it had mutually agreed with the owner for the 9F to move to another railway for completion. In April 2018 the locomotive returned to the North Yorkshire Moors Railway, which had been its home base when it was first rescued from the famous scrapyard at Barry in South Wales.

Unique Caprotti valve gear fitted BR Standard 5, 4-6-0 No. 73129 visited the ELR on a couple of hire periods courtesy of the Midland Railway Butterley, with the locomotive proving extremely popular on passenger services and photographic charters.

BR Standard 5, 4-6-0 No. 73156 was purchased from Woodhams Scrapyard by the Bolton Steam Locomotive Company and brought to the ELR in 1986 for restoration to working order. However, it was moved to the Great Central Railway in 2002 for completion of its restoration and it returned to service in early 2018.

Both surviving BR Standard 7 'Pacific' 4-6-2 locomotives, No. 70000 *Britannia*

BR Standard 4 Tank 4-6-0 No. 80080 was a regular performer on the ELR between 2011 and 2016 before returning to its Swanwick base for overhaul. The locomotive is due to return to the ELR during 2018. No. 80080 departs from Irwell Vale station to Rawtenstall on June 5, 2016. LIAM BARNES

and No. 70013 *Oliver Cromwell*, have visited the ELR, although No. 70000 was only on the railway for contract repairs by Riley and Son (E) Ltd at the Locomotive Works and did not see any use on ELR services. No. 70013 was loaned to the railway for a steam event in 2010 and returned to the railway again in 2013 for a further visit, courtesy of the National Railway Museum and the 5305 Locomotive Association, who are the custodians of the locomotive.

The ELR was also home for a number of years to unique BR Standard 8 'Pacific' 4-6-2 No. 71000 *Duke of Gloucester*. The locomotive first arrived on the railway in 1994 and remained part of the resident fleet until 2012, operating both on main line charters as well as running on the ELR.

OTHER

Three former United States of America Transportation Corps S160 2-8-0 locomotives have run on the ELR, with the first being the Keighley and Worth Valley Railway's No. 5820 *Big Jim*, arriving in Lancashire for a four-month hire period in 1992.

The powerful and imposing locomotive provided quite a contrast to the usual steam locomotives that worked between Bury and Rawtenstall.

No. 5197 also spent a number of months working on the railway, on loan from its usual base on the North Staffordshire Railway, while the Mid Hants Railway also loaned their S160, No. 3278 *Franklin D Roosevelt*, for a steam event.

Powerful War Department Austerity 2-8-0 No. 90733 was also loaned to the ELR at short notice from the railway's neighbours on the Keighley and Worth Valley Railway for a steam event in January 2010, making the first and only visit of one these locomotives to Lancashire.

JOANNE CROMPTON

FIREMAN

NIGEL VALENTINE

How did you get interested in railways?
"I wasn't really interested in railways as a youngster, although as a child I spent a lot of time with my grandad, a skilled engineer and steam modeller who built 3½ inch gauge steam locomotives and was passionate about his hobby. After he passed away, his collection was sold and as I grew up I didn't really have any interest in railways, as none of my family or friends were connected with them.

"On September 21, 2011, I was commuting to Preston and I remember standing on the platform at Leyland station and A1 4-6-2 'Pacific' No. 60163 *Tornado* came to a stand on the opposite platform. It was the first time I had ever seen a full-sized steam locomotive and I had no idea that such things still existed. As soon as I saw it I was mesmerised and just stared at it for a while, but there was something about it that fascinated me. I then boarded my train to Preston and when I arrived at the station *Tornado* was standing on Platform 7 taking water, so I went over to take a closer look at her.

"The sight and smell took me back to my childhood and those times with my grandad and his model steam locomotives. I watched the fireman on the footplate for a few minutes and at that moment I decided that's what I wanted to do, although at the time I had no idea how I could achieve this new ambition. I had no railway knowledge and no understanding of what was involved, but I just knew that I wanted to be on the footplate.

"I ended up being late for my job as a book-keeper and immediately went on the internet to find out more about these locomotives, quickly finding out just how many steam locomotives were still around. A colleague then told me there was a steam railway based in Preston, so shortly afterwards I joined the Ribble Steam Railway, where I initially worked as a ticket inspector and also in the cafe. However, I really wanted to be on the footplate, as the pull of steam was too great. I quickly got involved in the steam department and was invited to fire Andrew Barclay 0-4-0 *John Howe* for a short time on a trip and it was everything I hoped it would be. I loved it."

When did you get involved in volunteering at the ELR?
"My interest in steam was growing and every time I saw one of the large steam locomotives working through Preston on main line tours I was fascinated by them. Then someone told me about the East Lancashire Railway and I went down one weekend with my husband, Mark, during the January steam event.

"Again, I found myself just staring at the engines and watching the footplate crews at work from the platform at Bury. One of Ian Riley's 'Black 5s' was in the station and the driver, Garry Laxton, invited me on to the footplate and offered me a footplate ride as far as Ramsbottom. After passing my bag to Mark I got on and after telling them about my

firing experience at Ribble, they invited me to fire the 'Black 5' for a short distance on the way to Ramsbottom. Garry told me that if I wanted to get involved in the railway I needed to join the society and could then volunteer in the steam department if I wanted to.

"I came back for another visit a few weeks later and this time I got chatting to another two steam volunteers, driver Malcolm Frost and fireman Ian Chapman, and they also encouraged me to join the railway and get involved, so I completed my membership form and started working as a volunteer in the steam department.

"My first cleaning turn on the railway came in March 2013, when the railway was hosting LNER K1 No. 62005 and during that first day I was given the chance again to fire the locomotive for a short time, which I managed okay. I spent a year learning about the railway and steam locomotives during my cleaning turns – I was a complete novice with no knowledge of railways and how they operated. Most people joining the railway as a volunteer are already enthusiasts with a knowledge and understanding as to how the railways work, but this was all very new to me. It was a steep learning curve, but every time I was on the footplate I tried to soak in as much knowledge as I could. The railway and the other steam department volunteers made me very welcome, although I think there was some scepticism as to whether I would continue volunteering for the long term.

"In 2014, I almost walked away because I was suffering from a bit of self-doubt about whether I would be able to make the grade, but one of the railway's firemen trainers, Paul Greaves, convinced me that I had a natural talent for firing and urged me to stick with it. Paul was very encouraging and we have become firm friends since that day. We had a great day working on Andy Booth's L&Y No. 52322 and following my chat with Paul, I found a new determination and enthusiasm for firing and the ELR. A year later, on September 20, 2015, I became the ELR's first ever female passed cleaner and on December 1, 2017, I was promoted on to the fireman's roster.

"I've also been lucky enough to spend some time working on locomotives on the main line, as part of the support crew for Chris Beet's LMS 'Jubilee' No. 45690 *Leander* and for West Coast Railway Company. I'm not actively involved in main line operation at the moment, but hopefully this is something I can do again in the future.

"Firing on the main line is a little different than on heritage railways, as firing on a heritage railway requires a bit more boiler management and with more frequent stops and starts to consider. On the main line everything is on a much bigger scale, but once you've got going, stamina comes into play, supplying sufficient steam and water to keep the locomotive running at much higher speeds. Volunteering has also become a real family affair, as my husband Mark is also

now a volunteer in the steam department at the ELR and he has recently qualified as a passed cleaner."

What can the railway do to attract more women into areas that are traditionally male dominated?
"I would like to think that I am leading by example. I believe there are not enough women volunteering on our heritage railways, especially on the footplate. All jobs on the railway can be done by both men and women and if I can help to inspire one woman to come down and join our volunteer crews then that's a success. At the ELR we do have another female cleaner who has recently started volunteering in the steam department and hopefully more will come and join us in the future.

"Some railways, such as the North Yorkshire Moors Railway, have more female volunteers in traditionally male roles, such as on the footplate, but women are still very much under-represented at the moment in the sector. Being a woman is no longer a barrier to progressing on heritage railways and I would recommend volunteering to any woman who was thinking about it. Railways may be traditionally male orientated, but the vast majority of the volunteers I have met during my time on the railway have been very welcoming and have encouraged me to get where I am now. The railway needs to attract younger volunteers and more females and I believe that women should be used to promote recruitment on the railway, showing other women that they can get involved. Women should be encouraged to have the confidence to get involved and by having other women at the forefront of volunteer recruitment that can only help to show others that they can do it too."

Which locomotive would you like to see on the ELR in the future?
"I've been fortunate to work on a number of locomotives of all sizes since I got involved in footplate volunteering, but I would love to see an Ivatt 2MT locomotive on the railway, as they are lovely looking locomotives. I wasn't involved in the ELR when No. 46441 was based on the line, but I'd love to fire one."

A Home for Wells

No. 34092 *City of Wells* fits well into the Lancashire countryside as it approaches Irwell Vale with a service to Rawtenstall on September 17, 2016. LIAM BARNES

In its quest to expand its home-based steam fleet, the East Lancashire Railway is currently raising funds to allow the railway to purchase ex-Southern Region Bulleid 'West Country' 4-6-2 No. 34092 *City of Wells*.

For several years the East Lancashire Railway has aimed to become more self-sufficient when it comes to the steam locomotives that work on the railway. With the railway opening to Ramsbottom as recently as 1987, the ELR wasn't fortunate enough to purchase any steam locomotives directly from British Rail when it was first formed in 1968. A member of the ELRPS purchased Stanier 5MT 4-6-0 No. 44806, which he brought to Helmshore for an Open Weekend visit in 1970, but due to there being no covered accommodation at the site and with no immediate prospect of any revenue-earning work for the locomotive, it never returned to ELR metals.

The ELR has three steam locomotives on its books, with ex-North Western Gas Board Andrew Barclay 0-4-0ST No. 1 and ex-Manchester Ship Canal 0-6-0T Hudswell Clarke No. 32 *Gothenburg* representing the industrial smaller locomotives, with No. 1 on static display inside Bury Transport Museum and No. 32 in regular use, including

appearances disguised as No. 1 Thomas the Tank Engine.

In 1996, the ELR purchased Hughes-Fowler 2-6-0 'Crab' No. 13065 outright from its former owner after a legal dispute into the ownership of the locomotive between the two parties. The purchase of No. 13065 (or No. 42765 as it was then numbered) gave the railway its first ex-British Railways steam locomotive, which saw regular use on the ELR between 1994 and 2003, and then returned to service on the railway once again between 2013 and 2018. It is currently out of service undergoing another boiler overhaul and it is hoped that it will be back in service in early 2019.

However, the ELR is still forced to rely on hired-in steam locomotives from private owners and other heritage lines to cope with its annual service requirements, particularly during the peak summer months when the supply of steam locomotives can sometimes not always meet the demand for them.

The railway is fortunate in having

very good relationships with various locomotive owners and heritage railways, resulting in many steam locomotives gracing ELR metals over the years. Some of these locomotives have been hired in for a few weeks, while others have visited for a number of years, before moving on to either their previous home railways or on to other hire contracts.

In 2017 it was announced that the ELR was in negotiations with the three owners of Bulleid 'West Country' 4-6-2 No. 34092 *City of Wells* to purchase the locomotive, which had spent long periods on hire to the railway since first arriving on the line during the summer of 2015.

Since arriving at Bury, No. 34092 had proved itself to be more than capable of handling the heaviest ELR services, while also being popular with locomotive crews and costs about the same to operate on a daily basis as a Standard 4 Tank. Since 2015 it has amassed over 16,000 miles of running on the ELR and has certainly proved its worth. Owned by Richard Greenwood, Graham Bentley and John Adams since being rescued from Dai Woodham's scrapyard in Barry, South Wales, its sale to the ELR will bring an end to their 47-year ownership of the locomotive, over three times the 15-year period it was in operation with British Railways from 1949 until withdrawal in November 1964.

Based on the neighbouring Keighley and Worth Valley Railway (KWVR) since it became the 17th locomotive to escape from Woodham's scrapyard in October 1971, No. 34092 has been a regular on the ELR's steam roster since it first visited the railway in summer 2015.

No. 34092 first returned to steam following restoration from scrap condition in 1980 and enjoyed many memorable operating days both on the KWVR and the main line, becoming known as 'The Volcano' due to its powerful exhaust. Following the end of its first period of operation in preservation, it underwent a protracted overhaul, which was completed at Haworth in the summer of 2014.

Spearheading the fundraising appeal is ELR volunteer John Stephens, who is also chairman of the Class 40 Preservation Society. John is a natural salesman and he has a proven history of leading fundraising initiatives for the CFPS, successfully raising the six-figure purchase price for 40106 *Atlantic Conveyor* at very short notice when it was offered to the CFPS by its previous owner.

His task with *City of Wells* is somewhat more ambitious than that of 40106 and the fundraising appeal aims to raise £340,920 towards the purchase price of the locomotive by the end of 2018. And he's clearly excited at the prospect of securing the future of No. 34092 for the ELR: "It just makes so much sense for the railway to buy it. It's a powerful locomotive that can handle any of the ELR service trains, it's in excellent condition following its last overhaul and it still has a number of years remaining on its boiler certificate before it will fall due for another overhaul. The railway would be mad to let the opportunity pass them by."

John Stephens also has extensive experience of organising main line railtours, with the CFPS flagship Class 40 locomotive, 40145, registered for main line running. The CFPS has promoted a number of very successful tours using its own locomotive, in conjunction with Carnforth-based train operating partner company, West Coast Railway Company. Profits generated by the tours have been reinvested into the three-strong CFPS locomotive fleet.

It is through his experience with the CFPS that John Stephens has been organising a trip from Bury to Holyhead in mid-September 2018, hauled by legendary LNER A3 4-6-2 'Pacific'

Shortly after its delivery to the Keighley and Worth Valley Railway, No. 34092 is shunted into Haworth Yard by BR Standard 4 2-6-4 No. 80002, with restoration work getting under way shortly afterwards and it returned to service in 1980. RICHARD GREENWOOD

During its first period of main line operation No. 34092 *City of Wells* stands at Scarborough, after working the Scarborough Spa Express, adorned with an appropriate headboard, along with its now-familiar Golden Arrow headboard and bodyside arrows. RICHARD GREENWOOD

During an evening photographic session in the Locomotive Works yard, No, 34092 poses for the cameras on March 11, 2016. LIAM BARNES

City of Wells runs around its train on September 5, 2015, while the ELR's civil engineering department volunteers take a break from trackwork at Rawtenstall. KEVIN DELANEY

No. 60103 *Flying Scotsman*, with all profits going towards the 'Home for Wells' appeal. 'The Wells Flyer' is aimed at enthusiasts and day trippers who want to enjoy a train journey behind *Flying Scotsman* from the ELR to the North Wales Coast.

Main line running in the future for No. 34092 itself is also not being ruled out by the ELR, despite it being primarily purchased for use on ELR services. The locomotive put in some stunning main line performances during the 1980s and its excellent condition means re-certifying it for main line running in the future shouldn't present too many problems for the railway should they decide to register it again.

The biggest expense involved in certifying it for main line running would be the fitment of the mandatory safety equipment now required by any locomotive operating on the main line network and, in anticipation of a possible main line return, the wiring required for the safety equipment was all installed by the locomotive's owners during its last overhaul.

John Stephens also thinks main line running for No. 34092 could help the ELR to exploit another very successful facet of its business, as he explains: "The ELR's 'Dining with Distinction' programme is hugely popular and has been voted the No. 1 restaurant experience in Greater Manchester on Trip Advisor on a number of occasions. The railway's Friday evening and Sunday lunchtime dining trains often run at capacity and, despite a fairly extensive timetable of services, at times the

railway cannot satisfy the demand from customers.

"Wouldn't it be great if some Sunday dining trains could venture off the ELR on to the main line for an afternoon excursion, with a leisurely lunch and tea served on board the train before it returns to the ELR later in the afternoon? Obviously, a number of obstacles would have to be overcome before such a train could run, but having a suitably powerful main line steam locomotive available means there could be new markets that the ELR can investigate and I truly believe the luxury dining train market could be one area that the railway can exploit to its advantage."

The deadline for the purchase to be completed is the end of December and, to date, around £220,000 has been raised since the appeal was launched a year ago – the most successful fundraising appeal that has been organised by the ELR so far.

While the railway has set up a dedicated fundraising appeal, with a range of benefits available for donors to the appeal, traditional forms of fundraising – such as the sale of raffle tickets on the railway and donation envelopes being left on trains – are helping to encourage ELR passengers to dig deep for the appeal.

The operation of *Flying Scotsman* on a main line fundraising special train will undoubtedly add another hefty chunk of money towards the appeal, but the railway is not complacent and is aiming to try and reach its target by the end of the year.

In perfect lighting conditions, No. 34092 *City of Wells* stands at the head of its train in Platform 3 at Bury Bolton Street station on May 6, 2018, during the ELR's Day Out with Thomas event. NIGEL VALENTINE

■ More information on the 'Home for Wells' appeal and how you can help the ELR purchase this locomotive can be found at *www.preservationforgenerations.co.uk*

JOHN STEPHENS

CFPS CHAIRMAN AND 'HOME FOR WELLS' FUNDRAISER

JOHN WANTLING

Where did your interest in the ELR come from?

"I've been actively involved in the Class 40 Preservation Society for a long time and I have been chairman of the CFPS for the past 12 years. I also man the CFPS sales stand at ELR events and other national events to help raise funds towards the operation and maintenance of our three locomotives.

"As the ELR is the home railway for the CFPS locomotives and is also only a few miles away from my home in North Manchester I've always shown a keen interest in the railway and how it has developed.

"I've watched the railway grow over the years and am incredibly proud of the ELR and how successful it has become."

What made you get involved in fundraising for the purchase of *City of Wells*?

"For me it was a no-brainer really and it was more a case of the railway couldn't afford not to buy it because the value of having it on the railway is massive. I raised the money required by the CFPS to buy 40106 in a very short time and while this appeal is quite a bit more it needs the same sort of gusto and enthusiasm to make it happen.

"To convince people to part with their hard-earned money to a fundraising appeal, it needs someone with passion and dedication. I am passionate about the ELR and really want the railway to be even more successful than it already is and having *City of Wells* as one of the mainstays of the steam fleet can only be a good thing for the railway that I love so much.

"I don't have the engineering skills to maintain or restore a locomotive such as *City of Wells*, but I do have skills when it comes to raising money and while it would be very easy for people to say the amount needed is too much to raise by an organisation like the ELR, it would be wrong if we didn't try to reach the target and the success of the appeal so far indicates that we should hopefully be fairly close to the target by the end of 2018 when the locomotive has to be paid for.

"The main difference between the fundraising for buying 40106 and the appeal for *City of Wells* is that the funds for 40106 were raised through the generosity of a few people who I took into my confidence, as we weren't able to go public about the purchase until it had been completed. We were also given a very generous interest-free loan to allow us to buy the Class 40, and after we had bought the locomotive we could then appeal to our members for donations, which then went towards paying off the loan and we did pay it off within the six-month period that had been agreed.

"With *City of Wells*, we were able to go public very soon after the terms of the purchase had been agreed with the owners, so while we have a longer period of time to raise the money the target amount we have set of £340,920 is still a huge sum of money to bring in. So far, almost £220,000 has been raised, which is a fantastic amount, but we aren't being complacent and need to keep the momentum going.

"I'd love to see it back on the main line too at some point in the future and the possibilities for trips on and off the ELR, hauled by our own locomotive, could open up some great potential opportunities to bring in additional revenue to the railway, as well as providing a big publicity boost for the ELR."

What fundraising initiatives are you currently trying?

"I'm so passionate about the railway and see it as being my own in many ways. I want to see it thriving and successful. The focus of my attention at the moment is obviously the CFPS and *City of Wells*.

"The railway launched the 'Home for Wells' appeal in 2017 and a range of benefits are available for people making various amounts of donations towards the appeal, but I have been focusing more on the donations that we can get from people travelling on the railway, or special fundraising events which can generate a larger lump sum.

"Over the summer we have been operating a fundraising raffle for the 'Home for Wells' appeal and more than 9000 tickets were sold, generating a decent profit for the appeal. The ELR is hosting LNER A3 'Pacific' 4-6-2 No. 60103 *Flying Scotsman* for a number of days in August and September 2018 and we will be holding another raffle throughout the autumn. Myself and my team of supporting volunteers will try and get out on the railway as much as possible to sell raffle tickets and try and beat the summer raffle total. While raffles may seem rather old-fashioned, they are an easy way of generating large amounts of money although it does need a lot of effort from everyone to sell as many tickets as possible.

"We've also had a good response from the donation envelopes which are being left on the trains for ELR passengers to place their loose change in. Again, it is the inexpensive fundraising ideas that tend to be the most successful and we have raised a considerable sum over the past few months from the generosity of passengers putting anything between a few pence and several pounds in those envelopes.

"At the moment I am busy organising a railtour off the railway in mid-September that will see *Flying Scotsman* travelling to North Wales. While organising a steam railtour is slightly different to operating our diesel locomotive, 40145, on the main line, I do understand the work that is required to make a railtour happen. Thanks to our partners at West Coast Railway Company and the co-operation of No. 60103's operator, Ian Riley, the unique opportunity to operate *Flying Scotsman* on a train running off the ELR should hopefully capture the imagination of the general public."

Which locomotive would you like to see on the ELR in the future?

"A highlight for me was the Class 40 reunion event, '40s@60', in April 2018, which saw six of the seven surviving Class 40s at the ELR. The only locomotive which was unable to attend was 40118, which is undergoing a comprehensive overhaul at Tyseley Locomotive Works and is not yet completed. I would love to see 40118 run on the ELR as a guest at some stage in the future once its restoration has been completed."

In November 2015 the Class 40 Preservation Society successfully purchased 40106 *Atlantic Conveyor* after a hurried fundraising campaign managed by John Stephens, who is also the chairman of the organisation. 40106 heads past Springside Farm on its way towards Bury on September 25, 2016. LIAM BARNES

FAREWELL TO THE DUCHESS

The East Lancashire Railway has always had a positive working relationship with the National Railway Museum and that relationship has seen most of the NRM's operational steam and diesel locomotives spend periods of time on loan to the ELR throughout the last 25 years.

Throughout the 1980s and 1990s the NRM's flagship steam locomotive was LMS Stanier Coronation Class 'Pacific' 4-6-2 No. 46229 *Duchess of Hamilton*, which saw extensive use on the main line, as well as visiting various heritage lines. In 1996 the locomotive paid a successful visit to the ELR and such was the popularity of the locomotive that the railway requested a further visit in the autumn of 1997.

However, by the time the locomotive arrived on the railway in September 1997 its maroon paintwork was in very poor condition and the locomotive itself was tired and coming to the end of its boiler certificate. A visit by the boiler inspector saw him state that No. 46229 would have to be withdrawn from traffic after a limited number of steamings due to the poor condition of the firebox crown stays in the boiler, which were suffering from wastage.

The ELR has had a number of proactive and enthusiastic lineside photographers among its supporters over the years and an approach was made to the NRM to see if they would

Looking suitably grubby and work-stained, No. 46229 *Duchess of Hamilton* stands at Bury Bolton Street in September 1997, while employed on a Driver Experience course. The poor condition of the paintwork is evident. MIKE TAYLOR

permit the locomotive to be repainted into BR green livery for a limited period of time, after which it would be returned to the NRM's preferred choice of lined BR maroon livery, with the costs of the work being met by the photographers.

The NRM agreed to the request after consulting with other interested parties and following the October 1997 steam event on the ELR, No. 46229 was taken into the Carriage and Wagon Department shed at Buckley Wells for work on the repaint to begin.

Work continued on the transformation

On February 24, 1998, No. 46229 crosses Brooksbottom Viaduct during a 26D Charters photographic charter using the locomotive, showing the BR green livery to good effect. The repainting of the locomotive generated a lot of goodwill for the ELR, NRM and the photographers who raised more than £3000 for the initiative. TERRY EYRES

No. 46229 powers through Burrs during a photographic charter on February 24, 1998, less than a month before the locomotive worked its final services. TERRY EYRES

over a period of weeks, with the locomotive completed in time for the ELR's BR Enthusiasts' Weekend on January 24-25, 1997. The appearance of a green 'Duchess' certainly attracted the crowds and the newly painted locomotive gained a lot of attention throughout the weekend.

Following the January event, the 'Duchess' was used on a number of photographic charters and at special events, but the condition of the boiler

caused the decision to be taken that the locomotive would work its final services on March 21, 1998 in a special 'Farewell to the Duchess' event, which was jointly promoted by the ELR and the Friends of the National Railway Museum. Again, the railway was very busy with enthusiasts coming to see No. 46229 in steam for the final time of its current boiler ticket and for the final time in BR green.

Although it wasn't realised at the time, this would be the last occasion that

No. 46229 appeared in steam, as although it has now been returned to its as-built streamlined condition, it has not been returned to service and remains on display at the NRM.

Following the event, the locomotive was repainted back into the maroon colours which it had previously carried, with the now-out-of-ticket 'Duchess' returning to York in September 1998 to take its place in the Great Hall as a static exhibit.

A poster produced by the ELR to promote the final day of service for No. 46229 on March 21, 1998.
EAST LANCASHIRE RAILWAY

Immaculately repainted into BR lined maroon livery, No. 46229 *Duchess of Hamilton* stands in the ELR Locomotive Works yard on August 27, 1998, just prior to the locomotive being returned to the National Railway Museum at York for static display. MIKE TAYLOR

Diesel Locomotives on the ELR

The East Lancashire Railway has become well known as probably the leading heritage railway when it comes to the preservation and operation of heritage diesel locomotives, with the first main line diesels arriving at Bury back in 1981, several years before passenger operations on the rejuvenated railway began.

When the fledgling East Lancashire Railway was first establishing a fleet of locomotives for use on the restored Bury to Rawtenstall line, it was quickly realised that the railway should not just feature historic steam locomotives, but also offer homes to classic diesel locomotives, which could be used on both passenger and engineering trains. By the late 1970s it was widely acknowledged that interest was growing in the preservation of former British Rail main line diesel locomotives, although the sector was very much in its infancy at the time with only a tiny fraction of preserved diesels, compared to the numerous former BR diesel locomotives now in private ownership on heritage lines across the country.

In 1980 the railway was asked to provide a new home to three former British Railways Western Region diesel-hydraulic locomotives, Class 42 'Warship' D832 *Onslaught*, and Class 52 'Westerns' D1041 *Western Prince* and D1048 *Western Lady*. The locomotives were to be displayed at the BR Horwich Works open day in August 1980 before being transferred to Bury. The need to provide some covered accommodation

Another early member of the diesel fleet to be based at Bury was 24054, which arrived in October 1983. The locomotive took part in works trains prior to the reopening of the line between Bury and Ramsbottom and is seen just south of Ramsbottom station in May 1987. It was returned to original BR green livery as D5054 in 1988. THE LATE DAVE DYSON, COURTESY OF TIM GRIMSHAW

for these locomotives saw a new three-road running shed being built at Castlecroft at the bottom end of the Bury Transport Museum yard, alongside the Bury to Rawtenstall line. Although D1048 subsequently moved to the now-

closed Steamport museum in Southport, D832 and D1041 were delivered to Bury by rail, being hauled along the now-mothballed Heywood to Bury line by 40115 in February 1981, and both locomotives have remained based at the ELR ever since.

Another Western Region diesel hydraulic locomotive also came to call the ELR home, when a member of the society purchased the derelict hulk of BR Class 35 'Hymek' D7076. The locomotive, which had been used by the BR Research Department at Derby, was one of two derelict Hymeks kept at Derby, with the other, D7096, providing many spare parts to benefit its sister locomotive. D7076 arrived at Bury in February 1983 and returned to service following restoration in October 1988 and it has remained an important and popular part of the diesel fleet ever since.

Next to arrive at Bury in October 1983 was BR Class 24, 24054, which had most recently been used for carriage heating duties and numbered TDB968008. The locomotive arrived at Bury in generally good condition, although it required new traction motors to replace those that had been removed by BR when

The second Class 33 to call the ELR home was 33109 *Captain Bill Smith RNR*, which arrived on the railway in 2007. The locomotive was repainted into engineers grey livery in 2017 and is shown approaching Burrs Country Park halt on March 29, 2018. EMMA SEDDON

LEFT: 45108 is owned by the Peak Locomotive Company and on long-term loan to the ELR. The locomotive is pictured approaching Ramsbottom station during the Spring Diesel Event on February 17, 2018. EMMA SEDDON

Former BR Western Region diesel-hydraulic Class 52 locomotive D1041 *Western Prince* crosses Calrows Viaduct at Burrs on June 18, 1989 while working a Ramsbottom to Bury service. D1041 was one of the first two former main line locomotives to be based on the embryonic railway. DAVID A INGHAM

it had been converted into a carriage heater. The Class 24 was used on various works trains in the run-up to the line being reopened to Ramsbottom in July 1987, but it entered passenger service on the ELR in 1988 freshly repainted in original BR green carrying its pre-TOPS number as D5054. The Class 24 provided many years' service on the railway before being taken out of service for an overhaul, which is now reaching its final stages. D5054 was named *Phil Southern* during the ELR's 20th anniversary celebrations in 2007 in recognition of one of the owning group's leading members and a former East Lancashire Light Railway Company director, who sadly passed away in 2004.

The next main line diesel locomotive to call the ELR home was of a type that was very familiar to the Bury to Rawtenstall line. The Class 40 Preservation Society (CFPS) bought

40145 from BR in December 1983 and they sought permission to base it on the ELR. The majority of the regular coal trains to Rawtenstall were hauled by Class 40s and it is possible that 40145 could have worked along the Bury to Rawtenstall line prior to its withdrawal by BR. The locomotive was in good overall condition and had been withdrawn following minor derailment damage, arriving on the ELR in February 1984. It entered service on the ELR on the first day of public services between Bury and Ramsbottom, July 26, 1987, and like all the other early diesel locomotives to be based on the railway, it remains at the ELR to this day. 40145 is also now registered for main line running on Network Rail, although it is due to have two new wheelsets fitted at Barrow Hill during 2018, as the tyres on these wheelsets are now close to scrapping size and the locomotive

cannot run on the main line again until these have been changed.

The CFPS purchased another locomotive, D335 (40135), in 1988 and then added a third, 40106 *Atlantic Conveyor*, in November 2015. All three Class 40s make regular appearances on the ELR, although 40135 is due to move to the Severn Valley Railway for a two-year hire period from summer 2018.

In 1985, the sole-surviving Class 15, D8233, was delivered to Bury. The Class 15 design had been one of the numerous diesel types to be built as a result of the 1955 British Railways Modernisation Plan, but the type was not deemed to be a success and the 44 locomotives were all withdrawn at a very early age with many having seen less than 10 years in service. D8233 survived thanks to it being selected as a locomotive to be used for carriage heating, gaining the departmental number ADB968001, being

The East Lancashire Railway is now home to three Class 40 locomotives, with 40145 arriving at Bury in 1984. The BR blue Class 40, owned by the Class 40 Preservation Society, entered service on the railway on July 26, 1987, the first day of public services between Bury and Ramsbottom. 40145 emerges from Nuttall Tunnel with a Bury to Rawtenstall service on June 4, 1996. NEIL HARVEY

Western Region diesel-hydraulic D7076 arrived at Bury in February 1983 in a derelict condition after being used by British Rail's research department as a 'dead load' locomotive at Derby. It returned to service in October 1988 and is still a popular performer whenever it is in use. D7076 passes through Little Burrs with a Bury to Rawtenstall service on June 11, 1994. NEIL HARVEY

47402 *Gateshead* is another locomotive which owes its survival to the efforts of Pete Waterman, who bought the locomotive from BR in 1993. During its first weekend in service on the ELR, 47402 double-heads with 50015 *Valiant*, passing through Little Burrs with a Rawtenstall to Bury service on June 6, 1993. MIKE TAYLOR

bought for preservation in 1984.

Following delivery to Bury the locomotive was painted into fictitious Railfreight grey livery, but its owners moved it to another site two years later.

However, after previous restoration attempts had stalled, the locomotive was subsequently purchased by the Class 15 Preservation Society and moved back to Bury in 2006, where its restoration to working order is continuing by an active group of volunteers. The engine has been started on a number of occasions, but no target date has been set for its restoration to be completed. As the only remaining member of the class, its return to service is eagerly awaited by many enthusiasts.

EXPANDING THE FLEET

In October 1987 the railway took delivery of another former BR Western Region diesel-hydraulic locomotive when Class 14 D9531 arrived at Castlecroft. The 56 Class 14 locomotives had an indecently short working life on

British Railways, with D9531 itself only seeing its career on BR lasting less than three years before it and a number of other locomotives were sold to the National Coal Board. D9531 saw use at NCB Ashington for 19 years before being sold into preservation under the auspices of the Bury Hydraulic Group who also maintain D832, D1041 and D7076.

D9531 entered service on the ELR in October 1988 at the railways first-ever diesel weekend and saw use regularly on passenger and works trains until 2002 when it was withdrawn for a major and rather protracted overhaul which took almost a decade to complete.

Since returning to service in 2012 D9531, now named *Ernest*, has proved once again to be a versatile member of the fleet and it has now been joined by another Class 14 locomotive, D9537, which was overhauled by the same team that had revived D9531. In 2018 D9537 made its debut in an attractive plain black livery, a colour scheme never

carried by Class 14s in BR service.

A third Class 14, D9502, has also now joined the fleet and is undergoing full restoration in the Locomotive Works at Bury. D9502, which at the time of its purchase still carried the original BR paintwork applied from when it was newly delivered to British Railways in 1964, has never run in preservation and is now undergoing an extensive overhaul at the Locomotive Works, which is reaching an advanced stage.

In 1988 the ELR took delivery of Class 25, 25909, which was the last locomotive to be built by BR at Gorton Works in Manchester. The Class 25 was also the first diesel locomotive to be bought for preservation by record producer and media personality Pete Waterman. Mr Waterman is perhaps one of the most well-known railway enthusiasts in the UK and has been a long-term supporter of the ELR.

25909 made its ELR debut in October 1988 and remained on the railway for a number of years. During its time on the

The ELR is now home to three Class 14 diesel hydraulic locomotives, with D9502, D9531 and D9537 all based on the railway. The first member of the type to arrive at Bury was D9531 in October 1987, having spent many years in service with the National Coal Board at Ashington Colliery, and it entered service almost exactly one year later. D9531 works a freight service through Burrs on March 7, 2015.
NIGEL VALENTINE

Celebrating its 50th anniversary during 2018, 50015 *Valiant* stands on Platform 2 at Bury Bolton Street, working the last service of the day to Heywood on February 17, 2018. EMMA SEDDON

Visiting from Crewe Heritage Centre for the 2017 summer diesel weekend is 47712 *Lady Diana Spencer*. The ScotRail liveried Class 47 is pictured passing through Burrs whilst working a service to Rawtenstall on July 8, 2017. NIGEL VALENTINE

railway it was repainted into original two-tone green livery as D7659, but eventually moved to Mr Waterman's engineering base at Crewe. However, the locomotive has now been out of service for a number of years and is currently being restored back to operational condition at Rowsley South on Peak Rail. Mr Waterman hopes that D7659 may be back in service at some stage during 2018.

INTO THE 1990s

Another Class 25 arrived on the railway the following year when locomotive engineer Harry Needle purchased 25901 from BR. Despite being in poor external condition, the locomotive was in very good mechanical condition and saw extensive use on the ELR during its time on the line. The locomotive was given a bodywork overhaul and repaint into two-tone green as D7612 but was subsequently sold by its owner and moved to the South Devon Railway in 1999.

Harry Needle also purchased derelict Class 45 'Peak' 45112 *Royal Army Ordnance Corps* from BR in 1991, with it becoming the final locomotive to be delivered to the ELR by rail along the then soon-to-be-closed Manchester to Bury line. The Class 45 was returned to working order in 1995 and subsequently moved to Barrow Hill roundhouse. It was later sold by Mr Needle and registered for main line running once more, although it has been out of use now for a number of years and is located at Nemesis Rail at Burton-on-Trent.

RIGHT: 50015 *Valiant* and 50008 *Thunderer* haul a Bury to Rawtenstall service through Burrs on October 4, 1992. Both Class 50s had been used by British Rail as dedicated railtour locomotives for the 18 months prior to their withdrawal and both were purchased by Pete Waterman. 50015 has remained based at the ELR ever since, but is now owned by the Bury Valiant Group. MIKE TAYLOR

An unusual visitor in 2014 was preserved Class 86 locomotive, 86259 *Les Ross*, which was coupled to the Class 40 Preservation Society's D335 to recreate a class electric 'drag'. The pair are pictured at Springside Farm, on the approach to Summerseat with a Bury to Ramsbottom service on September 27, 2014. The Class 86 was on the railway for contract repairs before resuming its main line career hauling charters. TOM MCATEE

In 1993, the ELR became the first heritage railway to reunite both surviving Class 42 'Warships' with D832 *Onslaught* being joined by the Diesel Traction Groups D821 *Greyhound*. The two locomotives depart from Ramsbottom, nearing Nuttall Tunnel, with a Rawtenstall to Bury service on October 3, 1993. NEIL HARVEY

Visiting from the Great Central Railway (Nottingham), 47765 hauls a train through Ewood Bridge on July 3, 2010. Despite looking rather decrepit in faded Rail Express Systems livery, the locomotive was a popular visitor. Now repainted into Scotrail livery the locomotive returned to Bury in April 2018 as a permanent member of the ELR diesel fleet. KEVIN DELANEY

Harry Needle went on to establish an engineering base at Barrow Hill, where his company maintains and restores railway locomotives, but he remains an active supporter of the ELR and he has supplied a large number of diesel locomotives to the ELR over the past few years, primarily Class 20s, 37s and 47s, for use at diesel events and also for general services.

In October 1992 the ELR took delivery of two Class 50 locomotives, 50008 *Thunderer* and 50015 *Valiant*. At the time the Class 50s were being run down by BR and the type had a huge enthusiast following during their twilight years. Both Class 50s had been used as dedicated railtour locomotives during their final 18 months' service with BR and it was, therefore, appropriate that both should be preserved together.

The pair were purchased by Pete Waterman, with 50015 placed into the care of the Manchester Class 50 Group. Both locomotives were serviceable when they arrived on the railway, with 50015 hauling a train just a few hours

after being unloaded from a low loader at Bury. 50008 saw some use on ELR services over the following year and was repainted into Large Logo livery on one side for a filming contract on ITV drama series Cracker, featuring Robbie Coltrane. It was subsequently moved to Crewe for a possible return to main line service, but 50015 remained on the railway and was sold to the Manchester Class 50 Group by Mr Waterman.

In 2004, 50015 was taken out of use due to it needing a number of repairs and remained in an increasingly derelict condition with no work carried out until being purchased by a consortium of ELR volunteers, known as the Bury Valiant Group, in 2007. It was quickly returned to service and has remained an important part of the ELR diesel fleet throughout the years.

As it is fitted with electric train heating, it can be used to haul services during the winter months, as the ELR maintains many of its Mark 1 carriages with electric train heating equipment. Despite numerous requests for the owning group to return 50015 into the

unique Civil Engineers yellow and grey livery, as carried by the locomotive prior to withdrawal, the owning group have so far resisted these requests and it remains in the popular Large Logo BR blue livery.

50008 was subsequently sold to Garcia Hanson and returned to the ELR for one of the railways diesel events and then it remained on the line for repainting into the BR Laira Blue livery that it carried for its final 18 months service on BR prior to its withdrawal in 1992. It has since returned to main line service, operating various trains for Devon and Cornwall Railways, LORAM and also Rail Operations Group.

FURTHER EXPANSION
Another Pete Waterman locomotive to arrive on the railway in 1993 was 47402 *Gateshead*. The second-built Class 47 'Generator' had recently been withdrawn by BR from Immingham and was rededicated upon delivery to Bury. The locomotive carried BR blue for a number of years before it was restored back into its original BR two-tone green livery

Another locomotive which formerly belonged to Pete Waterman was Pilot Scheme locomotive 31101, which arrived on the railway in 1994. The distinctively painted locomotive is pictured approaching Ewood Bridge with a Bury to Rawtenstall service shortly after it made its home in Bury. The Class 31 was restored to original condition as D5518, but was subsequently sold in 1996 and is now based on the Avon Valley Railway. MARTIN LOADER

Diesel hydraulic Class 35 Hymek D7076 has always been popular whenever it is in service on the railway and for many years out of the four preserved Class 35s it has been one of only two operational Hymek locomotives, with D7017 on the West Somerset Railway being the other. In 2014 D7076 was repainted into BR blue and it is pictured hauling a demonstration freight train through Burrs on March 7, 2015. NIGEL VALENTINE

The ELR has hosted most of the diesel locomotives belonging to the National Railway Museum over the past few years. 50015 *Valiant* leads the NRM's 50033 *Glorious* through Townsend Fold on July 11, 1998. 50033 has since being disposed of by the NRM and is now owned by Tyseley Locomotive Works, but currently undergoing restoration by the Class 50 Alliance at the Severn Valley Railway.
MIKE TAYLOR

as D1501. During 2017 it underwent an engine overhaul and other maintenance before being repainted again into its original livery.

Mr Waterman also previously had other locomotives from his collection based on the railway, including 31101 and 47117 (one of the 10 former Class 48 locomotives, but converted back into a standard Class 47). He also supplied several other locomotives from his base at Crewe for diesel events, including 20042, 20188, D172 *Ixion*, D120 and various DMU vehicles, although many of these were sold in 1996 following a rationalisation of his collection.

In March 1997, Roland Hatton, an active volunteer on the railway, purchased 33117 from English Welsh & Scottish Railways (EW&S). At the time a number of other Class 33s were being purchased by preservationists, but 33117 successfully became the first member of its class to haul a train in preservation four months later in July.

Another Class 33, 33109 *Captain Bill Smith RNR* was purchased for the

ELR MAIN LINE DIESEL FLEET SUMMER 2018

CLASS	NUMBER	NAME	LIVERY	STATUS SUMMER 2018
14	D9502	*Kerys*	BR green	Undergoing Restoration
14	D9531	*Ernest*	BR green	Operational
14	D9537	*Eric*	Black	Operational
15	D8233		BR green	Undergoing Restoration
20	20087		BR blue	Stored awaiting sale
20	20110		BR green	Stored awaiting sale
24	D5054	*Phil Southern*	BR green	Undergoing repairs
25	D7629		BR green	Operational
28	D5705		BR green	Undergoing Restoration
33	33046		Blue	Spares Donor
33	33109	*Captain Bill Smith RNR*	Engineers Grey	Operational
33	33117		BR blue	Undergoing Restoration
35	D7076		BR blue	Undergoing repairs
37	37109		BR blue	Operational
40	40012	*Aureol*	BR blue	Operational
40	40106	*Atlantic Conveyor*	BR green	Operational
40	40135		BR blue	Operational
40	40145		BR blue	Operational
42	D832	*Onslaught*	BR green	Operational
45	45108		BR blue	Operational
45	45135	*3rd Carabinier*	BR blue	Undergoing repairs
47	D1501		BR green	Operational
47	47765		Scotrail	Operational
50	50015	*Valiant*	Large Logo Blue	Operational
52	D1041	*Western Prince*	BR blue	Undergoing Restoration
56	56006		BR blue	Undergoing repairs

Notes:
- 20087 and 20110 are owned by HN Rail and have been made available for sale. Both locomotives are currently unserviceable and likely to leave the ELR.
- 33046 was purchased as a spares donor locomotive for 33109 and 33117. It is unlikely that this locomotive will ever be returned to an operational condition.
- 40012 is on loan to ELR for the summer 2018 season from the Class 40 Appeal.
- 45108 is on loan from the Peak Locomotive Company.
- 56006 is on a three-year loan from The Class 56 Group.

Another 2017 arrival on the railway was the Class 56 Group's 56006, with the locomotive shown departing from Ramsbottom with a service to Rawtenstall on July 8, 2017. 56006 was one of the locomotives which took part in the EWS Classic Traction Event in 1999, featuring a number of main line locomotives which were due to be withdrawn. 56006 was subsequently bought for preservation and is on a three-year loan to the ELR. TOM MCATEE

Class 25, D7629 is one of two new permanent members of the diesel fleet, having been relocated from the Great Central Railway (Nottingham) by its owner along with 47765. On July 8, 2017, D7629 arrives at Ramsbottom with a Rawtenstall to Heywood service. TOM MCATEE

railway in 2007 and has been a regular performer on the railway since its arrival. 33117 was taken out of service for an overhaul in 2004, but has not yet returned to use.

A third Class 33, 33046, was also purchased, but this has been acquired as a source of spares for 33109 and 33117 and it is not planned that this locomotive will be returned to service.

Another now-unique diesel locomotive arrived at Bury in 1998, when the sole-surviving Class 28 Co-Bo D5705 was delivered to the ELR. The Co-Bo was another design to come from the 1955 British Railways Modernisation Plan which was not deemed to be a success by British Railways and all 20 examples had been withdrawn from traffic by 1969. Again, the locomotive owes its survival to it being used as a carriage heating unit before being bought for preservation in 1980.

D5705 is another locomotive that has not yet run in preservation and its return to service is eagerly awaited. Its restoration is progressing well under the auspices of the same team who are restoring D8233, but it is not yet known when the Co-Bo will run under its own power again.

In 1999, the ELR's resident diesel fleet was boosted by the arrival of a Class 20, two Class 31s and two Class 37s. A Manchester businessman, Mike Darnell, had purchased 20087, 31435 and 31467 from national freight operator EW&S, whilst Bury-based engineer Ian Riley had bought 37038 and 37197 from the same EW&S tender list.

Of the five locomotives, both Class 37s were returned to main line action for spot hire work, with another Class 37, 37261, also following in 2004. 20087 and 31435 both returned to service on the ELR, with both repainted into BR green livery as D8087 and D5600 respectively. 31467 was used as a source of spare parts and Mr Darnell also bought another Class 31, 31556, which also moved to the ELR. Both 31467 and 31556 were eventually scrapped after all reusable spare parts had been recovered.

D5600 moved to the Embsay and Bolton Abbey Railway in 2007 to join its owner's other locomotives based on that line, while 20087 has since been sold to

Harry Needle's HN Rail business, but he has since offered 20087 and 20110 (which is also stored at the ELR) for sale to preservationists.

Ian Riley subsequently sold his Class 37 locomotives to West Coast Railways and all of them ended up being acquired by Direct Rail Services, although 37197 was used as a source of spares and eventually scrapped without ever hauling a train for DRS. He also bought 37518 from its previous owner in 2012 and returned it to main line use, but it has also since been sold to West Coast Railways.

ENTER THE DELTICS

The railway has hosted a number of diesel locomotives belonging to the National Railway Museum for both diesel events and for extended loan periods. NRM locomotives which have been hosted on the ELR have been pioneer Class 20 D8000, Class 40 D200, Class 31 D5500, Class 50 50033 *Glorious*, Class 52 'Western' D1023 *Western Fusilier*, and Class 55 'Deltic' 55002 *Kings Own Yorkshire Light Infantry*.

The ELR has played host to every preserved member of the legendary Class 55 Deltic locomotives that were famed for plying the East Coast Main Line until they were withdrawn at the start of 1982.

In 1995 D9019 *Royal Highland Fusilier* was loaned to the ELR by the Deltic Preservation Society and it was joined a year later by the National Railway Museum's 55002 *Kings Own Yorkshire Light Infantry*, which was returned to service on the ELR after a long period of inaction.

In 1997 the railway hosted a special event, 'The 3 Deltics', featuring 55002, D9019 and 55015 *Tulyar*, which was loaned to the railway for the event by the Deltic Preservation Society – an event which proved to be hugely popular and brought together three operational preserved 'Deltics' for the first time since the locomotives had been withdrawn by BR. A fourth 'Deltic', pioneer D9000

Immaculately restored to original condition, the second-built Class 47, D1501, departs from Irwell Vale with a Rawtenstall to Heywood line on May 28, 2018. LIAM BARNES

Royal Scots Grey, was also in action on the Saturday of the special event, hauling a main line railtour into Manchester Piccadilly to link up with the event taking place at Bury.

In late 2004 ELR diesel department volunteer and then-chairman of the Class 40 Preservation Society, Martin Walker, bought the pioneer Deltic, D9000 *Royal Scots Grey*. The locomotive had spent much time on the main line hauling passenger services under its previous owners, D9000 Locomotives Ltd, before being laid up awaiting major repairs to its generators and in need of a bodywork overhaul.

The locomotive was extensively overhauled at Barrow Hill, including the complete renewal of the outer and inner skin of bodywork, by the commercial division of the Deltic Preservation Society. It was also re-registered for running on Network Rail, but after returning to service in 2006 disaster struck in October that year when it suffered a severe engine failure to one of its two engines while working a main line passenger railtour.

Although it still had one operational engine, a replacement power unit would be needed to replace the seriously damaged engine and a Napier Deltic marine engine was subsequently modified for use in the locomotive, but this too proved to be problematical.

Mr Walker purchased a second Deltic, D9016 *Gordon Highlander*, in late 2009, with it arriving at Bury in January 2010. Both D9016 and 55022 moved away from the ELR in 2013, with 55022 continuing to find use on main line duties (albeit restricted to running on one engine which precluded its use on passenger railtours) and also on the North Yorkshire Moors Railway, while D9016 saw use on the Great Central Railway, before moving to the Washwood Heath works of Boden Rail Engineering to begin an extensive bodywork overhaul

Normally based at the Midland Railway Butterley, 20048 leads ELR resident 20087 through Burrs with a Bury to Ramsbottom shuttle service on July 2, 2011, during the annual summer diesel event. 20087 is now owned by Harry Needle, but has been offered for sale and its future is unclear. TOM MCATEE

to address severe corrosion that the locomotive had been suffering from.

However, in November 2017, Mr Walker sold both locomotives and a huge quantity of spare parts to Locomotive Services Ltd at Crewe, with the aim being that they will both return to the main line at some stage in the future.

Another arrival in 2006 was the Pioneer Diesel Group's Class 45 'Peak' locomotive 45135 *3rd Carabinier*, which joined the home-based fleet, having previously been based on Peak Rail in Derbyshire.

The locomotive was used on services for three years before being taken out of service for an engine overhaul in 2009. The 'Peak' has not yet returned to service although repairs on it are advancing. In its place, the ELR is currently the base of 45108 which has been loaned to the railway by the Peak Locomotive Company.

The latest additions to the ELR diesel fleet have been Class 25, D7629 and Scotrail liveried 47765, which both belong to preservationist Mark Fowler and had previously been located at the Great Central Railway (Nottingham).

D7629 arrived at the railway in 2017 for the summer diesel event and remained on the line for a longer loan period before the owner decided to seek permission to also relocate his Class 47 to the line alongside the Class 25, with both now classed as permanent members of the ELR home fleet.

As well as the preserved diesel locomotives a number of main line freight and passenger operators have loaned locomotives to the railway for special events, with a number of Class 37, 47, 57, 60, 66 and 67 locomotives having also graced ELR metals.

As can be seen from this chapter, the ELR has been home and host to the widest possible collection of former main line diesel locomotives and it is unsurprising that the railway has a reputation as one of the leading heritage lines catering for diesel enthusiasts. The railway hosts various diesel events and theme days throughout the year, attracting visiting locomotives to enhance the extensive home fleet, with the railway's main annual diesel event taking place over the first weekend of July each year.

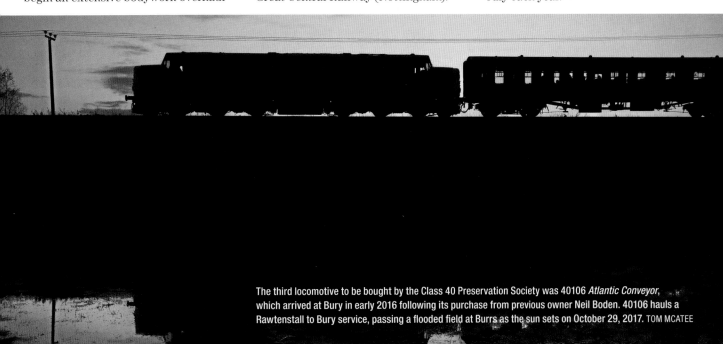

The third locomotive to be bought by the Class 40 Preservation Society was 40106 *Atlantic Conveyor*, which arrived at Bury in early 2016 following its purchase from previous owner Neil Boden. 40106 hauls a Rawtenstall to Bury service, passing a flooded field at Burrs as the sun sets on October 29, 2017. TOM MCATEE

The Reunion Line

The East Lancashire Railway has always had a good reputation for its popular diesel events which usually take place in March, July and October. However, in recent years the railway has gained an enviable reputation for reuniting preserved examples of various specific classes of diesel locomotives.

Since the advent of diesel galas on the railway back in October 1988, the ELR's reputation as one of the leading UK heritage lines for diesel enthusiasts has grown, with more ambitious events and a quest by the organisers to hold events that prove attractive to enthusiasts at all times.

However, the ELR has also become very adept at organising special events which bring together a number of preserved locomotives from a particular type and these reunions have got even more ambitious in recent years, creating some memorable events for visitors to the railway and photographers at the lineside.

In March 1997, the ELR was the home base for the Deltic Preservation Society's D9019 *Royal Highland Fusilier* and also the National Railway Museum's 55002 *Kings Own Yorkshire Light Infantry*. The DPS offered to bring 55015 *Tulyar* to Bury from its usual base at the Midland Railway Butterley for a reunion event, which would be one of the last working appearances for 55015 before it was to be withdrawn for a major overhaul and rebuild.

'The 3 Deltics' event saw 55002, 55015 and D9019 working in various combinations throughout the weekend of March 8-9, 1997, with the highlight of the event being a triple-headed service where all three 'Deltics' hauled a seven-coach rake of coaches along the railway, something which was believed to have

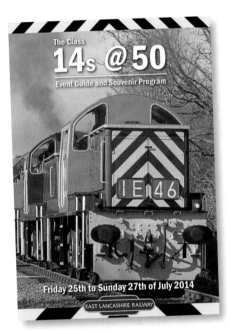

never happened before throughout the history of the 'Deltics'.

Additionally, on the Saturday of the event main line registered Deltic 9000 Locomotive Ltd's pioneer D9000 *Royal Scots Grey* hauled the 'West Coast Deltic Pioneer' railtour from London Euston to Manchester Piccadilly. Many of the tour participants then made their way to Bury for the ELR event, before returning to London behind D9000 later in the day. This was believed to be the first time in preservation history that four of the surviving preserved 'Deltic' locomotives

had worked trains on the same day.

Just four months later, the ELR operated another triple-header, this time using the Class 40 Preservation Society's D335 and D345, which were joined by type pioneer D200, visiting from the NRM. Again, this was the first time that three preserved Class 40s had worked on the same day in preservation and the opportunity to run all three on the same train could not be resisted.

The final diesel event of 1997, saw newly preserved pioneer Class 26, D5300, visiting the ELR for the autumn diesel weekend, where the opportunity was taken to operate a Sulzer Type Two triple-header along with Class 25, D7612, and Class 24, D5054. However, the event was overshadowed with the failure of the Class 26 and it was unable to operate under its own power for most of the weekend.

By 2009, the ELR was home to three Class 37s in the shape of 37109, 37418 *Pectinidae* and 37901 *Mirrlees Pioneer*. 37109 had arrived in the railway at the end of 2007 and had recently undergone an extensive bodywork overhaul and repaint into BR blue livery, while 37901 (fitted with an experimental Mirrlees power unit and Brush electronic equipment) had arrived on the ELR during 2008. The final member of the Class 37 trio to arrive on the line was 37418 (the former *East Lancashire Railway*), which had been purchased from former owners English, Welsh and

LEFT: In September 2012, five of the six surviving Class 55 'Deltics' were brought together on the ELR for a special Deltic Reunion event. On the evening of September 21, 2012, 55022 *Royal Scots Grey*, 55019 *Royal Highland Fusilier*, 55002 *Kings Own Yorkshire Light Infantry*, D9016 *Gordon Highlander* and D9009 *Alycidon* stand in the sidings adjacent to the Locomotive Works beneath the moon during an evening photographic charter, with their exhausts highlighted by floodlights. TOM MCATEE

RIGHT: A visit to the railway by the National Railway Museum's pioneer Class 40, D200, saw the railway create a BR green triple-headed Class 40 service during the summer 1997 diesel event, providing one of the highlights of the event. D335 leads D200 and D345 through Burrs on July 9, 1997, with a heavily loaded train of enthusiasts enjoying the spectacle. MIKE TAYLOR

Scottish Railways and had been newly returned to service by its new owner, resplendent in EW&S maroon and gold colours.

On May 30, 2009, with all three Class 37s now returned to operational condition, the opportunity was taken to operate the Class 37s on two of the railway's three timetable diagrams, supported by LMS 3F 0-6-0 No. 47324 on the remaining (steam) diagram. Again, various single and double-headed combinations were operated throughout the day, before the final train of the day was operated as a very colourful triple-header with 37418 leading 37901 and 37109 at the front of a modest, but rather packed four-coach train. Glorious weather conditions had ensured that the lineside photographers also came out in force to capture some precious memories.

Having successfully operated 'The 3 Deltics' event 15 years earlier, the railway was now the home base for pioneer 55022 *Royal Scots Grey* (formerly D9000) and D9016 *Gordon Highlander*, both of which were now owned by ELR volunteer and former Class 40 Preservation Society chairman, Martin Walker.

In September 2012, a special reunion event was organised, again in association with the NRM who supplied 55002 *Kings Own Yorkshire Light*

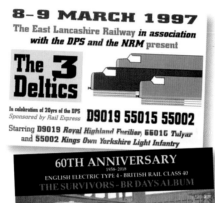

Infantry and the DPS who brought D9009 *Alycidon* and 55019 *Royal Highland Fusilier*, with the three visiting locomotives also joining Martin Walker's ELR based 'Deltics'.

Six of the legendary East Coast Main Line locomotives had survived into preservation and the ELR event brought together five of the survivors, with just the DPS's D9015 *Tulyar* missing from the celebrations, due to its ongoing rebuild at the DPS Depot at Barrow Hill. The event proved to be phenomenally

popular, with thousands of enthusiasts visiting the railway throughout the weekend, and proving that the 'Deltics' are just as popular now as they always have been.

Perhaps the most ambitious reunion event operated by the ELR came in 2014, when diesel department volunteers organised an event to bring together 10 Class 14 locomotives to commemorate the 50th anniversary of the design. With two Class 14s based on the line at the time, D9531 and D9537 (a third, D9502, arrived for restoration following the event), the event would see eight other Class 14s moved to the ELR for a 10-engine event.

Visiting the event were D9513, D9520, D9521, D9523, D9526, D9539, D9555 and 14901 (D9524). Throughout the weekend the locomotives worked on a variety of single and double-headed combinations, although D9523 failed with engine problems on the first day of the event and spent the rest of the celebrations

BELOW: In what is believed to have been the first-ever 'Deltic' triple-header 55015 *Tulyar* leads 55002 *Kings Own Yorkshire Light Infantry* and D9019 *Royal Highland Fusilier* through Burrs on March 9, 1997, with the three legendary East Coast Main Line 'Deltics' leaving behind a smokescreen as they make their way from Bury to Rawtenstall. This event was jointly organised between the ELR, the NRM and the Deltic Preservation Society. MARTIN LOADER

Pioneer Class 26, D5300, leads Class 25, D7612, and Class 24, D5054, through Burrs on a Rawtenstall to Bury service on September 7, 1997. THE LATE DAVE DYSON, COURTESY OF TIM GRIMSHAW

With three Class 37s based on the railway, the opportunity was taken to operate a special and rather colourful triple-headed train on May 30, 2009, when 37418 *Pectinidae* leads 37901 *Mirrlees Pioneer* and 37109 through Burrs with a Bury to Ramsbottom service. The three locomotives were more than able to manage the train of four Mark 1 coaches. TOM MCATEE

on static display on Platform 1 at Bury Bolton Street station.

Despite the expense of bringing in so many visiting locomotives for the event, it proved to be a successful weekend and did turn out to be a profitable event for the railway.

April 2018 marked the 60th anniversary of the introduction of the first English Electric Type Four locomotive, pioneer D200, into service on the Great Eastern Main Line. To celebrate the anniversary, the CFPS sought to bring together as many of the seven surviving Class 40s as they could for another reunion event.

With the ELR being the home railway for 40106 *Atlantic Conveyor*, 40135 and 40145, it was natural that a celebration event for this significant anniversary should be held on the railway. The CFPS has close links with the other owners of preserved Class 40s and agreement was quickly reached for D213 *Andania* to return to Bury from Barrow Hill for its second working visit, with the Class 40 Appeal's 40012 *Aureol* accompanying it from Barrow Hill for a first visit to the ELR by that particular locomotive.

However, with the event being held primarily to celebrate the introduction of D200 into service, it was also essential that the preserved pioneer could also attend. D200 has been out of service for a number of years at the NRM in York, awaiting repairs to the locomotive's main generator. In 2016 it was repainted at the NRM by Heritage Painting to bring its bodywork back to an exhibition standard.

Agreement was reached between the CFPS and the NRM for D200 to attend the event, where it would be placed on display in Platform 1 at Bury Bolton Street throughout the weekend. During the lead-up to the event, CFPS chairman, John Stephens, and engineering officer, Lee Kenny, made several trips to York to carry out work on D200 to make it fit for

In November 2015 the Class 40 Preservation Society bought 40106 *Atlantic Conveyor* from its former owner, Neil Boden, and moved it to the ELR to join their other two locomotives. The following September, the owner of D213 *Andania* brought his immaculate locomotive to the railway for a working visit, bringing together four Class 40s for the first time in preservation. The quartet are seem during a photographic evening at the Locomotive Works on September 23, 2016. TOM MCATEE

movement by rail to Bury.

Only missing from the party was 40118, which is undergoing a comprehensive rebuild at Tyseley Locomotive Works by the 16SVT Society. 40118 has not yet run in preservation, but its restoration is steadily advancing and it is certain to be a popular locomotive when it returns to service following the completion of its rebuild.

On April 9, 2018, the Deltic Preservation Society's main line registered D9009 *Alycidon* was dispatched to the Great Central Railway (Nottingham) to collect new ELR resident 47765, before running to Barrow Hill to collect D213 and 40012 and then continuing its journey to York to collect D200 from the NRM. Once all the locomotives had been collected, the BR blue 'Deltic' hauled the convoy of classic locomotives to Bury.

Two days later, the CFPS held two sold-out photographic events at the Locomotive Works, with the six Class 40s lined up for the photographers in the sidings.

The main event ran from April 13-15, 2018, with all five operational Class 40s seeing extensive use throughout each of the days, supported by D9009 and ELR resident 50015 *Valiant*. As intended, D200 was displayed at Bury Bolton Street, carrying a replica of the

The ultimate event for Class 40 followers was held in April 2018, when six of the surviving Class 40s were brought together for the first time in private ownership to celebrate the 60th anniversary of the English Electric Type Four. During a photographic session on April 11, 2018, the six locomotives are posed for the cameras, while being fired up for the assembled photographers. From left to right are D200, D213 *Andania*, 40106 *Atlantic Conveyor*, 40012 *Aureol*, 40135 and 40145. TOM MCATEE

Perhaps the most ambitious reunion event organised by the ELR was the 14s@50 event, which saw 10 Class 14s in use on the railway. The highlight of the event was an evening special when nine of the locomotives hauled a train up the line, pictured heading through Burrs on the evening of July 26, 2014. The 10th locomotive, D9523, could not take part in this train as it had suffered a failure earlier in the day. TOM MCATEE

headboard it had carried when it worked its first train on the Great Eastern Main Line 60 years earlier.

Following the event, D200 and D213 were returned to their respective homes by D9009, although 40012 has remained at the ELR on an extended visit, where it is due to stay until the autumn of 2018.

The CFPS and ELR gained plaudits for organising such an excellent event and, as with the previous reunion events, it proved that this style of event is becoming increasingly popular.

It will be interesting to see what the next reunion event on the ELR will be in the future.

A perfect reflection on a type of locomotive celebrating its 60th anniversary. The six Class 40s are reflected in a puddle at the Locomotive Works sidings on the evening of April 11, 2018. TOM MCATEE

TRACEY PARKINSON

ELR GENERAL MANAGER

ANDY COWARD

Where did your interest in railways come from?

"My parents used to take me walking in the North Yorkshire Moors and railways were always a little peripheral, with us sometimes coming back on the train, but it wasn't until I did a work placement from university at the National Railway Museum in York that I started to gain an appreciation for railways. Listening to an explanation about how a steam locomotive works by Dave Mosley really captured my imagination and was a real inspirational moment for me.

"After university I got a job with the NRM and while visiting the North Yorkshire Moors Railway, my mum entered me in a competition to win a footplate ride and I won a ride on No. 34101 *Hartland*. I didn't want to get off the footplate when we got to the end of the line – I ended up spending the whole day on the footplate. It was absolutely brilliant and my love for steam and heritage railways started then."

What made you decide to apply for the ELR general manager's job when it was advertised?

"I was working as general manager of the Talyllyn Railway and was very happy there, with plenty to do looking after that wonderful little railway which runs through some beautiful countryside, but much as I loved working on the narrow gauge line I was more used to standard gauge lines and their operations. The opportunity to take charge of a railway the size and profile of the ELR doesn't come around very often.

"I also knew that I had many of the skills that would be required for the job and thought I had absolutely nothing to lose from applying for the position. I didn't ever think I would get the job, but was absolutely delighted when I did.

"I'd spent some time on the ELR previously, visiting with NRM locomotives, such as *Green Arrow* and the *Duchess*. Whenever I'd been here I loved it. I had been made to feel very welcome by the volunteers and I knew that leading a railway like the ELR would be a challenge, but would also get me

Tracey Parkinson believes that Lancashire & Yorkshire Railway locomotives are so authentic to the ELR she would like to see more L&YR locomotives gracing ELR metals in the future. Carrying BR unlined black livery, L&YR Class 27 0-6-0 No. 52322 heads a demonstration freight through Burrs during a photographic charter on February 12, 2018. EMMA SEDDON

back working on a standard gauge line with a huge amount of potential."

What does the job of ELR general manager involve?

"There are some real challenges facing the ELR at the moment which need addressing to safeguard the future of the railway. Perhaps the biggest of these is the development of Buckley Wells and the Locomotive Works. The Locomotive Works is ageing around us rapidly and we need to ensure that this wonderful facility can continue to serve the railway well for many years to come.

"We also need to protect the assets that we have. Our carriage fleet really needs a shed where they can be kept safely undercover when not in use, to protect them from both the Lancashire weather, but also from the threat of vandalism. We haven't been the only heritage railway to have suffered from vandal attacks on our coaching stock in recent times, but we are located in a very urban area and we need to do all we can to minimise the risk of our assets being damaged by vandals, while dry undercover stabling would also assist with keeping our coaches in good condition for longer between overhauls.

"I'm also keen to attract more young volunteers on to the railway, as if we get them early enough then they gain a level of enthusiasm that means they are likely to stay with us for many years, as those teenage years are when they are forming the friendships and interests they are likely to keep into adult life.

"Recently we hosted a group of scouts who came down to volunteer at Rawtenstall station and do some jobs around the station as part of one of their badges – they did a fantastic job and seemed to really enjoy themselves. Hopefully we can forge links with similar organisations for our mutual benefit and to show that volunteering on heritage railways can be a fun and useful pastime.

"The average age of volunteers on heritage lines is a concern to lot of railways and youngsters can become valuable additions to our team if they are given the correct amount of supervision and encouragement. It's my quest that we have younger volunteers getting involved in the railway from our local community doing proper engineering projects that can make a real difference to the railway, while giving them the skills and experience they need that can also serve them well in the future.

"The other aspect of my job involves looking after our staff and volunteers. The people working on the railway are our biggest asset and we want to look after them, whether they are a paid member of staff or a volunteer. I have a great team of people here at the ELR and they are generally very supportive. Other things I get involved in are safety matters and ensuring

our people are safe and continue to work safely when they are on the railway. I also monitor revenue streams coming in and out of the business, look at future developments to the railway, co-ordinating our operations and engineering departments to ensure that everyone can do the work they need to do. We also have two pubs that need looking after and are now starting work on a new 10-year strategy for the ELR Trust.

"It's a wide and varied remit and no two days are ever the same."

What are the priorities facing the ELR at the moment?

"Buckley Wells and its development is definitely the priority at the moment. We need a carriage shed as a matter of urgency and we also need to secure the long-term future of the Locomotive Works building. Additionally, the improvements at Rawtenstall should start coming together soon with work on the installation of a canopy at the station.

"Obviously the main focus of our fundraising efforts at the moment is on purchasing *City of Wells* and while it is going well, we can't be complacent and need to keep the money coming in. John Stephens is doing a fantastic job spearheading the fundraising for *City of Wells* and I am so grateful to him for taking on this crucial role for us."

Which locomotive would you like to see on the ELR in the future?

"I would go for absolutely anything from the Lancashire & Yorkshire Railway. We have an L&YR carriage here at Bury which is crying out for restoration and I would love the ELR to have its own vintage train at some point in the future. No 52322 has obviously run on the railway on a number of occasions over the past few years and it just feels so right seeing it working on the ELR. Having an L&YR locomotive at the head of a vintage train in firm L&YR territory would be a fantastic achievement and a real attraction for the railway. Other lines have made a real success of operating vintage trains on pre-advertised dates and this is something I would like to see us do in the future."

DAVID LAYLAND

ELR FINANCIAL CONTROLLER AND DEPUTY GENERAL MANAGER

How long have you been a member of the railway?

"I joined the ELR in 1989, following a chance conversation with Peter Lord, who was membership secretary for the society at the time and also one of the founding members of the ELRPS. Peter worked for the Midland Bank, where I also worked at the time and from conversations we had, he knew that I'd had a lifelong interest in railways.

"Shortly after meeting him, Peter told me all about the railway, which was still very much in its operating infancy at the time, and he handed me a membership form. I joined initially as an 'armchair' member for a number of years, mainly due to me playing a lot of cricket at the time which restricted my availability for volunteering, before finally getting actively involved in 1998."

Where did your interest in railways come from?

"I was born and brought up around Wigan and my great-grandad used to live in a house that backed on to the West Coast Main Line and he often walked me down the road to watch the trains go past when I was a toddler, so I used to see various LMS 'Pacifics' and some of the earlier diesel designs hauling trains along the WCML.

"As my childhood interest in railways grew I spent time visiting the local signalbox at Rylands Sidings and on my 11th birthday I was taken on a visit to Wigan Springs Branch Depot and had a footplate ride on English Electric Type Four D211 *Mauretania*, a 'Black 5' and a Sulzer Type Two diesel.

"Although I desperately wanted to work on the railways, after university I started a career in banking with the Midland Bank, where I worked for many years, although I still followed the railways, especially those around my home town of Wigan."

What roles have you carried out for the ELR?

"In 1999 on a visit to Bury Bolton Street I saw an advert asking for a volunteer who may be willing to become the membership secretary for the ELRPS and a week later I met with the then-membership secretary,

One of David's earliest memories is being given a cab ride in English Electric Type Four D211 *Mauretania* during a visit to Wigan Springs Branch Depot. In 2018, the ELR brought together six of the preserved Class 40s for a special reunion event, with the locomotives displayed on the sidings alongside the Locomotive Works. EMMA SEDDON

David Flood, who told me about the role and I subsequently offered to take on the role.

"I remained membership secretary and also became a trustee of the East Lancashire Railway Holdings Company, which is the charitable organisation of the railway, until November 2008 when I started full-time employment with the railway as the ELR's financial controller and volunteer financial director for the East Lancashire Light Railway Company.

"The sheer amount of work involved in my new role meant that I had to give up the membership secretary role for the ELRPS.

"In 2017, I was also asked by the company to be deputy general manager to help and support our general manager, Tracey Parkinson. I'm now in the 10th year working for the ELR and I have to say it is the best job I have ever had, although it can also be rather frustrating at times.

"It's now a major business and so much more than those founding members can have ever imagined."

What would you say are the greatest achievements of the railway?

"Every heritage railway is different because of the way they've been set up, but due to our location our business is about so much more than just running a train service, with special events, footplate experience, Santa Specials and dining services providing much of our income. It is also interesting that almost a quarter of our income each year now comes from the operation of our two pubs, which are seen as very much community assets as well as being facilities that are used by visitors to the railway.

"The railway has achieved many things over the years. When the railway first started running Santa Specials it was a very small operation in Bury Transport Museum yard with a steam-hauled brake van ride. However, in 2017 we carried more than 40,000 passengers on our Santa Specials, which demonstrates just how much the ELR has grown from those humble beginnings. I think those founding members of the railway, a lot of whom are now sadly no longer with us, would be amazed to see just what has been achieved from their vision.

"The *Flying Scotsman* effect since it first returned to service in 2016 has been very beneficial for the railway and we are grateful that we have been allowed to operate the locomotive on a number of occasions in 2016 and 2018. Whenever the locomotive runs on the ELR there is a great interest in it and it continues to bring in visitors who may not normally come to the railway, as well as generating useful income that we can use to invest in improving the railway.

"Every penny we make in profit goes back into the ELR. We have no shareholders, but we are very lucky to have the support of our local councils, who manage the budgets for maintaining the numerous structures along the line. The Board is now investing more in

NIGEL VALENTINE

our rolling stock than ever before and our carriage and wagon department are turning out some fantastic coaches for our visitors to travel in.

"This is just part of a huge planned increase in the amount of money to be invested in our traction and rolling stock department, which encompasses steam, diesel and coaching stock.

"The *Flying Scotsman* visits, *Tornado* operating for five days over Easter, the popular 'Class 40s@60' diesel event and a record breaking 1940s event means 2018 is already showing signs of being a fantastic year for us, with more exciting events to follow later in the year."

Where would you like to see the ELR in 10 years?

"We have achieved our aim of carrying more than 200,000 per year in 2016 and look set to beat that figure in 2018, and while we would like to carry more there are still things we can improve to make it a better day out for our visitors. We offer a good family day out, but we need to improve the yield that we generate from our visitors to provide us with more income, which can then be reinvested in the railway.

"I would like to see a much more stable home fleet of steam locomotives, as we still struggle sometimes during the peak periods with steam locomotive availability. We are actively looking at ways of improving this situation and key to this has to be having more locomotives that can remain on the railway throughout the year, supplemented by visiting locomotives for special events or loan periods.

"The railway is already in a strong position, but we can still do better and I'd like to think that in 10 years' time the ELR will be an even more popular attraction, helping to tell the story of our railway heritage to a modern audience."

Multiple Units on the ELR

A significant part of the story of Britain's railways can be devoted to the various types of multiple units that were constructed from the mid-1950s to help to transform the fortunes of many lines across the country. Throughout its operating history the East Lancashire Railway has operated a varied fleet of multiple units and they remain an important and valuable part of the railways collection.

In addition to the steam and diesel locomotives that haul trains between Heywood and Rawtenstall, the East Lancashire Railway has a first class reputation for the restoration and operation of various types of historic multiple units.

The first multiple unit to call the ELR home was the former BR Research Department two-car Derby Lightweight Battery Electric Multiple Unit, *Test Unit Gemini*, made up of Driving Motor Brake vehicle Sc79998 and Driving Trailer Sc79999, which arrived at the ELR in 1989.

The unit was converted into a battery unit in 1958 using banks of batteries which could be recharged and it was used on passenger services between Aberdeen and Ballater in Scotland, before being rendered redundant with the closure of the Ballater line in 1966. It was then transferred to BR's Research Department and used at the Railway Technical Centre in Derby until it was withdrawn.

It was then purchased for the now-closed Transperience Museum in Bradford, but was loaned to the ELR, whose electrical department successfully revived the unit to allow it to be used on services on the railway. It had the seating in its passenger

On November 3, 2017, the Llangollen Railway's Class 109 DMU stands in Platform 2 at Bury Bolton Street, while the Class 105 'Cravens' DMU stands in Platform 3 during a 3P20 Parcels Group photographic charter. The Class 105 is carrying the headboard which was used on the final train from Bury to Accrington on December 3, 1966.
TOM MCATEE

compartments reinstated and was then repainted into original BR green livery, with the unit mainly seeing use during diesel events. Although a BEMU, the sight of a BR green Derby Lightweight was appropriate for the Bury to

Rawtenstall line, as one of the identical diesel multiple units was allocated to the Bury to Bacup line when services went over the DMU operation in 1956.

Following the collapse of the Transperience Museum, items from the collection were offered for disposal and the BEMU was subsequently sold for use on the Royal Deeside Railway, where it remains, although it is currently unserviceable.

In 1990 ELR member Allan Schofield purchased a two-car Class 110 'Calder Valley' DMU from BR. The unit, consisting of vehicles E51813 and E51842, had been identified as being in good condition out of the withdrawn Calder Valley sets that were examined at Neville Hill Depot in Leeds. The owner wished to restore the unit to original condition but it operated for a couple of years in as-withdrawn blue and grey Metro-Train livery before work started on returning the set to original BR green. Mr Schofield subsequently also acquired a trailer car, vehicle E59701, to reform the unit as a three-car set.

The Class 110 unit saw regular use on the ELR for a number of years, but left the railway in 2003 for a new home on the Wensleydale Railway, where it saw intensive use for a number of years before being taken out of traffic

LEFT: The highlight of the 2017 Scenic Railcar Weekend was the eagerly awaited return to service of the two-car Class 105 Cravens DMU, consisting of vehicles SC51485 and E56121, after a lengthy 21-year restoration to as-built condition. The unit passes over Brooksbottom Viaduct with a service from Bury to Rawtenstall on November 5, 2017. KEVIN DELANEY

RIGHT: Visiting the 2017 Scenic Railcar Event from the Llangollen Railway was the sole surviving two-car Class 109 DMU. The unit is paired with the Class 104 on the approach to Ramsbottom, with a service from Rawtenstall to Heywood on November 5, 2017. KEVIN DELANEY

requiring engine and other repairs.

The unit returned to the ELR in 2016 where it underwent a general overhaul and the rebuilding of its cabs, prior to being repainted into BR green with small yellow warning panels. It is now once again part of the ELR home-based DMU fleet, although it has also paid a working visit to the Llangollen Railway in June 2018 as part of that railway's annual DMU gala.

The closure of the Bury to Manchester electric line on August 16, 1991, saw the end of the two-car Class 504 EMUs which had almost exclusively plied the line since the summer of 1959. Powered by a unique side-contact 1200v DC third rail, the closure of the route for conversion to the first phase of the Manchester Metrolink tram system rendered the vintage EMUs redundant.

Two Class 504 were bought for preservation, with 504451 (consisting of power car M65451 and trailer car M77172) purchased by the Class 504 Group and 504461 (M65461 and M77182) bought by Harry Needle, with both sets being delivered to Bury on the morning of August 17, 1991.

504461 was subsequently acquired by the ELR from Harry Needle, but due to a shortage of siding space and with

ELR MULTIPLE UNIT FLEET SUMMER 2018

CLASS	VEHICLE NUMBERS	LIVERY	STATUS
104	M50455 & M50517	BR blue	Operational
104	M50437, M59137 & M50494	NSE/green/blue	Undergoing Restoration
105	SC51485 & E56121	BR green	Operational
110	E51813, E59701 & E51842	BR green	Operational
121	W55001	BR blue	Operational
122	W56289	BR blue	Undergoing Repairs
207	S60130, S70549 & S60904	BR green	Awaiting Bodywork Overhaul
504	M65451 & M77172	BR green/GMPTE	Undergoing Restoration

another Class 504 already safely based on the railway, the unit was offered free of charge to anyone wishing to take it on, providing it was removed from the railway to a new home. Despite some enquiries, no feasible offer was forthcoming and the unit was scrapped in October 1994, donating many spare parts to the other surviving set.

The Class 504 Group carried out a great deal of restoration work on trailer M77172, but after some use at various ELR events, the unit was vandalised and spent almost 20 years coupled to its unrestored power car, with the whole unit presenting a sorry sight. In 2015 a

new group, the Class 504 Preservation Society, was set up to take on the stalled restoration of the now-unique EMU set. Work is now well under way on the restoration of M77172 with the society aiming to have the complete unit restored towards the end of 2019 to coincide with the 60th anniversary of the unit's introduction into service and the 140th anniversary of the Bury to Manchester line.

In 1997, the ELR took delivery of a two-car Class 105 'Cravens' DMU, a type which had been common around Bury and which saw extensive use on the lines that now make up the heritage

Relocated from the former Transperience Museum at Bradford, the two-car Derby Lightweight Battery Electric Multiple Unit operated at the ELR for a number of years. The BEMU, which had finished its working life on BR as part of the Research Department, was known as *Test Unit Gemini* and had its interior restored for passenger operation. The unit passes through Burrs on August 30, 1993. It was later repainted into BR green, but was subsequently moved to the Royal Deeside Railway. MIKE TAYLOR

The first diesel multiple unit to be based at the ELR was Class 110 'Calder Valley' DMU vehicles E51813 and E51842, which arrived on the line in 1990. The pair are pictured passing over Townsend Fold level crossing while working a Rawtenstall to Bury service on June 5, 1993. A centre car for the '110', vehicle E59701, was subsequently added and the unit was repainted into original BR green livery. MIKE TAYLOR

The National Railway Museum's Class 101 two-car DMU were delivered to Bury in 2005. The vehicles, M51192 and M56352, had been selected from different Class 101 sets with one painted in Strathclyde PTE livery and the other in Regional Railways colours. Both were returned to service quickly and repainted into BR green livery with small yellow warning panels. The Class 101 heads through Burrs as the sun sets on January 3, 2010. The set is now based on the North Norfolk Railway. NIGEL VALENTINE

ELR route, with the final train from Bury to Rawtenstall on June 3, 1972, being handled by a 'Cravens' unit.

The unit purchased for the railway consisted of Driving Motor Brake Second Sc51485 and Driving Trailer E56121 had originally been preserved by the West Somerset Railway, but had been taken out of service in need of a full overhaul. The unit was also extensively contaminated with blue asbestos behind the wall and ceiling panels, which would need to be removed by specialist asbestos contractors.

Following asbestos stripping the vehicles were left as essentially bare bodyshells requiring complete rebuilds. Such was the level of work required that each vehicle has been completely rebuilt mechanically, electrically and with complete bodywork refurbishment, with the interiors returned to as-built condition. The project to restore the 'Cravens' unit took 20 years to complete, but it is understandable when the level

of work carried out is considered.

After one of the most comprehensive DMU rebuilds in preservation history, the Class 105 returned to service on the ELR over the weekend of November 3-5, 2017, with many passengers praising the high standard of restoration. Every detail of the unit has been perfectly restored, with attention to detail clear throughout. The Class 105 has now settled into normal use and has operated on a number of running days and special events since then.

A highlight for the dedicated team who had restored the set, headed by ELR traction and rolling stock director Graham Thornton, came when it was announced the Class 105 'Cravens' unit had won the 2017 Heritage Railway Association Modern Traction Award, sponsored by *Rail Express* magazine, a fitting recognition for more than two decades of dedication in rebuilding this DMU which could so easily have been scrapped.

The next multiple unit to arrive at Bury was a three-car Class 207 'Thumper' Diesel-Electric Multiple Unit that had been built for the Southern Region and spent most of their working lives working commuter services in and around the South East. Although not at all local to East Lancashire, upon withdrawal in 2004, a number of withdrawn 'Thumper' units were offered for sale to heritage railways by owner Porterbrook Leasing for a nominal £1 each.

The ELR successfully applied for one of these units and 207202 *Brighton Royal Pavilion* was delivered to Bury a few weeks later in Connex livery, but covered in copious amounts of graffiti. The unit was quickly repainted into BR green livery and numbered 1305 and saw use for a number of years. Its relatively modern commuter-style interior also proved popular with filming companies and the unit was used for a number of filming contracts while it was operational on the ELR.

On August 17, 1991, newly delivered Manchester to Bury Class 504 Electric Multiple Unit sets 504451 and 504461 are shunted at Bury South. The two EMUs had originally worked out of Bury Bolton Street between summer 1959 and the closure of the station in March 1980. 504461 was scrapped in October 1994, but 504451 is now being restored to original condition at Bury. THE LATE DAVE DYSON, COURTESY OF TIM GRIMSHAW

In December 1997 the railway took delivery of former BR Research Department Wickham *Laboratory 20*, vehicle number 999507. Painted in research colours, the unit is pictured shorty after delivery in Castlecroft Yard in Bury. ANDY COWARD

A two-car Class 117 DMU consisting of vehicles W51339 and W51382 arrived at Bury in 2012 for a five-year loan, seeing regular service at special events throughout the period of its hire. The Class 117 departs from Summerseat station on August 24, 2016. EMMA SEDDON

Class 121 'Bubble Car' W55001 arrived at Bury in a stripped condition in 2008 and was extensively rebuilt over a period of a few months, making its debut in service on the railway in November 2008. The vehicle was completed in BR blue and was joined by trailer car W56289 in 2009. W55001 passes beneath Alfred Street bridge while working a service from Bury to Heywood (displaying the wrong destination on its blind) on January 4, 2015. NIGEL VALENTINE

The 'Thumper' remains at Bury but has not been in service for several years, as it now requires an extensive bodywork and mechanical overhaul, which should take place over the next few years.

The ELR has also hosted two DMU sets belonging to the National Railway Museum, with the first to arrive on the line being a two-car Class 101 DMU in summer 2005. The Class 101 design bears a striking similarity to the early Metropolitan Cammell DMUs which debuted on the Bury to Bacup line in 1956. The two Class 101 vehicles selected for the National Collection had come from different units, with vehicle M51192 painted in Strathclyde Passenger Transport orange and black livery and M56352 carrying Regional Railways colours.

The Class 101 DMUs had worked all across the rail network, but the type spent their final days working suburban services in and around the Manchester area before the final examples were withdrawn from service at the end of 2003, so the decision by the NRM to base their unit on the ELR was appropriate.

The Class 101 unit was quickly returned to service, making its debut along the line in November 2005. It was subsequently taken out of service for repainting into BR green and saw regular use on the railway for a number of years, but was subsequently moved to the North Norfolk Railway in 2012.

The railway also provided a home to the NRM's Class 108 two-car DMU, formed of vehicles 51562 in BR blue livery and 51922 in BR green colours, between 2011 and 2014, where it saw

use on a number of occasions, before moving to a new home on the East Kent Railway, although it has since returned to the NRM in York.

Class 122 'Bubblecar' vehicle W55001 arrived at Bury during 2008 and arrived from its previous home at the Northampton and Lamport Railway in a stripped condition, requiring a number of mechanical components to return it to service. The Bury Unit Team, who collectively maintain the ELR's DMU fleet, purchased a Class 108 vehicle from Peak Rail, which donated many spare parts towards the Class 122s restoration before being scrapped.

Following reinstatement of its interior, W55001 returned to service resplendent in BR blue during 2009. A Class 121 trailer car, W56289, was also purchased in 2009 to provide additional capacity whenever the Class 122 was in use. While W55001 remains operational at the time of writing, the trailer is undergoing an extensive bodywork overhaul.

Between 2012 and 2017, the railway also had use of a two-car Class 117, formed of vehicles W51339 and W51382, and belonging to Mike Thompson. The unit was used at special events and

summer midweek services and was repainted into original BR green livery while based on the line. For a period of time it also ran with Class 110 'Calder Valley' centre car E59701, although this vehicle has since being reformed with the other Class 110 vehicles based on the railway. The Class 117 remains at the ELR at the time of writing, but its loan agreement has expired and it is expected to leave the railway in the near future.

In 2014 the Birmingham Railcar Workgroup relocated one of their two car Class 104 DMU, vehicles, M50455 and M50517, from the North Staffordshire Railway to the ELR, with the unit seeing use on the railway for a short period before it was withdrawn from service to undergo a major overhaul. The restoration of this unit was also completed to a very high standard after three years, with it finished just hours before the ELR's November 2017 Scenic Railcar Weekend. The same group also has a second three-car Class 104 awaiting restoration stored on the ELR and it is not yet known what sort of timescales are envisaged for the completion of this second DMU. The owners of the Class 104 units have also

RIGHT: After leaving the ELR for the Wensleydale Railway in 2003, the three-car Class 110 unit returned to Bury in 2016 to rejoin the DMU fleet, where it then underwent extensive restoration work before returning to service at the 2017 Scenic Railcar Weekend. Guard Stuart McDonald chats to the driver of the freshly repainted Class 110 at Bury Bolton St Station during a 3P20 Parcels Group charter on November 3, 2017. EMMA SEDDON

In 2014 the Birmingham Railcar Workgroup moved Class 104 vehicles M50455 and M50517 to the ELR. The unit then underwent an extensive refurbishment, which was completed just in time for the 2017 Scenic Railcar Weekend. The immaculate unit departs from Burrs Country Park station halt working a service to Rawtenstall on November 4, 2017. NIGEL VALENTINE

become active members of the Bury Unit Team, assisting with the other multiple units based on the railway. In addition to the home-based fleet, the ELR has also benefited from visiting DMUs to some of its diesel events, principally a three-car Class 117 DMU and Class 122 'Bubblecar' which belonged to Pete Waterman, which visited the line for the 1994 summer diesel week.

The railway has also hosted modern DMU sets which have visited the line for testing purposes, with a couple of Northern Rail Class 158 units formerly belonging to Central Trains tested on the railway in connection with Network Rail railhead treatment trains in 2008.

The biggest event organised by the ELR to celebrate the humble DMU to date came in November 2017, when the ELR's annual Scenic Railcar Weekend saw several restoration jobs completed in the run-up to the event, making it one of the most successful such events held at the railway, with many trains fully loaded with only standing room.

The 2017 Scenic Railcar Weekend saw the successful relaunch into traffic of the ELR's Class 104, Class 105 and Class 110 DMUs after major restoration work, with the highlight undoubtedly being the return to service of the Class 105 Cravens DMU after a complete rebuild and restoration spanning more than 21 years. The event also featured a visiting DMU, with the appearance of the sole-surviving Class 109 unit from the Llangollen Railway.

With a proactive and skilled team of volunteers, the Bury Unit Team has gained an enviable reputation for their work in maintaining and operating these unsung heroes and often overlooked vehicles, which are an important part of the rich history of Britain's railways.

Visiting the ELR for the summer 1994 diesel week, Pete Waterman's Class 117 three-car DMU passes through Burrs on June 10, 1994. The Class 117 was visiting for the event, along with a Class 122 single car unit. MICHAEL RHODES

It's not just heritage DMUs that have run along ELR metals, with the railway hosting a couple of Class 158 units which were brought on to the line in connection with testing of Network Rail's railhead treatment trains. The units underwent adhesion testing on Broadfield Bank on the line between Heywood and Bury, with former Central Trains 158851 pictured descending Broadfield Bank on May 13, 2008. NIGEL VALENTINE

Restoring Bury's rail heritage

One of preservation's forgotten projects is now progressing well, after a group of enthusiasts got together to safeguard the future of the sole-surviving Class 504 EMU, which is historically significant to both Bury and the East Lancashire Railway, but came perilously close to scrapping less than three years ago.

In 2015, a somewhat derelict two-car electric multiple unit sat in the sidings alongside the ELR carriage and wagon department shed at Buckley Wells, seemingly forgotten and waiting for the inevitable call for scrapping to put it out of its misery. However, this was not just any electric multiple unit; it was the sole-surviving Class 504 Bury to Manchester unit, 504451, which had originally been preserved in August 1991. Restoration of the set by its owners, the Class 504 Group, had stalled almost two decades previously and it now presented a very sorry sight to anyone who saw it.

The fate of the unit seemed sealed when the ELR's then-general manager stated that a survey of privately owned vehicles of the railway had identified several for which there were no restoration agreements in place and little or no work had been carried out on them for a number of years – the Class 504 unit was one such example.

ABOVE: Two Class 504 units were bought for preservation following the closure of the Bury to Manchester line, with 504451 bought by the Class 504 Group and Harry Needle acquiring 504461. During the October 1991 diesel weekend, the two Bury line units were coupled and through-wired to Harry Needle's Class 25, 25262, allowing the units to be driven from the '504' cabs. 504461 was subsequently scrapped in October 1994. MIKE TAYLOR

Attempts to contact the owning group had resulted in nothing and if contact and mutual agreement could not be made seeking a way forward then the unit would be removed from the railway, including the possibility it could be sent for scrapping.

However, unbeknown to the ELR management at the time, behind-the-scenes discussions had been taking place between the members of the original owning group and a number of enthusiasts who wanted to safeguard the future of the unit. This new group, which included some of the original owners, sought to get the unit transferred into their ownership on condition that it would be restored and then maintained in good condition. Agreement was subsequently reached and the unit was transferred into the ownership of the newly created Class 504 Preservation Society.

A committee for the new society was formed and a meeting was then arranged with the ELR general manager and the ELR traction and rolling stock manager. At that meeting the group presented a plan for how they intended to tackle the restoration and they also gave assurances that work would be done immediately to improve the condition and appearance of the unit quickly. It was agreed that the society could keep the unit on ELR premises providing that

suitable progress was made within six months. After a long period of inactivity and uncertainty it seemed that the future for the sole-surviving Class 504 Bury EMU was looking much brighter.

Delivered new to Bury Electric Car Sheds (now the ELR Locomotive Works) during 1959, the 26 units were unique in that they were powered by 1200v DC side-contact third rail electrification. This form of electrification was unique to the Bury to Manchester Victoria line (the neighbouring Bury to Holcombe Brook line had also been fitted with the same form of electrification, but this had been discontinued in 1951, a year before that line was closed to passenger services) and the sets worked intensively on the popular commuter line throughout their working lives.

Following rationalisation of some services on the line and the withdrawal of Sunday services in the late 1960s, eight of the original 26 units were deemed to be surplus, taken out of service and subsequently scrapped after donating spares for the remaining examples.

From their introduction in 1959, through to 1980, the units operated out of Bury Bolton Street station, which is now home to the ELR and the railway's main operating base. Following the closure of the Bury to Rawtenstall line to passengers in June 1972, the electric

Class 504 Driving Trailer Car M77172 stands inside the ELR Locomotive Works building in May 2018, returning the vehicle to the building that had been its home depot for 32 years between 1959 and 1991. PAUL LAMBERT

For 32 years the Class 504 exclusively worked on the Bury to Manchester electric line until the line was closed to BR services in August 1991 for conversion to Metrolink services. Towards the end of BR operations, the units were often covered in graffiti and the line had a run-down appearance due to weeds on the trackbed being untreated. On August 8, 1991, one week before services ended, 504456 calls at Heaton Park working a truncated Bury to Crumpsall service. TERRY EYRES

train service to Manchester was the only remaining passenger service to use the station. However, coal traffic continued to run through Bury Bolton Street station to Rawtenstall until December 1980, outlasting the electric trains (which were moved to a new terminus at Bury Interchange in March 1980) by nine months.

In October 1989 it was announced that the Bury to Manchester and the Manchester to Altrincham lines would be converted to form the first phase of the Manchester Metrolink tram system, which would link the two lines by a section of street running tramway through the city centre of Manchester. Although no exact date was announced at the time, the two lines would both be closed during the course of 1991.

By this stage the Class 504s, as they had been classed under the TOPS numbering system, were more than

30 years old and were getting close to the stage where they would need to be replaced, despite enviable levels of reliability. The unique Lancashire and Yorkshire Railway electrification system, which dated back to 1916, was also starting to show its age and had the route not been earmarked for Metrolink it would have eventually needed to be either re-electrified, or possibly given over to DMU operation.

The Bury to Manchester line closed in two stages, with the Crumpsall to Manchester Victoria section closing on Saturday, July 13, 1991, before the final Bury to Crumpsall services were withdrawn five weeks later on Friday, August 16, 1991.

Two Class 504 units were transferred into preservation the following morning, with the pair being propelled over Buckley Wells Level Crossing by 31306 before an ELR Sentinel shunting

locomotive was attached to the other end of the units to drag them on to the railway and into preservation. 504451, consisting of driving motor coach M65451 and driving trailer M77172, had been bought by the Class 504 Group, while locomotive owner Harry Needle had purchased last-built 504461 (M65461 and M77182).

Both units were hauled to Rawtenstall on a volunteers' special that same evening, becoming the first electric trains to have travelled along the ELR route. They were then through-wired with Harry Needle's Class 25, 25262, for the ELR's October diesel event, with the Class 25 sandwiched between the two Class 504s, where they could be driven from any of the six driving cabs within the train, providing a unique and memorable formation.

Following their preservation the trailer car of 504451, M77172, did receive some restoration work by its owners, with the vehicle receiving bodywork repairs and reinstatement of the two former First Class compartments, which had been removed from the units in the late 1960s, when the units were de-classified. The vehicle was painted into plain unlined green on one side and BR blue with a wrap-around yellow cabside and front end on the other. However, after use as hauled stock at a couple of events in the mid-1990s, the unit was targeted by vandals who smashed a number of windows and covered the vehicle in copious amounts of graffiti. It was not used again by the ELR and was eventually re-coupled to the unrestored M65451 and stored at Buckley Wells, where it remained virtually untouched for almost two decades.

The fate of the other preserved Class 504 was even more unfortunate. It was acquired by the ELR from Harry Needle, but with siding space at a premium and another Bury electric train preserved on the railway, the ELR offered the unit free of charge to any group wishing to take it

504451 stands in the once-familiar surroundings of Platform 4 at Bury Bolton Street on November 5, 2017 during the ELR Railcar Weekend, showing both progress made by the Class 504 Preservation Society to date, as well as the task ahead to get the unit back into original condition. The unit is carrying the headboard which was carried by 504456 on the last evening of services between Bury and Crumpsall on August 16, 1991. SIMON THOMAS

on, providing it was removed from Bury. No suitable agreement was reached, despite a number of enquiries, and the unit was scrapped at Bury in October 1994, donating many spare parts to the surviving unit.

The long drawn-out saga of the preservation history of this unique survivor has now turned the corner and under the auspices of the Class 504 Preservation Society, the unit's fortunes have certainly improved significantly, with work on the restoration of the trailer car now reaching an advanced stage and plans are also being put in place to tackle the more major task of rejuvenating the power car, which is largely untouched and in need of major bodywork attention and full restoration.

The new society quickly made a start on making the unit more presentable, with a large quantity of spare parts and other items stored inside the passenger saloons removed from the unit and placed into storage. A lot of rubbish, debris and broken window glass was removed, while on the outside graffiti was removed from one side of the unit and a number of broken windows were replaced.

A BRIGHT FUTURE

Regular working parties soon started on the restoration, with initial efforts concentrated on the trailer car, which was seen as being much easier to make presentable in a relatively short period of time. Agreement was also reached with the ELR for the unit to be moved nearer to the carriage and wagon department shed at Buckley Wells, allowing it to be closer to an electricity supply. The movement of the unit also allowed a large amount of graffiti to be removed from the side of the unit which had not been accessible in its former resting place.

During the hugely successful ELR Scenic Railcar weekend in November 2017, the Class 504 was brought into Platform 4 at Bury Bolton Street station for the first time in many years. This gave visitors a chance to see the restoration work that had been carried out so far, but also provided an idea of the level of work remaining before the unit could be used on the railway once again. Originally it had been hoped that the trailer car could have been outshopped in a quick coat of BR blue, but time ran out for the group prior to the event and it remained in a patchwork of BR green and grey undercoat on the side visible on the platform. As it was paired with M65451, the comparison between the partially restored trailer and the unrestored power car was also striking.

In May 2018, following an offer by the railway of four months' undercover accommodation, the trailer car was moved into the ELR Locomotive Works

Graphically illustrating the effects of more than 25 years' storage out of use, power car M65451 is moved for the first time on October 16, 2016. The movement of the unit was to allow the Class 504 Preservation Society to be closer to an electricity supply as they progressed the restoration of the unit, with this side of the unit having previously been inaccessible due to its former storage location. SIMON THOMAS

building to allow bodywork welding repairs to be carried out, as well as providing the opportunity to repaint the roof of the vehicle and paint the bodysides into undercoat. Once the bodywork repairs have been completed and the undercoat has been applied the vehicle will be stored under a tarpaulin until the power car is in a similar condition, when both vehicles will be glossed at the same time to return the unit into its original BR green livery.

Once work on M77172 has been completed, it will be the turn of the power car to receive attention, which is a much bigger task, as the bodywork is now in poor condition some 27 years after the unit was withdrawn. The power car has received no major restoration work externally since arriving on the ELR in 1991 and the society is not underestimating the level of bodywork repairs needed on M65451.

Class 504 Preservation Society welder Mark Griffiths working on bodywork repairs on M77172 on May 17, 2018. PAUL LAMBERT

The society has secured the services of an enthusiastic and skilled welder, who has already worked wonders on arresting the areas of corrosion on M77172 and who is keen to play his part in transforming M65451 to a similar high standard. Internally, both vehicles have been rewired and while some of the wooden and Formica wall and roof panelling is in need of replacement, the saloons are in a reasonable condition and should be relatively easy to make presentable once again, although it is likely all the seating and trim will require new upholstery material.

Both cabs also require restoration work and rewiring to be completed, with the guard's compartment also requiring repainting and general restoration. New destination blinds, featuring both Bury line and ELR destinations, and new route indicator blinds, have been produced by a society member and these will be fitted when the unit's restoration has been completed.

The 60th anniversary of the introduction of the Class 504s into service will be marked in 2019 and it is also the 140th anniversary of the opening of the Bury to Manchester line.

The Class 504 Preservation Society is working hard to complete the restoration of the unit in time for the autumn of 2019, when it is hoped the completed unit can be unveiled in original lined BR green livery. It is also hoped that a series of special events can be organised to celebrate both of these significant anniversaries.

After so many years stored out of use, the Class 504 Preservation Society is working hard to ensure that the last remaining 'Bury Lecky' unit gets its chance to shine in the limelight once again. Although it will never work under its own power again, it should be possible to through-wire it, so that it can work in a push-pull format, probably alongside one of the ELR Class 33s at special events.

2017 SCENIC RAILCAR WEEKEND

The introduction of Diesel Multiple Units (DMU) by BR during the 1950s and 1960s did much to transform the fortunes of many railway lines. Indeed, the Bury to Bacup branch was one of the first lines in the country to see its services go over to DMU operations in 1956, providing a much more frequent level of service to that which had been previously provided by steam services on the line.

The modern-day ELR is now home to a number of DMU vehicles and each year the railway holds an event to celebrate these unsung heroes of the railway world.

The most memorable of these events was the 2017 Scenic Railcar Weekend, which took place over the weekend of November 4-5, and the return to service of three DMUs that had spent lengthy periods of time out of service.

The event also coincided with the annual convention of the Railcar Association, which took place on the railway throughout the weekend.

Although the two-car Class 109 DMU was brought in as a visitor from the Llangollen Railway, it was an ELR resident unit that was destined to steal the show.

The Cravens Class 105 DMUs were once a common sight all across the

With the Peel Monument on top of Holcombe Hill clearly visible in the background, the immaculately restored Class 105 Cravens DMU heads through Burrs on November 4, 2017. The unit had been restored from near-scrap condition over the previous 20 years by the Bury Unit Team in a project managed by ELR volunteer Graham Thornton. NIGEL VALENTINE

network, but the units were also widely used on the network of lines around Bury and Rossendale throughout the 1960s and early 1970s. Indeed, it was Class 105 units that formed the final trains on both the Stubbins to Accrington line in 1966 and the Bury to

Rawtenstall route six years later.

In 1996, a two-car Class 105 unit was offered for sale by the West Somerset Railway, who no longer needed it, and it was bought by members of the ELR.

However, following asbestos stripping the vehicles were in very poor condition

The Calder Valley Class 110 departs from Ramsbottom heading towards Rawtenstall on November 5, 2017. KEVIN DELANEY

The pride of the ELR DMU fleet, as the Class 105 unit emerges from Brooksbottom tunnel on November 4, 2017, heading a service to Heywood, rather than York as indicated on the destination blind. EMMA SEDDON

and have had to be completely rebuilt. The restoration of this two-car set has taken 20 years to complete, but no detail has been left out and, after testing, the unit entered passenger service over the weekend, with most of its trips fully loaded with passengers keen to sample one of these popular DMUs once more.

Also returning to service for the first time in more than two years was the Birmingham Railcar Workgroup's two-car Class 104 DMU, which had been extensively overhauled and repainted into BR blue livery, with work on its restoration only completed hours before the start of the event.

The three-car Class 110 'Calder Valley' DMU was also making its first working appearance at the ELR for a number of years.

Having previously been based on the railway, the unit moved to the

Wensleydale Railway for a number of years, but returned to Bury in 2016.

Following its return to Bury the unit has undergone engine repairs, as well as a bodywork overhaul and repaint into BR green with small yellow warning panels.

Also making an appearance at the event on the Sunday was the Class 504 electric multiple unit, 504451, which is undergoing overhaul by the Class 504 Preservation Group.

The unit was displayed on Platform 4 at the station, giving visitors a chance to take a look at the unit and view progress, as well as seeing the level of work required before it is completed.

With a supporting cast of the Class 117 DMU and Class 122 Bubblecar, the event had been the most ambitious such event held at the ELR and it proved to have a winning formula that saw record numbers of visitors.

On the evening of November 3, 2017, a photographic charter event took place at Bury Bolton Street, using the DMU fleet as a preview to the forthcoming event. The opportunity was taken for the Cravens Class 105 DMU to be posed in Platform 3 carrying the headboard which had been carried on the last service train along the Stubbins to Accrington line on December 3, 1966, which was worked by a pair of Class 105 units. LIAM BARNES

Recreating a classic DMU 'drag' is 40135 along with the two-car Class 104 DMU, seen heading through Burrs. The Class 104 had returned to service following a two-year overhaul and repaint into BR blue. NIGEL VALENTINE

Having returned to the ELR from the Wensleydale Railway in 2016 after a number of years away, the three-car Class 110 'Calder Valley' DMU underwent an extensive overhaul and repaint into BR green with small yellow warning panels. The DMU calls at Ramsbottom station on November 4, 2017. LIAM BARNES

LMS Stanier 'Princess Royal' 4-6-2 'Pacific' No. 6201 *Princess Elizabeth* stands in the Locomotive Works alongside LMS 3F 0-6-0 'Jinty' No. 47324 on June 26, 2006 on the running side of the building. While No. 6201 has since left the railway, No. 47324 remains part of the fleet and is undergoing an overhaul to return it to service for a further period of operation on the ELR. NIGEL VALENTINE

THE Locomotive Works

The he East Lancashire Railway Locomotive Works building is located on Baron Street in Bury, a short distance from the town centre. The building was formerly the traction maintenance depot for the Bury to Manchester electric trains until it was closed by British Rail in September 1991. The steam shed at Bury (26D) was located alongside the electric depot and following closure as a steam shed, it was used to store various electric locomotives and stored Bury electric units until it was demolished in 1976.

The TMD building was used for maintaining and stabling the electric trains which ran on the Bury to Manchester electric line and was often

The East Lancashire Railway boasts one of the biggest and most well-equipped railway workshops in the heritage railway sector, after the railway took over the former BR Bury Traction Maintenance Depot in 1993.

referred to as Bury Electric Car Sheds. The building was originally constructed as part of the original East Lancashire Railway Locomotive Works in 1856 and it is believed that some locomotives built for the original ELR were constructed at Bury. The southern end of the depot workshop is higher than the rest of the building and this section of the building contains an overhead crane to assist with the movement of heavy components. The workshop building

was shortened by British Rail in 1976, which explains the modern frontage to the building on the yard side.

The Locomotive Works and its stabling yard that make up the complex contains six tracks, Road One which stops immediately outside the building, Roads Two to Five within the building, while Road Six runs alongside the outside of the workshop building. Roads Two and Three are both equipped with inspection pits and there are also two additional pits located outside the depot building.

Bury TMD was officially closed by BR on September 20, 1991, just over a month after the final Class 504 electric units had been removed for scrapping. Following the removal of the last EMUs on August 17, 1991, depot staff were retained by BR to manage the clearance of spares and other ancillary jobs which were required before formal closure.

LEFT: A number of locomotives stand in the yard at the Locomotive Works during a photographic evening as part of the ELR's Lostock Hall themed spring gala on March 9, 2017. NIGEL VALENTINE

The building is located on a large plot of land and, following closure, BR was keen to dispose of the land, which they saw as being a prime commercial development site for either housing or retail units. As well as the maintenance building and yard, there is also an extensive parcel of land containing a number of sidings and allotments on the west side of the building and further land to the east of the depot.

However, the ELR was also keeping a close eye on the future use of the BR depot, as it would make an ideal engineering base for the heritage railway and its growing collection of locomotives, with siding space on the railway at a premium. The boundary between BR's land and the ELR was the former Buckley Wells level crossing on Baron Street, with the ELR's carriage and wagon department maintenance shed located on the opposite side of Baron Street to the BR depot. While BR saw the depot land as commercially valuable, both the ELR and Bury Council saw it as being strategically important to the future of one of the area's leading tourist attractions.

Bury Council was also concerned about the site being developed for

The ELR Locomotive Works was formerly the British Rail traction maintenance depot for the Bury to Manchester Class 504 electric train fleet. A number of Class 504 stand in the depot yard awaiting their next duties in summer 1990. The Bury to Manchester line was closed on August 16, 1991, with the depot officially closing on September 20, 1991. TERRY EYRES

Owned by the Keighley and Worth Valley Railway, but currently operated by Riley & Son (E) Ltd, Stanier 5MT No. 45212 stands inside the Locomotive Works undergoing maintenance on February 4, 2017. EMMA SEDDON

The newly preserved building was opened to the public for the ELR's Festival of Steam in August 1993, where a number of diesel locomotives were on display in the yard, with steam locomotives not in use on the railway displayed inside. The main attraction on view in the shed was Stanier 'Duchess' 4-6-2 No. 6233 *Duchess of Sutherland*, which had been loaned to the railway by then-owner Bressingham Steam Museum. On August 11, 1993, No. 6233 is on display inside the building, with the tender of under-overhaul GWR 'Manor' 4-6-0 No. 7828 *Odney Manor* visible to the left. NEIL HARVEY

The Locomotive Works oozes the atmosphere of a typical depot from the days of steam. During a winter photographic charter inside the building in January 2017, Stanier 5 MT 4-6-0, No. 44871 stands in steam, with Class 40, D335 alongside to help give the feel of a 1960s shed scene, as a young trainspotter admires the locomotive. Behind No. 44871 was another Stanier 5MT, No. 45407. LIAM BARNES

Alongside the Locomotive Works is an area of vacant land which was where the Bury Steam Shed (26D) was located. The building was demolished in the mid-1970s, after being used for storing various Woodhead and WCML electric locomotives and redundant Bury line EMUs. The ELR now plans to erect a new shed on this site, which will serve as a running shed for the steam fleet. A pair of Bury EMUs pass the still-active steam shed in October 1964. COLOUR RAIL

and a large number of locomotives had been hired to take part in the festival. Following extensive work to bring the trackwork up to a suitable standard, the building was ready to become the centrepiece of the steam festival.

During the steam festival, the Locomotive Works building was opened to the public with various locomotives that were not in use on the railway displayed in the building and yard, with Stanier 'Duchess' 4-6-2 No. 6233 *Duchess of Sutherland* on static display inside the shed and under-overhaul GWR 2-6-0 'Manor' No. 7828 *Odney Manor* on display with its boiler removed from the frames.

Between 1993 and 2015 the building was co-occupied by Riley & Son Engineering, which overhauls and operates steam locomotives in the UK. Ian Riley has been actively involved in the development of the ELR since its days at Bury Transport Museum and was also the railway's chief mechanical engineer for a number of years. The movement of his business to Bury in 1993, from his previous base in Kirkby, allowed him to expand and a large number of locomotives were overhauled in the Works while he was based at Bury.

Perhaps the most high-profile of these overhauls was the return to steam of the National Railway Museum's LNER A3 'Pacific' 4-6-2 No. 60103 *Flying Scotsman*, which was also the last locomotive to be completed by Riley & Son (E) Ltd before the company relocated to a new base close to the ELR at Heywood.

Even though his business has now moved to a new more modern facility, the ELR still hosts Ian Riley's Stanier 5MT locomotives, as well as *Flying Scotsman*, when they are not in main line use and the Works is still used for running repairs and maintenance by Riley & Son (E) Ltd when it is not practical for them to be moved by road to Heywood. The depot now houses an extensive range of tools and specialist

housing or retail, due to the existing residential communities surrounding the depot and the unsuitable local roads leading to the site, with the surrounding roads requiring significant upgrading if a commercial development occupied the site. There were also concerns about a significant increase in traffic in an area that was not really suitable for a major increase in vehicles using the roads and close to several local schools.

An interesting and rather unexpected development for the depot came in early 1992, when GEC Alsthom took out a short-term lease from BR on the depot yard and building, to assist in the commissioning of the then-new Metrolink tram fleet.

For nine months the depot played host to many of the 26 new Metrolink light rail vehicles, which were moved to Bury from Metrolink's depot at Queens Road and worked on by GEC Alsthom engineers to commission and modify the newly delivered vehicles, to allow them to enter service on the newly converted line. All of the trams had to have new window seals fitted, among other jobs that had been found following their delivery from Italy before they

could be accepted for service by Greater Manchester Metro Ltd.

SECURING THE FUTURE

Meanwhile, the ELR was working alongside its local authority partners at Bury Council to seek listed building status from English Heritage for the depot building due to its historic importance to Bury. The application for listed building status was based on the information that the lower part of the workshop building was believed to be the oldest surviving Locomotive Works in the UK, having been built by the original East Lancashire Railway.

The application for listed building consent was successful and the building was given Grade II Listed status in early 1993. Subsequently Bury Council purchased the depot building and land from BR and then leased it to the ELR, with the preservationists taking control of the depot in June 1993.

The transfer of the building and yard to the ELR was particularly timely, as the railway was organising a huge Steam Railway Festival to mark the 25th anniversary of the end of steam on British Railways in August 1993

The empty depot yard in March 1993, a few months before the ELR took occupation of the building. As well as the spacious yard in front of the workshop building, a number of sidings were also located out of view to the left of this picture. MIKE TAYLOR

A profile of the Locomotive Works building in March 1993 before the preservationists took over. The lower part of the building was constructed by the original East Lancashire Railway and was one of the reasons the building was given a Grade II listed status by English Heritage. MIKE TAYLOR

engineering equipment, allowing the ELR to restore and maintain its fleet of railway vehicles, a facility that many heritage railways would be envious of. The depot also has an extensive sidings area, where restoration work can be carried out.

The Locomotive Works is now one of the largest maintenance depots in the heritage railway movement and continues to prove invaluable for the maintenance and overhaul of the ELR's steam, diesel and carriage fleets. As with most heritage railway depots, the workshop building is not open to visits by the general public, although pre-organised group visits are often given a tour of the facility under the supervision of trained ELR guides.

The building is not without its problems though, with the roof requiring replacement over the next few years which will cost a considerable sum. The ELR and Bury Council are working on various options to safeguard the long-term future of this historic building, as well as developing the land around the Works to provide a new running shed on the site of the former Bury steam shed and a carriage shed, among other facilities, leaving the Works building eventually to be used solely for the restoration of steam and diesel locomotives for the ELR and other railways on a contract basis.

In the past 25 years the ELR Locomotive Works has certainly proved its worth and is sure to continue to do so for many years to come.

BELOW: In the days of steam, Bury would have never played host to LNER Gresley A4 4-6-2 'Pacifics', but the ELR had both No. 60007 *Sir Nigel Gresley* and No. 60009 *Union of South Africa* as guests at the autumn 2014 steam event. During a photographic evening on the depot on October 17, 2014, the two former East Coast Main Line stalwarts pose for the cameras. No. 60007 was previously based at the ELR for a number of years before relocating to the North Yorkshire Moors Railway. NIGEL VALENTINE

Between 1993 and 2015, the Locomotive Works building was occupied by both the ELR and Riley & Son (E) Ltd, with Riley's carrying out locomotive overhauls and other railway engineering in half the building, with the ELR running and restoration fleet contained on two of the internal roads. With unique BR Standard Class 8 4-6-2 'Pacific', No. 71000 *Duke of Gloucester* receiving attention, the well-equipped workshop is shown to good effect in September 1994. MIKE TAYLOR

The National Railway Museum's LMS Hughes-Fowler 'Crab' 4-6-0 No. 2700 spent many years allocated to Bury Steam Shed prior to its withdrawal by British Railways and it arrived back at Bury in 1996 on loan from the NRM, while the ELR investigated as to whether it was viable to return the locomotive to service. No. 2700 stands inside the Locomotive Works on January 26, 1997, although it was eventually moved to Barrow Hill when it was found that the cost of overhauling the 'Crab' would be prohibitive. MIKE TAYLOR

STEAM ON THE MET!

Steam locomotives have rarely worked on the Bury to Manchester commuter line since it was electrified in 1916. However, two ELR steam locomotives have worked along the route – for very different reasons – since the line has been operated for Metrolink services.

The close working relationship between the ELR and Metrolink has seen the heritage line gaining some occasional contract work providing locomotives to Metrolink for various infrastructure projects on the northern section of the Bury line, with the most notable project coming in early 2010 when four ELR diesel locomotives were employed on infrastructure trains in connection with the renewal of a mile of track between Radcliffe and Whitefield. But it hasn't just been diesel locomotives that have graced Metrolink metals.

Back in May 1994, then-operator Greater Manchester Metro Ltd organised an open day at Queens Road Depot to showcase its facilities and give the local and wider community a chance to see behind the scenes.

In addition to the Metrolink T68 tram fleet, the ELR was asked to supply ex-Manchester Ship Canal 0-6-0T No. 32 *Gothenburg*, which was carrying its light blue livery, as No. 1 *Thomas*, to haul trains down one of the stabling sidings in the tram depot yard.

Once it was established that the locomotive could travel along the Metrolink line without fouling either platforms or overhead line equipment, it was arranged for it to travel down to Queens Road overnight after the Metrolink services had finished for the

The early hours of September 27, 2015, and Hunslet 0-6-0ST No. 2857 WD75008 *Swiftsure* stands in the Bury-bound platform at Radcliffe station with a ballast train. The unsocial hours meant that there were very few people around to witness this unique event. NIGEL VALENTINE

evening. The locomotive then travelled down to the Queens Road Depot under its own power, alarming the few people who witnessed the spectacle.

However, in September 2015 the ELR had been asked to supply a locomotive to haul a ballast train between Bury and Whitefield.

Due to additional height restrictions and tightened platform clearances on Metrolink there are now only a few members of the ELR fleet that are suitable for venturing out on to Metrolink metals.

With resident Class 03, D2062 undergoing repairs and no other suitable locomotives available, it was decided to

use Hunslet 0-6-0ST No. 2857 WD75008 *Swiftsure* to haul the ballast train.

Although several ELR-based diesel locomotives have been employed on Metrolink infrastructure projects over the years, this was the first time that steam had been employed on such a job.

In the early hours of September 27, 2015, the 1943-built steam locomotive headed out on to Metrolink hauling a water tanker and three ballast hoppers, dropping ballast between Hagside Level Crossing and Whitefield.

The use of the steam locomotive was deemed to have been successful but, to date, it has not been repeated.

Looking somewhat out of place surrounded by all the fixtures of a modern Metrolink tram stop, Hunslet 0-6-0ST No. 2857 WD75008 *Swiftsure* poses for the camera before continuing with its ballast dropping duties on September 27, 2015. NIGEL VALENTINE

The crew of the locomotive, driver Garry Laxton and fireman Jonathan Valentine, are bathed in steam at Radcliffe while working a Metrolink ballast train. NIGEL VALENTINE

Liquid stop off anyone...

It isn't just train services that are operated by the East Lancashire Railway. The railway now also operates two highly acclaimed real ale bars at Bury Bolton Street and Rawtenstall stations. What started as a project to make better use of the former cafe building at Bury has turned it into a much-valued community pub and a vital source of revenue for the railway.

The Trackside.

Buffer Stops. ALL IMAGES: EAST LANCASHIRE RAILWAY

The ELR now has two public houses on the railway, with The Trackside bar on Platform 2 at Bury Bolton Street station and Buffer Stops in the main station building at Rawtenstall. Both of these pubs are recognised for the quality and variety of the real ales and ciders on offer.

The Trackside was established in 2004 using the former cafe building on Platform 2, which had previously proved expensive to operate and unprofitable. However, following a suggestion to convert the cafe into a public house, the building was found to be ideal for its new use and a cellar and bar were installed, with the newly converted bar able to offer up to nine real ales, along with a full range of alcoholic and non-alcoholic drinks. The kitchen which was used when the building was in use as a cafe was retained and bar meals and snacks are served five days a week at lunchtimes.

The Trackside quickly proved to be popular with regulars and ELR visitors alike and, in 2015, the building was extended to provide a new cellar area and the bar was relocated to make better use of the internal space and

create additional seating areas. The addition of the former Oldham Mumps station canopy on the exterior of the building fronting on to Platform 2 has also helped to boost trade, as customers at the pub can now sit outside on the platform, protected from the elements whatever the weather.

The Buffer Stops bar is a smaller pub, situated in another former cafe premises within Rawtenstall station building and opened in 2013. While the bar itself is small with only limited seating in the main bar room, external seating is also provided and the station waiting room and entrance hall are also used for additional indoor seating areas.

Again a wide range of real ales and ciders are offered, with a full range of alcoholic and non-alcoholic drinks available. The Buffer Stops bar has successfully appeared in the CAMRA Good Pub Guide on a number of occasions.

Such has been the success of Buffer Stops, the ELR is keen to expand the facilities, but this is tied in with the planned construction of a new building at the station which will contain a shop, community space and toilets. When

this building has been completed, the existing station toilets will be removed and the main bar and seating area will be expanded. The ELR is investigating funding options to allow this project to go ahead.

The ELR is due to install the remaining part of the former Oldham Mumps canopy at Rawtenstall station, with the work due to start in early 2019. This will also provide much-needed protection from the Rossendale weather at the station and will provide further undercover seating areas for pub customers and railway passengers, while also transforming the appearance of the northern terminus, which would certainly benefit from a canopy.

Both pubs are open all year throughout the week and they help to keep the income coming into the railway at times when the trains are not operating, with the pubs accounting for more than 20% of the railway's annual income.

The ELR has proved that operating pubs on its stations can prove to be a useful additional source of revenue and they have become very popular in their own right.

PETER DUNCAN

SIGNAL ENGINEERING DIRECTOR AND FORMER ELR CHAIRMAN

NIGEL VALENTINE

How long have you been a member of the railway?

"I joined the ELRPS in 1977, but had been a regular visitor to Bury Transport Museum since it had first opened in 1972. I'd started working for British Rail in Liverpool in 1973, but moved to British Rail in Manchester (which was nearer my home in Middleton) in 1977 where I met Phil Bailey, who has been a volunteer at the ELR since the very early days and who remains active on the railway.

"After Phil told me more about the railway's plans I decided to join as a volunteer, but as there wasn't much happening at the time with the railway I volunteered to look after the road vehicle exhibits on display and undergoing restoration at the museum. In those early days, we kept amassing things that might come in useful when we did get an operational railway to run, but there was an air of despondency which must have also been felt a few years beforehand at Helmshore, as it seemed as if the coal trains to Rawtenstall would never end and we couldn't envisage the coal depot at Rawtenstall ever closing.

"As the railway prepared for opening I became the ELR's signalling director, a position which I still hold, although now also with responsibility for telecoms. It was my responsibility to deliver the complete re-signalling of Ramsbottom station in 1991, along with the restoration of the level crossings at Townsend Fold and Rawtenstall West to allow the railway to extend to Rawtenstall. In 1999 we began the huge task of re-signalling in and around Bury Bolton Street station, which was completed in various phases over a 15-year period.

"I also served as the ELR chairman for 15 years between 2001 and 2016, which was a huge period of change for the railway, as we developed the ELR into the thriving business it is today."

What has been your involvement in the railway?

"Through my job on BR, I was actively involved in the project to transfer train services from Bury Bolton Street to the new station at Bury Interchange in March 1980. As part of my job I was tasked with disposing of redundant assets to reduce BR's ongoing liabilities, and spent a lot of time demolishing closed signalboxes and removing disused bridges.

"After the final coal train had run to Rawtenstall coal yard, a Redundant Assets Walkout was convened to conduct a survey of the line from Heywood Green Lane to Rawtenstall to identify all of the redundant assets along the line, listing all the things that needed to be taken down and scrap that could be sold to realise some monetary value. Obviously I was involved in the railway as a volunteer, so I knew the line relatively well, but all items on the route that could raise revenue for BR had to be identified and

listed. After we had conducted a full walk out along the line I went to see my boss and explained that there was a good chance that, due to ongoing discussions with Greater Manchester Council, the line could possibly be sold as a complete railway, with the assets still in place which would save BR the cost of removing them. It could also raise potentially more than the monetary value which would be raised from the scrap and would ensure the liabilities that BR could not remove, such as certain bridges and tunnels for which they would still need to provide some maintenance, would be transferred to a new owner.

"I had been tasked with demolishing the remaining signalboxes, along with Bolton Street station, but my boss agreed to a six-month stay of execution to allow serious discussions to take place. At the time the only interest was in the Bury to Rawtenstall line, so that section was temporarily safeguarded, although a bridge at Pilsworth Road was removed on the Heywood line following closure, as the ELR had no plans to restore that line at the time.

"That six-month delay was essential, as without the trackwork, signalboxes and Bolton Street station, the project would have been extremely hard, if not almost impossible to achieve.

"As part of the ELR I got involved in the conversations with GMC, who were extremely supportive of our idea to restore the railway and myself, our legal adviser Dave Canavan and Phil Bailey compiled a report for GMC with input from all the departmental directors, detailing how the railway could be operated. Rossendale Council was also supportive but it was a local authority which wasn't cash rich, so GMC took the lead on the project. GMC then approached BR about purchasing the line using derelict land grants and other grant funding. GMC commissioned a report which established it would be cheaper to restore the railway as a heritage line than to reopen it as a cycle path, which was the other alternative under consideration at the time.

"The vast majority of the major works required on the line were on the northern section between Stubbins Junction and Rawtenstall, which had been a lower category of line almost from the date of construction, with the line from Bury to Accrington having Main Line status. A lot of bridge upgrading works on this section had previously been done by the LMS in the 1930s, with a number of new bridge decks being installed.

"However, north of Stubbins some of the structures were in a very poor condition and these had to be dealt with before regular passenger trains could use the line again. Two river bridges between Irwell Vale and Ewood Bridge needed replacement, along with another river crossing close to Rawtenstall West level crossing.

"After a great deal of hard work by the

local authorities with input from ourselves, derelict land grant funding was secured and a rolling programme of works was started, but it was agreed the railway should be opened in two stages, as it was clear the bridge replacement works north of Ramsbottom would take some time to be completed.

"As part of my role as S&T director for the company I had been busily acquiring signalling equipment from various parts of the BR network, which our volunteer gangs helped to recover, with enough equipment amassed to re-signal the railway to Ramsbottom. We were fortunate to get the services of John White, who designed both the signalling plan and electrical and mechanical interlocking for Ramsbottom and without whom it would have been impossible to complete. John has since been the designer on all our other signalling projects and is an invaluable member of the team.

"To start services, our signalling was basic, with ground frames installed at Bury North, Bury South and Ramsbottom, to control points for locomotives running round their trains.

"When it came to re-signalling Ramsbottom in preparation for the reopening to Rawtenstall, we were fortunate to recover all the equipment from Burn Naze signalbox, both from the operating floor and all the equipment underneath the box, which was virtually identical to Ramsbottom box. The under-portion of Ramsbottom had been completely stripped out by BR following closure, so the Burn Naze equipment was transferred straight into the box as a direct replacement. Missing levers for the frame were recovered from Thorpes Bridge signalbox and with the signals we had also recovered from various locations, we managed to get Ramsbottom fully re-signalled in time for the reopening of the line to Rawtenstall in April 1991.

"n 2001 I became chairman of the ELR operating company, which is a role I also carried out for 15 years, before standing down at the end of 2015. During my time as chairman I had a very supportive team of directors, but I should probably single out the late Malcolm Vickers for attention, as

Malcolm was always incredibly supportive to me, had a fantastic commercial understanding, and worked tirelessly to help the railway grow into the thriving attraction it is today.

"I still get a huge amount of enjoyment from the signalling side of my volunteering and I can be regularly found in our workshops at Bury, along with a great team of supportive volunteers."

What would you say were your greatest achievements?
"I would say that during my time as ELR chairman there were three significant achievements and I am equally proud of all of them. The first was getting the line from Bury to Heywood completed to passenger-carrying standards and opened in September 2003, which was such a big project for us as at the time and the effort taken to reopen that section of line cannot be underestimated.

"Securing lottery funding to enable the restoration of Bury Transport Museum was also a highlight of my time in office. In some ways the project proved to be problematical for us as a company and caused several problems along the way, but as our home base since 1972 it was essential that the building was restored, as without that work it is doubtful it would have survived much longer. It is now an important part of our visitors' day out and we get a lot of very favourable comments about the museum.

"The other significant achievement that I am incredibly proud of from my time as ELR chairman was leading the company through a period of huge growth and turning it from a loss-making organisation to a business that regularly records a profit, which is all reinvested back into the railway.

"It required a lot of hard work from our volunteers and staff to turn the railway around, but I am extremely proud that we have a railway that is relatively debt-free and profitable because of careful and structured management.

"In terms of the signalling department the biggest achievement has to be the completion of Bury South in 2014. From start to finish the Bury South re-signalling project took us over 15 years to complete, but when you consider that everything has been installed from scratch and we have done the work in stages around a fully operational railway, to see it now finished gives me an enormous sense of satisfaction, although we couldn't have done it without the help of a fantastic team of volunteers."

Which preserved locomotive would you like to see run on the ELR?
"I'd love to see BR Standard 9F 2-10-0 No. 92220 *Evening Star* run on the railway but that seems unlikely. As a shareholder of the Bury Standard 4 Group I'm really looking forward to seeing No. 80097 return to service in the near future."

RE-SIGNALLING BURY BOLTON STREET

In 2014 work was completed on a major 15-year project to re-signal Bury Bolton Street station and its approaches. Following closure by British Rail in 1980 all signalling equipment from the station was removed and the signalbox at Bury South quickly became derelict and vandalised. Under the leadership of Peter Duncan and using a design created by John White, Bury South signalbox has also been fully restored from derelict condition.

Bury South signalbox was closed by British Rail on March 14, 1980, when Bury Bolton Street station was closed. Over the following decade the structure became derelict and on February 15, 1989, the building stands looking only fit for demolition. Restoration of the building started in 1992 and was brought back into use from July 6, 2004. However, it would be a further decade before the full signalling scheme was completed. DAVID A INGHAM

A view of the beautifully restored interior of Bury South signalbox on July 20, 2018, showing the 65-lever frame, signalbox diagram and instruments to good effect. The project to completely re-signal Bury was completed in 2014, with all movements controlled from Bury South, which is one of the largest operational signalboxes in preservation. RORY LUSHMAN

One of the largest signal gantries in preservation spans the platforms at the south end of Bury Bolton Street station to control movements at the southern end of the station. The gantry was recovered from Lostock Junction and was extended before being installed. 40012 *Aureol* stands beneath the gantry on May 6, 2018. NIGEL VALENTINE

Semaphore signals also control train movements at the north end of Bury Bolton Street, with these two starting signals protecting movements from Platforms 3 and 2 respectively. Stanier 4-6-0 'Jubilee' No. 5690 *Leander* approaches Platform 2 having arrived with a service from Rawtenstall in July 2004, shortly after the signalling here had been commissioned. NIGEL VALENTINE

The Class 104 DMU has the signal to depart from Platform 2 at Bury Bolton Street on December 2, 2017, while working a shuttle service to Heywood. 45108 stands on the rear of a Santa Special service in Platform 3. The impressive ex-Lostock Junction gantry dominates the south end of the station. NIGEL VALENTINE

Another smaller gantry has been installed on the curve alongside Bury South signalbox to control movements on to the Heywood line. Visiting Class 47, 1842, heads towards Heywood on July 9, 2017, with both the home and distant semaphore signals showing proceed aspects for the inner curve. NIGEL VALENTINE

DAVID WRIGHT

ELRPS CHAIRMAN – THE VIEW FROM THE OTHER CHAIR

ANDY COWARD

Where did your interest in the ELR come from?

"I come from a railway family and was brought up in Clapham Junction. My dad was a guard working out of London Victoria and my grandfather's house backed on to Nine Elms steam depot. As a teenager I rode out with my dad on Saturdays travelling around the railway network close to our home and that's where I developed an interest in railways.

"After studies I didn't join the railway, but joined the forces and served in Army logistics for many years. My final tour was at Fulwood Barracks in Preston from 1987 until 1989. I visited Ramsbottom one day in 1988 when the station was just a simple single platform with a run-round loop. I remember watching one of the Santa Special trains come into the station and I decided then that I wanted to join the society, although at that time I wasn't able to commit to any volunteering due to my job and family life.

"In 1997 I decided that I wanted to become a volunteer on the railway. All I really wanted to do was to be a guard and I have remained an active guard on the railway ever since.

"In 1999 I was employed by the East Lancashire Light Railway as its site manager

and stayed with the company until I retired in 2008. As well as being a guard on the railway I am now a responsible officer and a signalman at Ramsbottom."

What is the purpose of the ELRPS and why is it still relevant 50 years after it was formed?

"I became chairman of the ELRPS in April 2013. The society has a history going back 50 years but the organisation now bears little resemblance to those pioneering volunteers back in 1968. In those days the volunteers were working against the odds to reopen the line through Helmshore, a goal which was ultimately unachievable. But if you fast forward to today the organisation is very successful and now plays a vital role in supporting the company in operating the railway by supplying the volunteer workforce that is the backbone of the ELR.

"The society is the recruiting arm of the railway and our volunteer liaison officer is very effective at organising monthly tours of the railway to attract new volunteers into our ranks. All volunteers enrolling into the railway's workforce also have to attend a basic safety course and pass a medical.

"In 2007 the society started to recognise

those volunteers who had completed 20, 30 and 40 years' service. It always gives me the greatest pleasure to present the long service certificates and appropriately embroidered society tie at our Annual General Meeting each April. For those busy volunteers who cannot attend the AGM, I always seek them out on the railway and make sure that they receive their award as a small token of our gratitude for the time they give up to help the railway.

"The ELRPS also purchases and issues

David Wright was brought up in a railway family, with his grandparents' house backing onto Nine Elms Shed. A former Nine Elms locomotive which survives in preservation is Southern Region Bulleid Merchant Navy 4-6-2 'Pacific' No. 35005 *Canadian Pacific*, which is seen running light engine through Buckley Wells ready to collect its train at Bury Bolton Street in August 1993. DAVID A INGHAM

the corporate black ties that are worn by operating staff on the railway when they are on duty. When we were honoured to be awarded the Queen's Award for Voluntary Service in July 2016 the society also sourced and distributed QAVS badges to every working member of the railway.

"Like most other heritage railways we also publish a magazine, ELR Review (formerly ELR News), to our members and supporters three times a year. Our magazine is currently undergoing a revamp under the guidance of our new editor, Rory Lushman. It is still the best way that we can share our information with the membership on a regular basis, although we also use social media to share news as and when necessary.

"The society also now manages the important function of organising and the scattering of persons' ashes whenever we receive such a request. Some families of a person who was very fond of steam locomotives or sometimes the ELR in particular will ask us if they can commit the ashes of their departed relatives into the firebox of the restored steam locomotive. We know how much comfort some families get from this and it is an honour to be able to carry out someone's final wish.

"Occasionally we receive bequests from members of the society who have sadly passed away and who want to be remembered through a donation to benefit the railway. Our bequest fund is quite healthy at this moment and we will ensure that all legacies are committed to a suitable project.

"However, with a lot of bequests there are specific caveats that stipulate the legacy should go to a specific project. If there is no such clause it is up to us as a Society Council to allocate their bequest to a project on the railway which we believe is worthy of entrusting such a gift.

"We have some 3500 members of the ELRPS. After annual running costs are taken into account the society usually has a surplus of around some £15,000 per annum, which we can then consider contributing towards an ELR project when the operating company submits a fully costed business case.

"The ELRPS has donated more than £350,000 to various railway capital projects over the past two decades and I believe that working in partnership with the company is where the strength of the ELRPS lies.

"We have supported the company with the refurbishment of coaching stock, including one of the coaches used on the ELR dining train. We have also funded boiler repairs for No. 32 Gothenburg and contributed towards the refurbishment of Bury Transport Museum, among many other smaller projects.

"We only consider requests from the company if the application is authorised by the company board, is fully costed and a business case is put forward detailing what our money is needed for. While this may seem laborious it has proved to be an effective way of allowing us to make an informed decision as to where we spend our members' money. All decisions are made at

The ELRPS has provided financial support to the ELR for the boiler overhaul of ex-Manchester Ship Canal 0-6-0T No. 32 Gothenburg. Seen heading towards Burrs along with Hunslet Austerity 0-6-0ST Sapper, the locomotive hauls a lengthy train on September 17, 2011. NIGEL VALENTINE

Council meetings whereby a majority vote is required. This democratic process is detailed in our Society Constitution and ensures we always act in what we believe are the best interests of our members.

"At the moment we are going through a transitional phase. For the past 50 years we have been an unincorporated association, essentially a club, which offers little protection to our trustees. So we have taken legal advice and are currently investigating becoming a company limited by guarantee, which I hope will be the springboard to us eventually becoming a charity in the future. This change may have some effect on how the Society Council is currently run but we are weighing up all the options and whatever we do has to be in the best interests of the ELRPS, its officers and members, and be fully supported by them.

"The ELRPS is still relevant as it offers members the opportunity to come along to our Council meetings and raise any concerns or items of interest that they may wish us to consider on their behalf. While we do not deal with items that are specific to the operating company of the railway we have a very good and close working relationship with the railway's Board of Directors. The chairman, Mike Kelly, and general manager, Tracey Parkinson, attend our Council meetings to update us on any relevant company matters that may affect us."

What do you see for the future of the ELRPS?
"The ethos of the society is changing all the time and this will change further if we do become a limited company over the coming months. We have a history stretching back

50 years and are a professional organisation already, but we need to ensure that we continue to run the society in a manner that represents and informs our members.

"One of the issues that currently can be a stumbling block to attracting more younger members is that membership cannot be instantly purchased online or by a phone app. We have to recognise that this is how many younger people manage their lives today.

"We cannot afford to let potential members slip away because they cannot enrol and renew their membership online. This is something we need to address very soon. Our website also needs to be overhauled to make it more user-friendly to give visitors the option to join us instantly and also to ensure it is regularly updated for our members.

"If we can recruit more young members who want to become actively involved in volunteering on the railway that will also be a success.

"The railway, like most other heritage lines, has a growing age profile for our volunteers and I see the recruitment of a new generation of volunteers as being key to the future of the railway.

"There is now a greater appreciation from the company of the work done by the volunteers. The railway's chairman and general manager are assiduous in praising and thanking the volunteers for their efforts particularly after very busy and demanding major events.

"It is vital that our 750-plus volunteers feel valued and appreciated for the work they do on behalf of the railway. The railway's full-time staff do an important job but without the volunteers we simply wouldn't have a railway to run."

FLYING SCOTSMAN

The much-anticipated return to service of world famous LNER A3 4-6-2 'Pacific' No. 60103 *Flying Scotsman* took place in January 2016 after a lengthy overhaul. With the majority of the repairs on the locomotive carried out by Riley & Son (E) Ltd in the Locomotive Works at Bury, it was decided that the locomotive would undertake its initial running-in trials on the East Lancashire Railway, bringing in thousands of visitors and media organisations to the railway to see the prestigious locomotive back in action.

Following its high-profile £2.31 million purchase by the National Railway Museum in 2004, *Flying Scotsman* soon disappeared from public view as work got under way on overhauling the locomotive for a further operating spell on the main line and at various heritage lines.

Much of the repair work was carried out by Riley & Son (E) Ltd at their base within the Locomotive Works on the ELR.

The engineering company was also awarded a contract to operate and maintain *Flying Scotsman* for the first two years after it returned to service. However, its overhaul was subsequently dogged with controversy and rising costs, mainly due to the poor overall condition of the locomotive at the time of its purchase and much more work was required than had originally been envisaged.

In addition to the overhaul of the locomotive's boiler, frames, wheelsets and motion, it was found additional and

The second weekend of the running-in trials for the locomotive saw wintry weather conditions descend on Bury and the Rossendale Valley. Despite this, most visitors who had booked to travel behind the world-famous locomotive managed to attend. With snow on the rails, *Flying Scotsman* brings its train into Ramsbottom on the final day of the running-in trials, January 17, 2016. NIGEL VALENTINE

costly work would be required to realign the frames, repair a cracked cylinder and attend to various cracks which had been discovered in the frames. The cost of the overhaul eventually topped £4.2 million, leading to fierce criticism of the project. However, the level of work carried out by Ian Riley and his staff has ensured that the legendary locomotive is now in the best possible condition and it is hoped that when it is next due for major overhaul, the costs involved in returning it to use again will be considerably less.

After the overhaul got under way it was agreed that following restoration the locomotive would undertake testing on the ELR, with some public trains included in these tests, which would undoubtedly prove to be popular. The ELR had previously hosted *Flying Scotsman* for a month-long visit in February 1993, while owned by the late Sir William McAlpine and Pete Waterman and that visit had attracted thousands of visitors to the railway.

During 2015, it was agreed between Ian Riley and the ELR that he would be leaving the Locomotive Works and relocating his engineering business to new premises towards the end of the year. This development would allow Riley & Son (E) Ltd to have bigger and more modern workshop facilities, while also freeing up a lot of space in the Locomotive Works for the ELR to maintain its own steam and diesel fleet. Suitable industrial premises were subsequently found in Heywood, close to the ELR's station, but the new Premier Locomotive Works base for Riley & Son (E) Ltd would not be rail connected.

The main line operating fleet belonging to Ian Riley or locomotives requiring more minor attention would still be accommodated in the ELR Locomotive Works, but the heavy engineering works would move to his new premises, with *Flying Scotsman*'s overhaul scheduled to be the final locomotive to be completed at Bury before the company moved. With work on the locomotive reaching an advanced stage it was targeted that its restoration would be completed towards the end of December 2015.

There are no other locomotives that seem to capture the general public's attention more than *Flying Scotsman* and if you ask someone to name a famous steam locomotive many would name the famous LNER 'Pacific'. The level of interest in its return to service was huge and when it was announced that the locomotive would be operating on the ELR over the first two weekends of 2016 the railway was quickly swamped by enquiries from visitors who were keen to travel behind it.

There was also a great deal of interest from local and national newspapers, radio stations and TV companies who were all keen to cover the return of the iconic locomotive. Indeed, a couple of TV documentaries were being filmed as the restoration was nearing completion, which would also include coverage of its maiden runs along the ELR, for

mainstream terrestrial TV channels, providing another huge publicity boost for the railway.

On the evening of Thursday, January 7, 2016, *Flying Scotsman* made its way from the Locomotive Works to Bury Bolton Street as it undertook its first powered tests following completion of works. However, issues with the locomotive's brakes saw it coupled to Class 31 diesel locomotive, 31466. It then undertook some test runs along the Heywood line, in preparation for its official unveiling the following morning.

Over the following three days the prestigious locomotive hauled trains along the railway, still coupled to either 31466 or Ian Riley's LMS Stanier 5MT 4-6-0 No. 45407, with thousands of people descending on Bury to travel behind it. In addition to those lucky enough to get tickets to ride behind *Flying Scotsman*, thousands more thronged around the stations and the lineside to capture photographs or just to witness the scenes.

While the first weekend of trials had highlighted some issues that needed attention, *Flying Scotsman* had performed generally well and the following weekend it once again worked along the railway, attracting the same

crowded scenes wherever it went. The railway had been covered with a reasonably heavy snowfall, but this did little to dampen the enthusiasm of visitors to the ELR.

After another successful weekend of running-in trials, No. 60103 retired back to the Locomotive Works, where Ian Riley and his staff worked on preparing the locomotive for its main line return, which would be hauling part of the Railway Touring Company's 'Winter Cumbrian Mountain Express' tour, with *Flying Scotsman* taking charge between Carnforth and Carlisle on February 6, 2016.

Following that inaugural main line tour the locomotive enjoyed a number of main line trips during the year, as well as spending time at the NRM and working visits to the North Yorkshire Moors Railway and Severn Valley Railway.

To round off a very successful first year back in action, No. 60103 returned to Bury for another working visit from October 13-16, 2016. As with the inaugural weekends in January when it had operated services on the line as part of its running-in trials, demand to travel behind the locomotive was phenomenal and the majority of trains it operated

Despite the poor weather conditions and with 31466 provided to assist with braking and train heating, No. 60103 shows off its powerful lines as it departs from Irwell Vale station on January 17, 2016. NIGEL VALENTINE

As daylight fades and with a heavy snowfall on the ground, *Flying Scotsman* runs around its train on the afternoon of January 16, 2016, during the locomotive's second weekend of running-in trials on the ELR. NIGEL VALENTINE

For its second working visit to the ELR during 2016, the A3 had been painted into lined BR Brunswick green by Heritage Painting, giving the locomotive a very different appearance to how it had been at the start of the year. On the evening of October 14, 2016, the locomotive stands at the head of a VIP Dining with Distinction service at Bury Bolton Street station, which it would haul to Rawtenstall later in the evening. NIGEL VALENTINE

were fully booked weeks in advance.

Since leaving the ELR in January 2016 the locomotive had been repainted into lined BR green by Heritage Painting. The company responsible for the transformation of the locomotive into BR colours has close links to the ELR, with its owner being an ELR volunteer. Heritage Painting has now been responsible for the repainting of many steam and diesel locomotives and has gained an enviable reputation for the high standards of work that have

been achieved. The locomotive was also chosen to haul the first ELR service to call at the brand-new Burrs Country Park halt, which had been constructed at a cost of £240,000 to serve the popular leisure amenity to the north of Bury, which also boasts a large Caravan and Motorhome Club camp site alongside the new five-coach platform.

The new station halt was officially opened by the Mayor of Bury, Coun Mike Connolly, on the morning of October 13, 2016, having been completed just

a few days beforehand. The visiting dignatories travelled behind *Flying Scotsman* from Bury and the train paused at Burrs while the opening ceremony took place. However, as the new station halt was not included in the ELR 2016 timetable, it was not officially brought into regular use until the new timetable was introduced in January 2017.

Over the next four days *Flying Scotsman* hauled more than 8500 visitors along the ELR and as well as operating standard passenger services along the line, the locomotive was also used to haul a premium black-tie and evening dress VIP Dining with Distinction service that was fully booked long before the train actually ran. It was clear from the second visit of the locomotive that interest in it had not waned.

Although No. 60103 didn't operate on the ELR during 2017, it returned to the railway for winter maintenance at the Locomotive Works on January 8, 2018. The NRM had announced towards the end of 2017 that it had awarded a six-year operating and maintenance contract to Riley and Son (E). This meant the locomotive would remain in the care of Ian Riley and his staff for the majority of its current boiler certificate and it would continue to be available for display at the NRM sites at York and Locomotion, along with static and operating days on heritage railways and regular appearances on the main line.

No. 60103 remained at Bury throughout the winter undergoing maintenance, before making its first appearances of the year on static display at Rawtenstall on March 10-11, 2018, when members of the public could visit the locomotive's footplate and learn more about it from knowledgeable guides. Another static display of the locomotive took place over the Easter weekend at Bury Bolton Street, which

In January 2018, *Flying Scotsman* returned to Bury for a period of winter maintenance by operators Riley & Son (E) Ltd. On the evening of January 8, 2018, the locomotive stands inside the Locomotive Works at Bury, having arrived on the railway earlier in the evening from the National Railway Museum in York. NIGEL VALENTINE

coincided with a working visit to the railway by new-build LNER A1 4-6-2 'Pacific' No. 60163 *Tornado*. Again, during 2018 the ELR has been fortunate to secure a number of operating days for the locomotive, which continues to prove extremely popular with the general public.

Having run services on the line over the weekend of May 12-13, it has also been booked for another eight operating days on the railway in late August and early September.

On September 15, 2018, the locomotive is to be used to haul a special railtour, 'The Wells Flyer', promoted by the ELR and operated by West Coast Railway Company, from Bury to Holyhead with profits generated from the trip going towards the ELR 'Home for Wells' fundraising campaign to allow them to buy Southern Region Bulleid 'West Country' 4-6-2 No. 34092 *City of Wells* from its current owners.

While its protracted and expensive return to service attracted a lot of negative headlines for its owners, since returning to service *Flying Scotsman*

In dramatic evening lighting, No. 60103 *Flying Scotsman* pauses at Ramsbottom station while working a VIP Dining with Distinction service between Bury and Rawtenstall on the evening of October 14, 2016. As with most services hauled by *Flying Scotsman*, the premium dining trains operated by the locomotive were sold out well in advance. LIAM BARNES

has proved itself to be a reliable and strong performer both on the main line and during its visits to various heritage lines, including the ELR.

Demand to travel behind the locomotive is as strong as ever and its operation has provided a welcome financial, visitor number and economic boost to those railways which have been fortunate enough to have hosted it.

◀ **PEOPLE PROFILE** ▶

LIAM BARNES

RAMSBOTTOM STATION STAFF

When did you join the ELR?
"I joined last September after my 16th birthday. I have been an enthusiast of steam and railways for many years, having gained my interests from my grandfather. I also have a passion for photography, which I share with my brother, so for the last three or four years before getting involved as a volunteer I have also been a regular face at the lineside honing my photographic skills as well."

What are your roles on the railway?
"At the moment I work at Ramsbottom

Liam Barnes is also a very talented photographer, who when he isn't volunteering on the railway can often be found with his camera at the lineside. On June 23, 2018, visiting Great Western 'Hall' 4-6-0 No. 6990 *Witherslack Hall* heads an evening dining train towards Burrs Country Park halt. LIAM BARNES

station, where I am a qualified platform dispatcher, booking office clerk and I spend as much of my spare time as possible on the railway, trying to work on the station at least one day each weekend, sometimes more, although I am studying for my A-levels so that is also important.

"I am aiming to start training as a guard over the winter after I get to 17 and when I reach 18 I would like to be a qualified guard. I would also like to start work within the steam department, as steam locomotives are my main interest and the reason I wanted to become a volunteer in the first place.

"Whatever roles I carry out on the railway in the future, I would like to keep working at Ramsbottom, as the volunteers on the station are a great bunch and I would miss working there. I would also like to become a duty station master at Ramsbottom after I become 18."

How can the railway engage with younger people to get more of them involved?
"It's difficult, because you have to get youngsters interested at an early age. While a lot of younger children love trains and railways, many of them get new interests, hobbies and pastimes as they get older and lose interest, so it's important to make them welcome and give them jobs to do that are fulfilling and interesting if they do show an interest in becoming volunteers.

"Station work isn't for everyone, but it

NIGEL VALENTINE

helps to grow your confidence and also provides some skills that will come in handy as you get older, such as dealing with the public. I was made very welcome by the team at Ramsbottom and really enjoy working on the station.

"It would be good if some of the volunteers could go and speak at local schools and six-form colleges to tell students more about the railway and what skills they could gain by joining as volunteers. Not everyone who joins as a young volunteer will stick at it, but if we can try and attract more youngsters that can only be good for the future of the ELR."

If you could choose any existing preserved locomotive to visit the ELR at some point in the future, which would it be and why?
"I'd love to see the Keighley and Worth Valley's BR Standard 4, No. 75078, or their LMS 4F, 43924 pay us a visit for a while. I wasn't even born when No. 75078 last visited the railway and both those locomotives would look very much at home here in Lancashire if they could be allowed to pay us a visit from Haworth."

Bury Transport Museum

Having been the hub of the East Lancashire Railway between 1972 and 1987, it is fair to say that the status of Bury Transport Museum was somewhat downgraded when the volunteers found themselves with an operational railway to run. However, a successful heritage lottery fund grant saw a project begin to return the historic Grade II listed building back to its former glory – opening it up to a whole new audience.

The survival of Castlecroft goods shed is somewhat remarkable. Built by the original East Lancashire Railway, it could so easily have been swept away beneath the network of dual-carriageway roads that surround Bury and which sprung up during the late 1960s and early 1970s. Indeed, Peel Way, which runs alongside the goods warehouse and yard, now covers about half of the original goods yard.

The warehouse was used as a depot for storing materials and equipment for the contractors building the local dual carriageways and was vacated by them during 1971, leaving it to an uncertain fate.

However, with it becoming increasingly apparent that the ELRPS would not be able to reopen the Stubbins Junction to Haslingden Grane Road section of railway line, the preservationists set about visiting a number of other possible new homes, with Castlecroft goods warehouse in Bury quickly rising to the top of the list.

The building was relatively large and offered undercover sheltered accommodation for the railway's rolling stock, while also offering additional

A plaque unveiled in Bury Transport Museum in 2013 to commemorate the opening of the museum back in August 1972, following the move of the ELRPS from Helmshore to Castlecroft Goods Warehouse.
ANDY COWARD

internal space for road exhibits and room to display the railway's growing collection of railwayana that had been collected by members. Outside, the yard had sufficient room to hold outdoor exhibitions and public steaming days would allow locomotives to move up and down the yard.

Crucially, at the bottom end of the yard was the Bury to Rawtenstall line, which was due to lose its passenger service imminently and the ELRPS initially hoped to be able to take over

passenger operations alongside the BR-operated freight trains which would still convey coal to the depot at Rawtenstall. The yard was not permanently connected to the BR line, but should the line ever become part of the ELR, then linking the two would be straightforward.

Another important factor in the preservationists' decision to move to Castlecroft was Bury Council's willingness to offer an immediate lease and an enthusiasm for the project that they hadn't witnessed before.

Over the first few months of 1972 the ELRPS relocated their collection and established Bury Transport Museum, mixing road and rail exhibits for visitors, with the building officially opened by the Mayor of Bury on August 26, 1972. While the new museum was somewhat primitive, the volunteers worked hard to tidy up the site and make it suitable for visitors, with a cafe, shop and exhibition room established in rooms on staging within the building, while on the other side, a volunteers' mess room and rest facility was created.

Over the following 15 years, running the museum and raising money were the main functions of the ELRPS volunteers.

The Bury to Rawtenstall line closed to freight in December 1980, but it would be another six-and-a-half years after that before they had an operational railway line to run.

Special events and regular steaming days were held for the public, with an annual historic vehicle cavalcade between Bury and Rawtenstall, using a convoy of historic buses, vans and wagons, becoming the highlight of the Bury Transport Museum annual events calendar.

However, in July 1987, the ELR reopened the line between Bury and Ramsbottom, with the focus of volunteer efforts moving away from running the museum to that of running a four-mile stretch of railway. While Bury Transport Museum was still open to the public, it was no longer the main focus of special events and became more of a place where visitors could go and wander around under their own auspices.

Historically, the volunteers of the ELRPS still appreciated the value of Bury Transport Museum, and road and rail vehicles were still maintained and restored inside the building, but the museum had clearly seen better days and if it was to remain part of the ELR something would need to be done eventually to bring the building up to a suitable condition.

By 2003, the directors of the ELR had some serious concerns about the deteriorating condition of the roof of the building and the decision was taken to close the museum building until such time as the roof could be repaired. To prevent further deterioration of the roof, scaffolding supports were installed within the building to help prop up the failing roof structure. While the building was still used by volunteers restoring road and rail vehicles, its days as a visitor attraction were over – for now.

The ELR and Bury Council both understood the importance of preserving the building and while the opening of the railway had changed the status of the museum from those early days, reopening it as a more modern facility which was still sympathetic to its history could help to make Bury Transport Museum an attraction in itself once again.

It was announced in November 2006 that the ELR had been awarded a Heritage Lottery Fund grant of £1.5 million towards the estimated £2.5 million projected costs of the

Some of the road transport exhibits on display inside Bury Transport Museum. ANDY COWARD

For many years a detailed model railway depicting the railways of Bury was on display at the nearby Bury Museum. However, when the museum was refurbished the model railway was put into store, before being released to the ELR for display on the staging inside Bury Transport Museum. The model has been rebuilt by volunteers and is fully operational on special event days. ANDY COWARD

Bury Transport Museum even has a small display dedicated to the Metrolink tram system, which only dates back to 1992. Having undergone a modernisation programme, an old obsolete ticket vending machine, station signs, photos and publicity leaflets make up the Metrolink display, with the equipment donated to the museum by Transport for Greater Manchester and Metrolink's then-head of engineering, Clive Pennington. ANDY COWARD

The museum also has a number of original signalbox name boards. Many of these are from the local area, including Helmshore Station, which was the first home of the ELRPS, along with Rawtenstall East and Stacksteads from the now-closed Rawtenstall to Bacup line. ANDY COWARD

Bury Transport Museum has a large number of former British Railways station signs on display, primarily from the local area and wider London Midland Region, although other regions are also represented on a smaller scale. The collection of station totem signs is one of the largest collections in the UK. ANDY COWARD

refurbishment of the building. When complete, the museum would feature a new entrance, interactive displays, and a new purpose-built education room.

21ST CENTURY MUSEUM

Work on the long-overdue renovation got under way in 2008, with contractors employed to refurbish the building. Over the preceding months, volunteers had been busy emptying the building, with the exhibits all placed in secure storage at a rented warehouse in Bolton.

Once the building was empty the contractors surrounded it in scaffolding and began the painstaking task of returning it to its former glory. The roof, walls and floor of the building were all given attention, with rotten roof beams replaced and renewed and all roof slates refurbished and refitted, or replaced, the walls were sand-blasted to bring the stonework up like new and then given a lime render to provide a bright, white interior finish. The stone setts on the floor were all lifted and relaid, while the wooden staging along both sides of the building were refurbished.

A new education and meeting room was also provided above the main entrance, with a glazed frontage to the room overlooking the main museum exhibition area.

A small kitchen area and toilets were also provided on the new education room level, while a lift and staircase from the reception area were provided to link the two areas.

As with all modern museum facilities, the refurbished building was designed to be fully accessible to all visitors, with lifts provided to help get wheelchair users from the floor level on to the staged walkways and exhibition areas. Specially constructed lifting platforms

were provided by two of the main external doors to allow road and rail exhibits to be removed from the building when it is not open to the public, but these platforms are lowered and part of the normal walkway system while the building is open to visitors.

The completed building was opened by the Duke of Gloucester on March 26, 2010, in front of an invited audience of the people who had been actively involved in the project to bring the building back to life.

As well as the Heritage Lottery Fund, funding for the museum refurbishment came from the Northwest Regional Development Agency, Bury Council, the East Lancashire Railway Preservation Society and various local businesses.

On the staging areas, toilet facilities have been provided inside the building for the first time in its history, while a mock-up of a goods warehouse manager's office is also provided to show what such an office would have looked like in days gone by.

A cab from a former Rossendale bus is also on display, along with an impressive model railway depicting the railways around Bury from the early part of the 20th century.

Since reopening, visitor numbers to the museum have been growing steadily year on year and the museum is free of charge for visitors, although donations are welcomed.

The buses and road exhibits are regularly swapped around to provide some variety for regular visitors and new smaller exhibits are always being added to the collection. The museum also hires out its education room and facilities to any organisation wishing to use the room, which is ideal for meetings.

The restored Bury Transport Museum yard at Castlecroft had all its stone setts replaced, providing a much improved appearance to the yard and making it even more suitable for photographic cameos. Chris Beet's ex-Yates Duxbury 0-4-0ST stands in the yard making a delivery of beer on February 19, 2012. NIGEL VALENTINE

LEFT: Somewhat far away from their traditional stomping ground, a gathering of former London Transport Routemaster buses are displayed in the museum yard on July 5, 2015. NIGEL VALENTINE

Bury Transport Museum is open between 10am and 4pm Wednesday to Sunday throughout the year, as well as Bank Holiday Mondays (excluding Christmas Day and Boxing Day).

BELOW: A display of former Yelloway road coaches in the museum yard at Castlecroft on July 5, 2015, during a gathering of vintage buses and coaches at the museum. NIGEL VALENTINE

THE 1993 STEAM RAILWAY FESTIVAL

To celebrate the 25th anniversary of the formation of the East Lancashire Railway Preservation Society at Helmshore in 1968, as well as to mark the 25th anniversary of the end of steam on British Rail, the ELR organised a month-long steam event. With 17 visiting locomotives brought in by road for the event, it was also one of the most ambitious steam enthusiast events ever organised in railway preservation history.

In summer 1993, when planning for the ELR Steam Railway Festival was at an advanced stage, news came through that Bury Council had successfully purchased the former Bury Traction Maintenance Depot from BR and the building would be leased to the ELR as its new maintenance facility. However, the period between the depot being secured and the start of the ELR festival was only a matter of weeks away, so there was a frantic effort to get the building and yard in a fit condition in time for the start of the event.

Once it was known that the depot building would be the operating base for the festival, it was decided that a number of locomotives should be displayed inside the building, which would be opened to the visiting public.

The star attraction for display in the newly-christened ELR Locomotive Works was LMS 'Coronation' Pacific 4-6-2 No. 6233 *Duchess of Sutherland*. The impressive Stanier-designed locomotive was owned by Bressingham Steam Museum and was being loaned to the ELR with a view to the railway assessing it for a possible return to steam.

Also on display would be GWR-

Making its second working visit to the ELR, Southern 'Pacific' No. 35005 *Canadian Pacific* departs from Ramsbottom on August 13, 1993. MIKE TAYLOR

designed 4-6-0 'Manor' No. 7828 *Odney Manor*, which was out of service undergoing a boiler overhaul. A number of ELR diesel locomotives, appropriate to the 1968-theme of the event, would also be displayed at the Locomotive Works, along with any visiting locomotives attending the event but not in use on a particular day.

It had been planned that the Heywood line would be completed to a standard where main line registered locomotives could attend the event using the reinstated extension. However, construction of a replacement bridge over Pilsworth Road at Broadfield had been delayed, meaning that the route would not be ready in time and all locomotives attending would need to be

brought in by road. This development immediately meant two of the planned star locomotives, LNER A4 4-6-2 No. 4498 *Sir Nigel Gresley* and unique BR Standard 4-6-2 No. 71000 *Duke of Gloucester,* would not be able to attend, as their respective owners were reluctant to bring the locomotives to Bury by road. However, both owners stated that they would be happy to bring their locomotives to Bury when the railway was reconnected to the BR network.

Thankfully, there were plenty of owners and railways that were willing to allow their engines to come to Lancashire for what was envisaged as being a ground-breaking event for the railway preservation movement.

Showing the fine lines of a Stanier 4-6-0 'Jubilee', No. 45596 *Bahamas* stands at Irwell Vale on August 28, 1993, ready to work its train to Rawtenstall. This was one of two 'Jubilees' to work at the August 1993 festival, with No. 5593 *Kolhapur* also visiting from Tyseley. DAVID A INGHAM

GWR heavy freight locomotive No. 3822 heads through Burrs on August 17, 1993, while hauling a record-breaking 23 coaches from Bury to Rawtenstall. The exhaust from the locomotive shows how hard it was working to haul its train up the Rossendale Valley. MIKE TAYLOR

Recreating a classic Somerset and Dorset Railway double-header, LMS 7F 2-8-0 No. 53809 and BR Standard 9F 2-10-0 No. 92203 *Black Prince* haul a train of maroon Mark 1 coaches away from Bury, heading towards Rawtenstall on August 13, 1993. MIKE TAYLOR

Chosen to bring down the curtain on the event was Keighley and Worth Valley Railway owned Stanier 8F 2-8-0 No. 48431 which was disguised as the last Copy Pit Banker locomotive No. 48278. The recreation had been done by photographers affiliated to the ELR and the locomotive is seen at Ramsbottom station bathed in steam before working light engine back to Bury. NEIL HARVEY

Naturally, there was a strong bias on the guest list for locomotives from the London Midland Region, with seven operational LMS locomotives taking part in the event. GWR heavy freight locomotive No. 3822 hauled 23 coaches from Bury to Rawtenstall, making it a record-breaking train, with the exhaust coming from the locomotive being particularly memorable as it worked its way up the Irwell Valley.

The appearance of David Shepherd's BR Standard 2-10-0 9F, No. 92203 *Black Prince*, allowed the organisers to double-head it with Somerset and Dorset Railway 7F No. 53809 for a recreation of 'The Pines Express' which regularly operated over the S&D route.

The event also featured the first double-headed train hauled by LMS 4-6-0 'Jubilees' in preservation, thanks to the arrival of No. 5593 *Kolhapur* at Bury in time for the final weekend of the festival, while the Bahamas Locomotive Society-owned No. 45596 *Bahamas* had been on site since the middle of August.

Another late guest at the event was Southern Region 'Urie' No. 30506, which

arrived from the Mid Hants Railway for the final weekend of the event. This was supplied as a replacement for BR Standard 5 locomotive No. 73096, which had originally been due to take part, but was unavailable at the time.

The end of the event saw Stanier 8F 2-8-0 No. 48431 disguised as No. 48278 for a recreation of the last Copy Pit Banker. Photos of the original No. 48278 were carefully studied and the work to recreate the paint markings on the locomotive were thanks to the efforts

of a group of photographers who were also supporters of the railway. After banking the last train of the day, the locomotive was detached from the train at Ramsbottom and worked light engine back to Bury, through clouds of drizzle, which seemed appropriate for the end of the month-long event. However, due to the very high cost of staging the event the railway suffered a fairly substantial financial loss and, as such, subsequent events organised by the ELR have been somewhat less ambitious.

RAISING THE ROOF

Between 2012 and 2016, the ELR organised an annual music festival at Bury Bolton Street station. Titled Raise the Roof, the event was designed to showcase a variety of local and national folk, alternative and tribute music acts, performing live to an audience watching from the opposite platform, while also raising funds for the railway to erect a new canopy over Platform 2 at the station.

The original aim of the Raise the Roof event was to raise funds towards the reconstruction of part of the former Oldham Mumps station canopy on Platform 2 at Bury Bolton Street station. The canopy had arrived on the ELR in 2010 following the closure of the Oldham Loop line for conversion into part of the Metrolink tram network.

It had always been the intention of the ELR to reconstruct part of the Oldham Mumps canopy over Platform 2, which would help to protect waiting railway passengers from the elements, but also customers of The Trackside bar which is also located on the same platform.

However, before the canopy could be refurbished and re-erected in its new location, funds needed to be raised to finance the costs of the works. A number of ideas were considered, including an appeal to members and supporters of the railway for donations.

However, another fundraising event organised to help finance the new canopy was Raise the Roof, which first took place in July 2012 and aimed to provide a music festival over two evenings at Bury Bolton Street station, with a wide and eclectic range of musicians and bands performing for an audience of people who had pre-purchased their tickets in advance of the event.

With The Trackside providing a licensed bar and plenty of room on the platform to host hundreds of spectators, the scene was set for the first event to get under way. Acts to suit most musical tastes were invited to join the bill and the two evenings proved to be a big success, with the musicians performing on Platform 3 beneath the original station canopy to an appreciative audience standing on the adjacent Platform 2.

Lighting and sound equipment were provided by Mainline Show Productions, which is a local company formed by a number of ELR volunteers, which hires state-of-the-art equipment to the entertainment industry for shows, events and music festivals.

Although it was originally envisaged that Raise the Roof would be a one-off event, the success and popularity of the event meant that a second event was organised the following year, proving to be even more successful than the first.

As the events progressed, the line-up proved to be even more ambitious, with the event becoming one of the highlights of the local music scene. By 2015, work on the erection of the former Oldham Mumps canopy was under way and for the 2015 event, the audience was able to enjoy Raise the Roof from beneath the new structure, although at the time it had yet to be glazed.

ALL PHOTOS: NIGEL VALENTINE

Following completion of the new Platform 2 canopy, the Raise the Roof events continued on an annual basis until 2016, but no event has been held in 2017 or 2018 and it is currently unknown if the event will return in future years. However, the events certainly helped to raise the profile of the ELR as a suitable venue for live music events.

The other East Lancashire Railways

Twinning a locomotive with a heritage railway is nothing new and several lines have seen their name applied to an active main line diesel locomotive. The East Lancashire Railway has seen its name applied to two diesel locomotives, along with a Manchester Metrolink tram. These are the other East Lancashire Railways.

The first locomotive to carry the name *East Lancashire Railway* was Class 37, 37418, which was named on April 22, 1994. The locomotive was one of a number of ETH-fitted Class 37/4s which had been allocated to BR passenger business Regional Railways and had been overhauled in preparation for its duties hauling passenger services around the North West and North Wales.

The immaculate locomotive, outshopped in the attractive Regional Railways dark blue and grey livery, travelled along the Heywood line to Bury for its official naming ceremony at Bury Bolton Street, before hauling a dining train for invited guests to Rawtenstall and back. Upon arrival back at Bury, 37418 immediately left the railway to resume its main line duties.

Following the privatisation of BR 37418 became the property of freight operator English Welsh & Scottish Railway (EW&S) and it was repainted into EW&S red and gold colours in early 1997, although it retained its name and, as an electric train heat-fitted locomotive, it remained mainly in use on locomotive-hauled passenger services. A move north came in 2000 when it was reallocated to Motherwell depot, where it regularly saw use hauling the Caledonian Sleeper, among other services. 37418 was withdrawn by EW&S in April 2005. After being offered for disposal, it was bought by preservationist Steve Beniston and moved to the ELR for a new life in preservation, although it received its previous name of *Pectinidae*, which it had carried while operating as part of the trainload freight fleet. It remained on the ELR until early 2018 when it was moved to Barrow Hill for a possible main line return, being placed on hire to Colas Rail. It is unknown if it will return to the ELR in the future.

In July 2007, as part of the ELR's 20th anniversary celebrations for the reopening of the railway between Bury and Ramsbottom, the Class 40 Preservation Society offered to name 40145, their main line flagship

During the 20th anniversary of the reopening of the railway celebrations, newly named 40145 *East Lancashire Railway* passes the National Railway Museum's celebrated GWR 4-4-0 No. 3440 *City of Truro* at Ramsbottom station on July 29, 2007. NIGEL VALENTINE

East Lancashire Railway

40 145

A close-up study of the *East Lancashire Railway* nameplate and the plaque above the nameplate dedicated to former ELR chairman, the late Trevor Jones, who lead the ELR board between 1974 and 2001 and remained a director of the company until his death in 2006. NIGEL VALENTINE

LEFT: 37418 stands at Rawtenstall on April 22, 1994, ready to return to Bury following its naming ceremony earlier in the day. Following its withdrawal by EW&S 37418 was preserved and spent many years based on the ELR. THE LATE MALCOLM ORRETT, COURTESY PETER M DUNCAN

On April 22, 1994, the newly named 37418 *East Lancashire Railway* runs round its special train at Rawtenstall station. The locomotive carried its name for 11 years, before being withdrawn by EW&S in April 2005. BRIAN SUTTON

locomotive, *East Lancashire Railway*, using the nameplates that had previously been carried by 37418 and which had been returned to the ELR after they had been removed from the Class 37 following its withdrawal by EW&S, the nameplates having originally been purchased by an ELR member on condition they were returned upon withdrawal.

As part of the 20th anniversary celebrations the Class 40 was repainted into BR Large Logo livery, which was a colour scheme that had not been carried by the type during their working lives on BR, although was carried by a large number of Class 37 locomotives, which had a similar English Electric body profile. 40145 had also previously carried Large Logo blue briefly in 1992, although it was also temporarily renumbered 40445 on that occasion.

Upon its naming, the locomotive also carried a crest above the nameplate dedicated to former East Lancashire Light Railway chairman, Trevor Jones, who had been a leading figure throughout the history of the railway prior to his death in 2006.

40145 regularly operated both on the main line and the ELR throughout the time it carried the railway's name on its bodysides, but it was repainted into

BR blue livery in summer 2013 and the nameplates were removed. They have not yet been reapplied to another main line locomotive.

Since its inception in the early 1990s, the ELR had enjoyed a close working relationship with the various Metrolink operators, who were responsible for operating services on the Bury to Manchester line and the wider Metrolink network. A number of past and present Metrolink employees were also ELR volunteers and so it was appropriate when then-Metrolink operator Stagecoach Metrolink Ltd offered to name one of its tram fleet after the railway. The tram chosen to carry the *East Lancashire Railway* name was Firema T68 tram No. 1007, which had been one of the original 26 trams delivered to Manchester between August 1991 and May 1992 for use on the original Metrolink Phase One route between Bury and Altrincham, with a spur line to Piccadilly station. No. 1007 had recently been modified to allow it to also be used on the Phase Two Eccles extension of the Metrolink network, ensuring it would be seen across both

core Metrolink routes. The naming of the tram took place at Bury Interchange on May 31, 2008, with the naming ceremony being carried out by ELRPS president Pete Waterman, witnessed by a small crowd of ELR volunteers.

However, the delivery of a new fleet of Bombardier/Vossloh M5000 trams from 2009 for the rapidly expanding Metrolink network spelt the premature end for the Metrolink T68 fleet, and all of the original T68 fleet were withdrawn from service between 2012 and 2014.

No. 1007 was one of the final three T68s to be withdrawn in February 2014 and it was also one of two trams (the other being No. 1016) used on a special farewell tour of some of the Metrolink network which took place on May 26, 2014. During this tour No. 1007 was formally handed over for preservation to the Greater Manchester Tramway Museum at Heaton Park by Transport for Greater Manchester, becoming the first second-generation tram to enter preservation. It is currently stored at Metrolink's Trafford Depot, awaiting movement to Heaton Park at some stage in the future.

Metrolink LRV No. 1007 *East Lancashire Railway* stands in St Peter's Square in Manchester city centre while being turned back during city centre track relaying works, before working a service to Eccles on September 17, 2009. ANDY COWARD

With less than a year in traffic before being withdrawn, LRV No. 1007 *East Lancashire Railway* makes its way down Mosley Street in Manchester city centre working an Eccles service on June 6, 2013. The tram is now preserved by the Heaton Park Tramway, but is currently still stored at Metrolink's depot at Trafford, awaiting movement to Heaton Park. NIGEL VALENTINE

In September 2014, Lime Pictures filmed explosive train crash scenes for their daily Channel 4 serial drama, Hollyoaks, where a train derailed after hitting a car blocking the tracks. For this, the production company produced a replica of Class 14, D9531, which was laid alongside a Mark 2 carriage on the Heywood line near to Roch Viaduct. This particular filming contract was one of the most ambitious ever organised on the ELR. Prior to filming starting Class 40, 345, heads a service from Bury to Heywood on September 27, 2014. TOM MCATEE

A perfect backdrop for drama companies, the East Lancashire Railway has hosted more than its fair share of filming contracts, providing a flexible and professional location which can provide the scenes that producers and directors are looking for.

The East Lancashire Railway has proved to be an extremely popular choice for filming companies seeking a rail-based location for both TV and film productions.

Its location in the heart of the North West and close to Manchester has proved to be an attractive proposition for filmmakers, while its size means the railway is able to supply a wide range of steam and diesel locomotives from various eras. On occasions, the main line connection at Heywood has meant that rolling stock can be brought on to the railway specially for filming purposes. The various ELR stations can be used to depict small country wayside stations from days gone by, or Bury Bolton Street's more modern appearance allows it to be disguised as a relatively modern main line station.

Filming has ranged from low budget short films produced by students through to advertisements, safety videos, promotional films, as well as prime-time TV dramas, comedies and films.

Popular mainstream TV programmes that have featured the ELR prominently as part of their storylines include Cracker, Cold Feet, Rik Mayall Presents, Coronation Street, Eric and Ernie, Life on Mars, Peaky Blinders, Coleen's Real Women, Waterloo Road, Hollyoaks, Mrs Biggs and Extreme Cakemakers.

The return to service of Gresley A3 'Pacific' 4-6-2 No. 60103 *Flying Scotsman* also attracted huge media attention, with national and local news broadcasts covering the event.

The railway also played host to an ITV film crew and TV personality Robson Green for an in-depth look at the locomotive's return to steam, with the railway featuring prominently throughout the programme.

When the A3 returned to Bury in October 2016, it was used to haul a special train for a touring version of Noel Edmonds' popular Channel 4 quiz show Deal or No Deal.

Various film companies have also used the ELR for locations in feature films, such as Danny Boyle's Millions and the film about the execution of Derek Bentley Let Him Have It! While Hughes Fowler 2-6-0 'Crab' No. 13065 has recently featured in the film Paddington 2, although the locomotive appears in the film superimposed on to the front of a circus train taking part in a race alongside the A1 Trusts, Peppercorn A1 'Pacific' 4-6-2 No. 60163 *Tornado*.

In September 1998, Granada Television filmed a science fiction drama about the end of the world, entitled The Last Train, which was shown on ITV. The plot saw a train coming to a stand in a tunnel and when the passengers emerged from the tunnel, this was the scene of devastation that greeted them. ANDY COWARD

Popular TV personality Noel Edmonds poses in front of *Flying Scotsman* at Bury during the filming of a touring version of Channel 4 quiz show Deal or No Deal. EAST LANCASHIRE RAILWAY

The familiar frontage of Bury Bolton Street station is disguised as Redhill Station for the filming of scenes for popular ITV drama series Mrs Biggs, about the wife of Great Train Robber Ronnie Biggs, starring Sheridan Smith. EAST LANCASHIRE RAILWAY

CORONATION STREET COMES TO THE ELR

Andy Coward gives an insight into the wedding on the 'Weatherfield Line' of popular Coronation Street characters Roy and Hayley Cropper in 2010.

Film and TV companies' love of heritage railways as locations is nothing new, with the irresistible combination of steam and nostalgia regularly providing a mouth-watering proposition for producers and directors.

The East Lancashire Railway became the Weatherfield Line briefly in 2010, with the railway used to film some hilarious, if slightly inaccurate, scenes for peak time ITV serial-drama Coronation Street in connection with the wedding of characters Roy and Hayley Cropper. Sadly the ELR's time on 'Corrie' was only brief, with the scenes being shown over two episodes in late August 2010, but the level of exposure from such a programme cannot be underestimated – with average audiences of more than seven million viewers. The filming and prominence of the railway certainly provided a short-term boost to the ELR in terms of publicity, while also providing a useful revenue source from the filming fees paid by ITV Granada for using the railway's facilities.

For the volunteers and staff, these filming contracts provide an interesting variation from the normal day-to-day business while the TV producers get a location that has the flexibility to give them exactly what they want, without the constraints that often face them if they are attempting to use the national rail network. So, how do our heritage railways plan and prepare for the arrival of TV and film cameras? The process for the ELR Coronation Street filming began as most other enquiries do – a phone call from a location manager enquiring about our facilities and a follow-up visit to the railway. As general manager of the ELR at the time, it was my responsibility to deal with these enquiries when they came in and to negotiate with the production company on how the contract could be managed.

Probably the hardest part was to accurately recreate what the script writers had written and what the director had pictured in his head for the scenes they were trying to create. This entailed searching for a suitable location, often from the briefest of

After the surprise choice of travel to his wedding is unveiled, Roy Cropper marvels at No. 44871 at Ramsbottom on June 28, 2010. ANDY COWARD

plots or description about what is required. Were they looking for steam locomotives and a vintage period set-up, or something more modern? Rural or built-up locations? Station scenes, open countryside, or a combination?

The first job after reaching agreement to host the filming was to identify a suitable location to match a scene being filmed at the picturesque Tatton Park, in Cheshire. For the story, two of the characters – Hayley Cropper and Mary Taylor – are looking at wedding venues and a steam-hauled train passes the back of the venue, giving Hayley the idea of a steam theme for the wedding. As many devotees of Coronation Street will already be aware, Roy Cropper is an unashamed railway enthusiast, with paintings and items of railwayana decorating his cafe and flat.

After walking several sections of the line with the director and production staff on a baking hot May morning, the chosen location for this particular scene was the open countryside alongside Irwell Vale station halt. Less than a week later, on May 26, 2010, visiting LMS Stanier 8F 2-8-0 No. 8624 was filmed passing through Irwell Vale, with the train then superimposed on to the Tatton Park backdrop for the final edit. It was also gratifying when the railway got a namecheck in the script during the episode when it was broadcast in July.

A further more detailed visit was then organised with the director Graeme Harper, assistant director Peter Shaw

On May 26, 2010, No. 8624 stands at Irwell Vale station, during filming of an initial set-up scene, where the railway and train were superimposed into a backdrop from Tatton Park in Cheshire. ANDY COWARD

No. 44871 *The Lancashire Fusilier* stands at Summerseat station on June 29, 2010, during filming for Coronation Street. The nameplates fitted to the locomotive are usually carried by Ian Riley's other Stanier 5MT No. 45407. ANDY COWARD

Upon realising that they have become separated from the main train, the bridal party look down the tracks from the observation coach. ANDY COWARD

LEFT: Julie Hesmondhalgh (Hayley Cropper), with her bridesmaids Katherine Kelly (Becky McDonald) and Jennie McAlpine (Fiz Stape) in the GWR observation coach. ANDY COWARD

and location manager Emma Smith attending, to decide what to film at the various locations around the railway and to look at the interiors of the railway's dining train and Pete Waterman's ex-GWR observation saloon which were to be used for the filming.

From this stage, it became apparent that this was going to be a major storyline with the ELR prominent throughout two episodes, and although some aspects of the plot could not physically happen in the real world and stretched credibility somewhat, the producer was keen to keep the plot light-hearted and of a rather slapstick nature. It was then agreed that the filming would take place over four days in June and July 2010, due to cast availability, with the programme to be broadcast on the August Bank Holiday Monday.

The first problem surrounded the steam locomotive to be used. As already mentioned, the character of Roy Cropper is an avid railway enthusiast and the scriptwriters intended giving Roy the ultimate wedding present of a steam footplate ride to take him to his wedding reception. For this, the director wanted a large named locomotive and on the dates that they intended doing the filming the only available large steam

locomotive on the railway was Ian Riley's unnamed Stanier 5MT 4 6 0 No. 44871. In the discussions that followed, the conversation turned to giving the locomotive a suitable name, so it could be referenced in the script. Originally, the plan was to name No. 44871 *The Manchester Mayflower* for the scenes, before Ian Riley mentioned that *The Lancashire Fusilier* nameplates belonging to his other Stanier 5MT, No. 45407, were in his stores at the Locomotive Works in Bury, as they had not been refitted to the locomotive before it had left the ELR for a spell working on hire to the North Yorkshire Moors Railway.

At this point, the director decided that as the name was usually fitted to No. 45407, we should use *The Lancashire Fusilier* nameplates and disguise No. 44871 as No. 45407 for the scenes.

Although another No. 45407 smokebox numberplate was ordered from Stephen Cliff at Procast Foundry to help with the disguise, the decision was subsequently taken to leave No. 44871 with its correct number, but to apply the nameplates from No. 45407. With the secret nature of the filming due to take place, it caused some speculation on

various internet forums when No. 44871 appeared in service in early July fitted with *The Lancashire Fusilier* nameplates.

With less than a week to go, the entire crew involved in the filming visited for a trip along the line in the Class 122 DMU, W55001, and stopped at a number of places along the route while they discussed what equipment would be needed at each location and to plan what scenes would be filmed on which date.

Due to the availability of No. 44871, the locomotive itself would only be available for the first two days they had chosen to film, with the final two dates being used for interior filming and exterior scenes that did not need the steam locomotive to be seen – with a diesel being used for these final two days. This meant the scenes filmed on the various days were rather disjointed and out of their natural order, but this would not matter when the final programme was edited.

The first days filming was Monday, June 28, and despite great secrecy the railway still managed to attract a large number of paparazzi and press photographers all keen to get a sneak preview of the scenes being filmed. By lunchtime, the train was at Ramsbottom for filming scenes at the station where Roy Cropper finally discovers what surprise has been arranged for his wedding. The message quickly spread around the town that Coronation Street was being filmed on the station and by early afternoon quite a crowd had gathered outside the station to catch a glimpse of their favourite characters. With more than 20 of the main cast members present, it was a good day to be an autograph hunter in Ramsbottom.

The following day featured lineside filming of the train passing through Burrs and then focused on its arrival at Summerseat – which was renamed as the fictitious Brookholme.

The script also called for a railway

ELR driver and locomotive owner Ian Riley and fireman Andi Moyes pose on the footplate of No. 44871 along with actors David Neilson (Roy Cropper) and Sam Aston (Chesney Battersby-Brown) at Ramsbottom on June 28, 2010. ANDY COWARD

Actors David Neilson (Roy Cropper) and Graeme Hawley (John Stape) receive instructions from director Graeme Harper and assistant director Peter Shaw at Summerseat on June 29, 2010. ANDY COWARD

Many prominent members of the Coronation Street cast gather for a group photograph on the last day of filming at Summerseat on July 26, 2010. ANDY COWARD

John Stape (Graeme Hawley) rushes to the back of the train when he discovers that the coach containing the bridal party is not attached to the train. ANDY COWARD

Every soap wedding has to have a twist and for Coronation Street the character of Mary Taylor interferes with the coupling on the rear coach, causing it to become separated from the train. Actress Patti Clare poses with the 'comedy' coupling at Ramsbottom on June 28, 2010. ANDY COWARD

pump trolley and sourcing one of these caused some problems, as the ELR didn't own one. For the story the bride and her bridesmaids – travelling in the observation saloon – became separated from the rest of the train after the coupling was sabotaged by another of the characters. While walking back along the track they stumble upon a permanent way pump trolley, which they then used to follow the train and catch up with the rest of the wedding party at Brookholme station. A number of railways were contacted in an attempt to source a suitable trolley, but there aren't many in a serviceable condition, with most restored as museum pieces rather than as working examples. The pump trolley used for the programme was loaned to ITV from the Nene Valley Railway and Phil Marshall from the NVR came along to provide some expert tuition to the actors charged with handling this beautifully restored item.

The sight of actors Katherine Kelly (Becky McDonald) and Jennie McAlpine (Fiz Stape) pumping the trolley up the steep gradient towards Summerseat station while bride Julie Hesmondhalgh (Hayley Cropper) stands on the side of the trolley looked fantastic, but it was clearly quite hard work. The pump trolley featured in several other scenes and Phil Marshall brought it back to the railway on July 5 for more filming with it at Ramsbottom sidings and also at Irwell Vale. Using the pump trolley caused some operational considerations, as it had to be removed from the tracks every time it wasn't in use to allow other train movements to take place and no train movements could take place while it was on the tracks due to single line working arrangements.

The final scenes were filmed on July 26, when 14 members of the cast returned to complete scenes inside the dining train carriages, while the train was stationary at Summerseat station. The whole cast were very friendly and

a lot seemed genuinely interested in the railway. The crew, led by Graeme Harper and Peter Shaw, were very professional and respectful of the ELR safety and operational instructions, put in place to ensure that the filming passed off without incident. And then it was all over with the words: "It's a wrap!" from Peter Shaw. All the scenes were done and the crew and cast left the ELR with some fantastic footage of the railway and some imaginative writing had produced an intriguing – if slightly unrealistic – story. On the side of the railway, the ELR had managed to get a high-profile advertisement on one of the country's best-loved prime time TV programmes.

Another unexpected boost from the filming was that Antony Cotton, who plays Sean Tully in the show, subsequently booked his birthday party on a private 'Red Rose Diner' train, with most of the cast returning again a few weeks later along with many of Mr Cotton's friends for a more leisurely evening out in an event that was featured in *OK!* magazine, bringing in yet more publicity for the ELR and the railway's facilities.

Bride Hayley and bridesmaids Becky and Fiz on a break from using the NVR's pump trolley at Irwell Vale on July 5, 2010. ANDY COWARD

Director Graeme Harper and assistant director Peter Shaw try their hand at working the NVR's permanent way pump trolley at Summerseat on June 29, 2010. ANDY COWARD

EXTENDING TO CASTLETON

With a busy 12-mile operational railway, the ELR is looking to a further extension of its route from Heywood to Castleton, where the railway hopes to have a cross-platform interchange with services on the national railway network. Additionally, the railway is planning a number of improvements to its existing facilities to help its long-term stability.

The ELR reopened the railway between Bury and Heywood in September 2003. Just beyond the station is Hopwood Junction, which is the current boundary between the ELR and Network Rail. When the railway line was open between Bolton and Rochdale, the next station along the line from Heywood was Castleton, which remains open to the present day due to it being located on the Manchester to Leeds Calder Valley line.

Beyond the ELR boundary at Hopwood Junction, a triangular junction links the line with the national network, with it currently possible for trains to run from either the Manchester or Rochdale directions towards the ELR. However, the ELR and Rochdale Council are both keen to extend the railway eastwards from Heywood towards Castleton, where it is hoped a cross-platform interchange station can be established, allowing ELR and Northern services to both use the station, while not operating on the same tracks.

Various options for the station are currently being investigated by the ELR, Rochdale Council and Network Rail, and it is hoped that progress on extending the ELR towards Castleton can take place over the next couple of years.

Castleton itself is a small town on the outskirts of Rochdale and the canal running through the town provides attractive walks for people. The council hopes that the arrival of the ELR can

These days, services on the Manchester to Leeds route are shared between Northern and Transpennine Express. On July 5, 2018, Northern Class 150 DMU 150136 stands at Castleton with a service to Manchester Victoria. Various options for a new station are being considered at Castleton, with one option being a new ELR platform being constructed in the area to the left of the picture currently occupied by a line of trees, providing a cross-platform interchange between the ELR and Network Rail. ANDY COWARD

help to revitalise the town in much the same way as the towns of Ramsbottom and Rawtenstall have benefited from the arrival of the railway. The project is seen as being a priority for all partners involved.

RAWTENSTALL

At the northern end of the railway there are ambitious plans to improve the passenger facilities at the station, as well

as expansion of the Buffer Stops bar. The station building at Rawtenstall was constructed in 1992 and has served the railway well in that time. However, since the opening of the Buffer Stops, the station has become much busier, with the bar proving to be more successful than could ever have been envisaged.

During 2017 the ELR submitted plans to Rossendale Council for a substantial redevelopment of the station, which is expected to cost in the region of £600,000, and planning permission for the development was approved in December 2017.

The first phase of the redevelopment will see part of the former Oldham Mumps station canopy erected on the station platform, providing some very welcome protection for passengers from the inclement weather conditions which can descend on the station. Modifications to the canopy will be carried out to allow it to be erected in an L-shape, spanning the entire width and length of the station buildings. Work on the erection of the canopy is expected to begin during the first half of 2019.

The railway also aims to build a second building at the station, again sympathetic to the style of the original East Lancashire Railway station designs, which will hopefully contain a cafe, community space, tourist information centre and toilets when completed. The railway has yet to

LEFT: Castleton station from a bygone era, as LNER Thompson B1 4-6-0 No. 61129 heads a Ramsbottom to Healey Mills train of coal empties through Castleton on June 2, 1965. The ELR and Rochdale Council aim to return regular steam services to the station over the next few years. RICHARD GREENWOOD

RIGHT: An artist's impression of how it is intended the terminus at Rawtenstall will look once completed, with its L-shaped canopy and new station building both prominent in the view. EAST LANCASHIRE RAILWAY

Another artist's impression of the new station building which is proposed for Rawtenstall station, with the ELR currently investigating possible sources of funding to allow the new building to be constructed. EAST LANCASHIRE RAILWAY

secure funding for this phase of the development, but is actively seeking ways of financing this project, which will help to transform the facilities available on the station.

Subject to the new station building being constructed, the toilet facilities in the existing building will be removed and the space will be used to allow the expansion of 'Buffer Stops'.

Outside the station, the forecourt area is to be landscaped, with new picnic areas and sheltered bicycle stands installed.

There is no target date set for the whole project to be completed, although it is hoped the construction of the canopy can be seen as a way of kick-starting the project and attracting possible funding towards the full station development.

BUCKLEY WELLS AND THE LOCOMOTIVE WORKS

Since the Locomotive Works building was first leased to the ELR by Bury Council in 1993, there has been a constant programme of inspections of the building, parts of which date from the 1850s. The condition of the roof of the building is the main concern and an application for National Lottery funding during 2009, which sought to completely develop the building and its surrounding area, proved unsuccessful.

However, the building continues to age and it is widely recognised that work will need to be done in the medium term to renew the roof to protect the long-term future of the building and both

the ELR Trust and the ELR operating company are actively seeking ways that the building can be re-roofed and receive the attention that it so richly deserves.

With the ELR taking on more of its own restoration and maintenance work in-house, the existing Locomotive Works building is seen as being ideal for this purpose. It is planned that a new running-shed for the operational steam fleet will be built alongside the Locomotive Works building on the site of the former Bury Steam Shed, which will free up more space inside the Locomotive Works for restoration projects and give secure storage and preparation facilities for the operational locomotives.

Additionally, it is recognised that the ELR desperately needs to build a carriage shed to house its operational

coaching stock fleet. Storing coaching stock outside throughout the year accelerates the rate at which a carriage deteriorates, while the railway's location in a heavily built-up area is also a problem, with the coaching stock being targeted by vandals on occasions.

The size of the ELR's site around the Locomotive Works complex at Buckley Wells means that a suitable location for a large carriage shed has been identified and, again, the railway is currently investigating ways in which it can finance the construction of a shed.

All of these projects are seen as being key to the future continued success of the railway and the completion of all of them will mean a heavy amount of investment will need to be made, but the railway believes that these are projects that it cannot afford not to do.

One of the biggest projects that the ELR has to address is the need to fit a new roof to the Locomotive Works, which is now starting to show its age. Giving a sense of the sheer size of the building, this photograph from May 29, 2006, shows unique BR Standard 'Pacific' 4-6-2 No. 71000 Duke of Gloucester inside the shed in the company of other steam locomotives. NIGEL VALENTINE

A PDF file of the development board produced by the ELR for the Rawtenstall station redevelopment. EAST LANCASHIRE RAILWAY

Dining with Distinction

As with most of the heritage railways in the UK, the East Lancashire Railway was keen to move into the luxury dining train market and has now built up its 'Dining with Distinction' brand to be top of the class and something that the railway can be justifiably very proud of.

The concept of luxury dining on board a train, hauled by a vintage steam locomotive, has always been popular and the operation of luxury dining services has become a valuable source of income for the ELR and also won the railway plaudits for the high quality of its dining services.

On Friday, May 4, 1990, the ELR operated its first ever dining train, with the company promoting 'The Presidential Diner'. The railway was keen to venture into the luxury dining train market as it sought to grow the business into areas that hadn't previously been explored.

At this stage, the dedicated dining coaches that are used these days for the services had not been restored, so two Mark 1 TSO coaches and a Mark 1 RMB miniature buffet coach were used for that first dining train, which was fully booked several weeks prior to it running, giving the ELR some confidence that there was a demand for such a service.

The catering for the train was to be provided by Bury College Caterers, with catering students and staff from the local college providing the food and table service for the evening, with ELR volunteers on hand to serve the wine and other drinks to the diners.

Priced at £15.50 per person, inclusive of wine, that initial dining train proved to be hugely successful and the partnership with Bury College had given the catering students a challenging training ground, while providing the ELR with a useful and promising new commercial opportunity. With the railway not yet open to Rawtenstall at the time, the train made two return journeys between Bury and Ramsbottom as 100 passengers enjoyed the experience of dining aboard a moving train, hauled by one of the railway's steam locomotives.

Another couple of wine and dine trains followed in 1990, although some changes were introduced based on the experience gained from the first train. For future services wine and other drinks could be purchased on board by passengers, but were not included in the ticket price for the train.

Work began on the restoration of a Mark 1 SO carriage that would be restored to umber and cream livery, in a similar style to Pullman livery, and the interior of this carriage would be more luxurious that the ELR normal passenger coaching stock, with it being dedicated solely for use as a dining coach.

By 1991, the first dedicated dining coach was completed and quickly proved to be popular with passengers. Although not a genuine Pullman coach, the Mark 1 SO coach had been restored to a very high standard with carpets, curtains and highly vanished wooden panelling, with lamps provided at every table in the interior, while on the exterior the coach was repainted into Pullman style umber and cream.

A second dedicated Mark 1 SO dining coach to match the first one was completed the following year and a Mark 1 BG coach was converted into a kitchen car for the train. The final coach was another Mark 1 BG which was used to carry the train's generator at one end, as well as providing a wine store and fridges at the other end.

From 1994, the Friday evening trains were promoted as the 'Red Rose Diner' and these generally operated once a month between March and October, as well as every Friday evening during December in the run-up to Christmas, serving a traditional festive menu.

Although the number of dining trains had been increased from those early days, the number of trains was limited due to the availability of the catering contractors from Bury College.

In 1998 the railway changed its catering suppliers, as Bury College

Severn Valley Railway-based Great Western Railway 0-6-0 Saddletank No. 813 hauls 'The Lancastrian' lunch train through Horncliffe, on the approach to Rawtenstall, on June 18, 2017. EMMA SEDDON

In connection with the visit of LNER A3 4-6-2 'Pacific' No. 60103 *Flying Scotsman*, the ELR organised a VIP black-tie Scottish-themed dining train, hauled by the legendary locomotive. The special train is pictured at Bury Bolton Street ready to depart on October 14, 2016. NIGEL VALENTINE

Catering for most of the 'Dining with Distinction' services is now provided by Lords Caterers of Rossendale, supported by the East Lancashire Railway dining train manager Andy McNamara and his staff, who look after the guests and serve the drinks. The Lords catering and waiting staff pose outside the train. EAST LANCASHIRE RAILWAY

ABOVE LEFT: The commemorative ticket for the ELR's first ever wine and dine train, 'The Presidential Diner', which took place on May 4, 1990, with the catering provided by Bury College Caterers. ANDY COWARD COLLECTION

There is no better venue for a meal than aboard a luxury train and the ELR's 'Dining with Distinction' trains have been voted the No. 1 restaurant on Trip Advisor for several months, with demand for the services remaining high. EAST LANCASHIRE RAILWAY

stated they no longer wished to provide the catering for the dining trains due to ongoing staffing problems with the Friday evening operation.

A new catering contractor, Percivals of Bolton, was appointed and the change of caterer also signalled the introduction of a new product. While the railway had operated a growing number of 'Red Rose Diner' services on Friday evenings, it was recognised that another, slightly cheaper, dining service may prove to be popular, so the railway introduced 'The Lancastrian' lunch service on selected Sunday afternoons.

While the 'Red Rose Diner' took about three hours from start to finish and operated to a more sedate, leisurely schedule, 'The Lancastrian' was attached to a lunchtime service train from Bury Bolton Street and a three-course traditional Sunday lunch was served while the train worked a round trip to Rawtenstall and back.

'The Lancastrian' quickly proved to be extremely popular and the Sunday lunch trains were often booked up months in advance. The 'Red Rose Diner' was also proving to be increasingly popular, with more and more evening dates added to the dining calendar each year to cope with the increased demand.

For the start of the 2015 season Lords Caterers of Rossendale became the main catering contractor for the dining services, while prestigious local chocolatier and caterer, Slatterys of Whitefield, provided the food for the afternoon tea and cream tea services.

The awarding of a new catering contract also coincided with the decision to market all of the railway's dining services under the 'Dining with Distinction' banner, and this now includes the full range of evening 'Red Rose Diner' services, themed dining trains, gin and whisky tasting trains, 'The Lancastrian' lunch trains, afternoon tea, cream tea, corporate hospitality, weddings and private

hire dining. Further coaches have been purchased by the railway to help increase capacity on the services and to allow the original coaches to be refurbished.

One of these coaches has been completed so far, to an even higher standard than the original dining coaches, and it is planned that the original dining coaches will eventually be overhauled and upgraded over the next couple of years. The addition of a third dining coach has allowed the ELR to increase the capacity on these services, which are often fully booked in advance. Under the leadership of

'Dining with Distinction' manager Andy McNamara, the ELR dining services have gained a first class reputation for the food and service.

Such has been the success of the services that they are often ranked in the top three of all restaurants in Greater Manchester on Trip Adviser, and have held the coveted No. 1 spot on a number of occasions.

As with the railway itself, the dining train services have grown from their rather humble beginnings into a much bigger operation, but the railway is focused on delivering a high-quality product at all times.

Illustrations of examples of the catering. All images EAST LANCASHIRE RAILWAY

ELR volunteers Stephen Lawton and Laura Duncan chose the ELR to give their wedding guests a journey from Ramsbottom to Rawtenstall and back when they got married in Ramsbottom on May 12, 2018. Stephen was formerly the station master at Ramsbottom, while Laura was passenger services manager for a number of years. The happy couple share a kiss from the footplate of *Flying Scotsman* during their wedding day celebrations. ANDY COWARD

Laura Duncan and Stephen Lawton pose for the cameras at Ramsbottom station on May 12, 2018, during their wedding day celebrations. OLIVIA WHITTAKER/EAST LANCASHIRE RAILWAY

A nice touch for the wedding of Stephen Lawton and Laura Duncan was specially prepared Edmondson card tickets which were handed to guests of the couple. OLIVIA WHITTAKER/EAST LANCASHIRE RAILWAY

Celebrate with steam

What could be more romantic than getting married on a heritage railway and then starting married life enjoying your wedding reception on board a steam or diesel-hauled dining train? In the past couple of years, the ELR has conducted a number of weddings on the railway, with the railway now able to provide bespoke packages for people seeking a wedding day with a difference.

Finding that wedding venue that has the added 'wow' factor is the quest of many couples, who want to give themselves and their guests a day to remember. Almost since the start of services on the ELR, the railway has played host to a number of weddings, with many couples choosing the railway as a way of transporting their guests to their wedding reception by train, or by holding their reception on board the dining train.

However, after receiving several requests, the railway decided to develop the packages that it can offer to couples and this involved taking out a licence on Bury Bolton Street station, meaning that happy couples can now exchange their

vows in front of a registrar beneath the glazed station canopy on Platforms 3 and 4 at the station. A number of couples have taken advantage of the ELR now being able to offer a complete wedding package, inclusive of the wedding ceremony itself.

The smallest wedding package offered by the railway includes a ceremony for up to 24 people, with the wedding party then enjoying an afternoon tea on board Pete Waterman's Great Western Railway observation saloon, while the railway can also cater for parties of up to 100 people, with the ELR's luxurious 'Dining with Distinction' coaching stock being used for a hot or cold wedding breakfast,

hauled by steam to Rawtenstall and back. The railway is also able to provide the station platform at Bury Bolton Street or the museum building at Bury Transport Museum as the venue for an evening reception and live bands or a disco can also be accommodated.

Whether it be a simple train ride following the wedding reception or an all-inclusive wedding package, the railway has something for almost every budget. The ELR prides itself on its flexible approach to weddings and the railway's wedding co-ordinator Nicola Wilcock always tries to do whatever she can to provide exactly what the bride and bridegroom want to make their special day pass off perfectly.

FOOTPLATE EXPERIENCE

Whether it be the opportunity to live out that childhood ambition, or for a special birthday, anniversary or retirement gift, the chance to take the controls of a vintage steam or diesel locomotive is an experience that will live in the memory of people for many years. The ELR offers a range of footplate experience courses for people who want an extra-special experience.

Footplate experience courses on the ELR have been run since the early 1990s and over the years they have become increasingly popular, with a wide range of locomotives being used for the courses. Locomotives are staffed by experienced ELR volunteer staff, offering guidance and training to participants, who on a steam course will spend time driving and firing the locomotive, before taking a turn in the carriages with the train guard. Locomotives used on the courses since they started have ranged from smaller industrial steam locomotives, through to high-profile 'Pacifics' such as the National Railway Museum's LMS 'Coronation' 4-6-2 No. 46229 *Duchess of Hamilton*. The ELR footplate experience courses also cater for modern traction enthusiasts, with various locomotives from the ELR diesel fleet used, with the Western Region diesel-hydraulics and Class 40s being particularly popular choices.

Most footplate experience courses also include a tour of the ELR site at Bury and lunch for the participant and any accompanying guests. Another additional extra is membership of the East Lancashire Railway Preservation Society, which has resulted in a number of former course participants becoming valuable members of the volunteer workforce on the railway, based on the enjoyment they experienced on their footplate course. Such is the popularity of these courses that they are often fully booked well in advance, so anyone wishing to book a place for a special occasion is encouraged to contact the railway as soon as possible before they make a booking.

The most popular footplate experience courses take place using mainly ex-British Railways main line steam locomotives, with participants given the opportunity to both drive and fire the locomotive. EAST LANCASHIRE RAILWAY

In addition to steam locomotives, the ELR's extensive collection of diesel locomotives are also used for footplate experience courses for those more interested in modern traction. During a footplate experience day, ex-Western Region diesel-hydraulic Class 42 'Warship' D832 *Onslaught* pauses at Ramsbottom station. LIAM BARNES

PHOTOGRAPHY

While many of us can take a perfectly nice photograph, there are many skills and tips that can help make someone a better photographer. Since 2015, the ELR has been hosting North West Photography Courses, who use the railway as one of the backdrops to their hugely popular photography courses.

The ELR photography courses are run to help people learn new skills, improve their photography, or just for the sheer enjoyment of it. The railway provides the perfect backdrop for photographers, giving a range of settings and effects that can help them hone their camera skills.

North West Photography Courses offer a wide range of photography experiences, with the ELR course being just one of a number of experiences that they offer for photography enthusiasts, with each designed to suit people of all skill levels.

The ELR photography course includes a tour of the railway, with photographers being given the opportunity to take their cameras to many parts of the railway that are often

A photographer gets a close-up photo of the wheels and motion of Hunslet Austerity 0-6-0 *Sapper*. NORTH WEST PHOTOGRAPHY COURSES

A participant of the ELR photography course takes a close-up image of L&YR Class 27 0-6-0 No. 12322 as it heads a train out of Bury EL Tunnel at Castlecroft. NORTH WEST PHOTOGRAPHY COURSES

The photography courses include a visit to the signalbox at Bury South, which is one of the largest operational signalboxes on a heritage railway in the UK. NORTH WEST PHOTOGRAPHY COURSES

out of bounds to the usual railway visitor. As such, they can enjoy a tour of the Locomotive Works, stations and signalboxes.

Since they were started, these courses have proved to be very popular and this is yet another way that the ELR facilities can be showcased to visitors. Photography and railways are natural partners, so the courses provide the perfect chance to combine the two for photographers of all levels.

DIESEL GALLERY

Crossing Brooksbottom Viaduct, former BR Western Region Class 35 diesel-hydraulic 'Hymek' D7076 heads a service from Bury to Ramsbottom on October 7, 1990, during the ELR autumn diesel gala. The 'Hymek' has been based on the ELR for the past 35 years and remains a popular member of the home diesel fleet. MARTIN LOADER

In September 1999, the ELR hired a number of diesel locomotives that were due to be withdrawn from freight company English Welsh & Scottish Railways. The EWS Classic Traction Event proved to be very popular with visitors and lineside photographers, but sadly made a financial loss, due to the high costs involved in staging the event. EWS owned 37351, the second built Class 37, leads ELR resident Class 40 D345 towards Irwell Vale station on September 12, 1999. MIKE TAYLOR

For a number of years Freightliner supported the railway by sending some of their locomotive fleet to the railway for diesel events, with the company supplying various Class 47, 57 and 66 locomotives. On September 13, 2003, 66524 hauls a train of Mark 2 coaches through Burrs working a Rawtenstall to Heywood service. NIGEL VALENTINE

Visiting the ELR in 2012 from its usual home on the Gloucester Warwickshire Railway was Class 24, 5081. The immaculate locomotive was used on a mixed freight train for an East Midlands Railway Photographic Society photographic charter on September 11, 2012. The train is seen passing through Pilsworth, between Heywood and Bury, in almost perfect weather conditions. TOM MCATEE

A BR type-two pairing of Class 24 D5054 and Class 25 D7659 approach Nuttall Tunnel in Ramsbottom on June 6, 1993, working from Rawtenstall to Bury. The Class 25 had recently been repainted into two-tone green livery. NEIL HARVEY